# DURKHEIM
# AND POSTMODERN CULTURE

# COMMUNICATION AND SOCIAL ORDER

*An Aldine de Gruyter Series of Texts and Monographs*

Series Editor

*David R. Maines, Wayne State University*

Advisory Editors

Bruce Gronbeck • Peter K. Manning • William K. Rawlins

David L. Altheide and Robert Snow, **Media Worlds in the Postjournalism Era**

Joseph Bensman and Robert Lilienfeld, **Craft and Consciousness: Occupational Technique and the Development of World Images** (*Second Edition*)

Valerie Malhotra Bentz, **Becoming Mature: Childhood Ghosts and Spirits in Adult Life**

Herbert Blumer, **Industrialization as an Agent of Social Change: A Critical Analysis** (*Edited with an Introduction by David R. Maines and Thomas J. Morrione*)

Dennis Brissett and Charles Edgley (*editors*), **Life as Theater: A Dramaturgical Sourcebook** (*Second Edition*)

Richard Harvey Brown (*editor*), **Writing the Social Text: Poetics and Politics in Social Science Discourse**

Norman K. Denzin, **Hollywood Shot by Shot: Alcoholism in American Cinema**

Irwin Deutscher, Fred P. Pestello, and Frances G. Pestello, **Sentiments and Acts**

Joo-Hyun Cho, **Family Violence in Korea**

Bruce E. Gronbeck, **Rhetoric and Socioculture**

Pasquale Gagliardi (ed), **Symbols and Artifacts: Views of the Corporate Landscape** (paperback)

J. T. Hansen, A. Susan Owen, and Michael Patrick Madden, **Parallels: The Soldiers' Knowledge and the Oral History of Contemporary Warfare**

Emmanuel Lazega, **The Micropolitics of Knowledge: Communication and Interaction in Work Groups**

David R. Maines (*editor*), **Social Organization and Social Process: Essays in Honor of Anselm Strauss**

David R. Maines, **Time and Social Process: Gender, Life Course, and Social Organization**

Peter K. Manning, **Organizational Communication**

Stjepan G. Meštrović, **Durkheim and Postmodernist Culture**

R. S. Perinbanayagam, **Discursive Acts**

William K. Rawlins, **Friendship Matters: Communication, Dialectics, and the Life Course**

Vladimir Shlapentokh and Dmitry Shlapentokh, **Ideological Trends in Soviet Movies**

Jim Thomas, **Communicating Prison Culture: The Deconstruction of Social Existence**

Jacqueline P. Wiseman, **The Other Half: Wives of Alcoholics and Their Social-Psychological Situation**

# DURKHEIM
# AND POSTMODERN CULTURE

Stjepan G. Meštrović

Aldine de Gruyter

New York

# About the Author

*Stjepan G. Meštrović*, is a native of Zagreb, Croatia, and is Professor of
Sociology at Texas A & M University. Widely published in scholarly
journals, he is the author of *Emile Durkheim and the Reformation of
Sociology* (1988) and *The Coming Fin de Siècle* (1991).

ALDINE DE GRUYTER
A division of Walter de Gruyter, Inc.
200 Saw Mill River Road
Hawthorne, New York 10532

The paper used in this publication meets the minimum requirements of American
National Standard for Information Sciences—Permanence of Paper Printed
Library Materials, ANSI Z39.48-1984. ∞

**Library of Congress Cataloging-in-Publication Data**
Meštrović, Stjepan Gabriel.
    Durkheim and postmodern culture / Stjepan G. Meštrović.
        p.    cm. — (Communication and social order)
    Includes bibliographical references and index.
    ISBN 0-202-30439-6. — ISBN 0-202-30440-X (pbk.)
    1. Sociology—Philosophy.   2. Durkheim, Emile, 1858–1917.
3. Postmodernism—Social aspects.   4. Culture.   5. Romanticism.
I. Title. II. Series.
HM24.M47215   1992
301'.01—dc20                                                    92-21616
                                                                    CIP

Manufactured in the United States of America

10 9 8 7 6 5 4 3 2 1

*To my darling Amber,*
*the love of my life*

# Contents

# Preface and Acknowledgments

The present work is an elaboration of my previous efforts in *Emile Durkheim and the Reformation of Sociology* (1988) and *The Coming Fin de Siècle* (1991) to demonstrate Durkheim's neglected relevance to the postmodern discourse. My aims include finding affinities between our *fin de siècle* and Durkheim's *fin de siècle*, and connecting the contemporary themes of rebellion against Enlightenment narratives found in postmodern culture with similar concerns found in Durkheim's sociology as well as in his *fin de siècle* culture. I hope that these aims will contribute to Durkheimian scholarship as well as to the postmodern discourse.

The distinctive aspects of the present study flow from the focus on culture, communication, and the feminine voice in culture. I approach Durkheim as a *fin de siècle* student of culture, and apply his insights to our *fin de siècle* culture. Furthermore, because Durkheim claimed that culture is comprised primarily of collective representations, he was a forerunner of the current, postmodern concerns with communication. Because Durkheim shall be read in the context of his *fin de siècle*, this book shall lead to the conclusion that Durkheim was a kind of psychoanalyst such that society is the patient, culture comprises the symptoms, and the sociologist must decipher, decode, and even *deconstruct* collective representations. Yet, the Durkheimian deconstruction I am proposing here is unlike the postmodern deconstructions, which criticize and tear apart a text without substituting a better meaning or interpretation. Some postmodernists claim that such exercises are liberating, while others regard them as nihilistic. Some would deny that anything like a postmodern *culture* could exist. Consider the anticultural stand in the following claim made by Jean Baudrillard, who is often referred to as the high priest of postmodernism:

> I went in search of astral America, not social and cultural America, but the America of the empty, absolute freedom of the freeways, not the deep America of mores and mentalities, but the America of desert speed, of motels and mineral surfaces. (1986:5)

My focus on postmodern *culture* is made in deliberate contradistinction to Baudrillard and other postmodern writers. On the one hand, such a focus violates the rules of the postmodern rebellion against origins, cultural roots, or any foundations for the circulation of fictions in society (Rosenau 1992:19). On the other, it is commensurate with postmodern claims of offering liberation from oppressive narratives, freedom, and choice (Bauman 1991). At this point, I wish to indicate merely that my focus on "postmodern culture" is not an accident.

Feminism has emerged as a dominant voice that has accompanied postmodern discourse. I intend to show that Durkheim was always mindful of the "left-handed," feminine aspects of society and culture, and that he sought to balance these with the "right-handed," masculine aspects that came to dominate modern social arrangements. But again, Durkheim's seemingly Jungian approach to culture shall be pursued in order to distinguish it radically from Baudrillard's postmodern approach:

> The more general problem is one of an absence of difference, bound up with a decline in the display of sexual characteristics. The outer signs of masculinity are tending towards zero, but so are the signs of femininity. It is in this conjuncture that we have seen new idols emerging, idols who take up the challenge of undefinedness and who play at mixing genres/genders. "Gender benders." Boy George, Michael Jackson, David Bowie. . . . Pushed to its logical conclusions, this would leave neither masculine nor feminine, but a dissemination of individual sexes referring only to themselves, each one managed as an independent enterprise. The end of seduction, the end of difference, and a slide towards a different system of values. (1986:47)

Overall, my strategy in this book is to use the postmodern method (for it has already become rigid and reified) at the same time that I intend to subvert postmodernism. Postmodernism encourages such subversion and explosion of boundaries and turf-barriers erected by academic disciplines (Lyotard 1984). According to Rosenau:

> Postmodern social scientists support a re-focusing on what has been taken for granted, what has been neglected, regions of resistance, the forgotten, the irrational, the insignificant, the repressed, the borderline, the classical, the sacred, the traditional, the eccentric, the sublimated, the subjugated, the rejected, the nonessential, the marginal, the peripheral, the excluded, the tenuous, the silenced, the accidental, the dispersed, the disqualified, the deferred, the disjointed—all that which "the modern age has never cared to understand in any particular detail, with any sort of specificity." (1992:8)

Along these lines, I shall take up many themes, theorists, and theories that have been repressed or otherwise obfuscated in modern discourse, from Arthur Schopenhauer to Henry Adams. But I shall also examine that which the *postmodern* age does not care to understand, especially the rootedness of culture.

Postmodern discourse has made respectable again the synthesis of multidisciplinary insights that was fashionable in Durkheim's *fin de siè-cle*. In following this postmodern strategy, this book is more than a book about Durkheim. It is also a book about his contemporaries, among them, Carl Gustav Jung, Thorstein Veblen, Henry Adams, Georg Simmel, and Max Weber. But again, I do not follow the postmodern strategy completely, because I find some common strands that bind these and other thinkers and their theories. The postmodern critique cannot be immune from the criticisms it makes of Enlightenment narratives. Like the Enlightenment, postmodernism is a narrative, a text, and a set of assumptions rooted in culture. Neither the Enlightenment nor the postmodern rebellion against it exists a priori, as a mere abstraction, self-begotten and rootless. And neither narrative is completely liberating. Indeed, the postmodern narratives are every bit as oppressive as the Enlightenment narratives, despite the claims to freedom made by their supporters. In particular, I shall argue that postmodernism betrays a Nietzschean attitude toward the world, a pitiless, aristocratic, and sometimes cruel stance toward the very poor and helpless that it sometimes purports to liberate. Baudrillard, for example, does not try to conceal his fascination with inhumanity, which is why he equates America with the dawning of the future, and the desert: "The inhumanity of our ulterior, asocial, superficial world immediately finds its aesthetic form here, its ecstatic form. For the desert is simply that: an ecstatic critique of culture, an ecstatic form of disappearance" (1986:5).

The almost exclusively Nietzschean tone of the postmodern discourse exposes the lacunae of our social theory and our days. The goal in this book is to account for these lacunae by opposing Nietzsche with his self-acknowledged master, Arthur Schopenhauer; and therefore the will to power of the former with the compassion espoused by the latter; the right hand with the left; and other neglected aspects of culture with the ones that are in the forefront of discourse.

Nowadays, anybody who dares to write about compassion, the feminine voice, Schopenhauer, or other things seemingly forbidden runs the risk of not being taken seriously. One is automatically presumed not to be politically correct—or worse. And this, despite the promise that postmodernism is liberating and allows free discourse (like President Bush's promise not to raise taxes). To the reader who is tempted to react in these predictable, knee-jerk ways to these topics, I offer the following explanations and caveats:

1. My use of the word *compassion* is not to be confounded with pity, socialism, nor any efforts to systematize charity of fellow-feeling, nor

any exercise in social engineering by followers of any religion, creed, or ideology. I mean to imply Plato's dictum that virtue cannot be taught, and to highlight Schopenhauer's focus on compassion versus Kant's duty and Nietzsche's will to power. I also wish to connect Baudrillard's cruelty with Nietzsche's philosophy—and point to a cultural alternative. If I am to be criticized for this move, I should be criticized in relation to these philosophers.

2. My use of Schopenhauer does not imply loyalty to his philosophy nor the implication that he influenced directly Durkheim or anybody else. The important point is that Schopenhauer is part of the lacunae in current social theory, in that intellectuals march routinely from Kant through Nietzsche to the present without mentioning him. And Schopenhauer is a significant philosopher, depicted by the sociologist-philosopher Georg Simmel ([1907] 1986) as more important than Nietzsche for understanding the culture of the previous *fin de siècle*. In sum, Schopenhauer is interesting only because he has been *repressed* in the present *fin de siècle*. Were he as popular as Nietzsche still is to the postmodernists, I would have had no reason to invoke him. If I am to be criticized for this move, I would like to be criticized vis-à-vis Georg Simmel's neglected argument in his *Schopenhauer and Nietzsche* ([1907] 1986).

3. I regard the terms *masculine* and *feminine* as arbitrary labels that have been attached by force of habit to phenomena that can be shared equally by males and females. These terms shall be used because a discussion of this sort must use them in order to make sense of history and culture, but always with the implication, following Jung and Durkheim, that feminine and masculine archetypes or representations are found in each gender. I should like to be spared the inane criticism of equating feminine with female—and hereby disavow this connection completely. If I am to be criticized, I ask to be read vis-à-vis Carl Gustav Jung's (1959) writings on archetypes.

Having made these defensive remarks, I acknowledge that in the postmodern era, readers presume to read a text in any manner that they choose. My remarks are aimed at readers who still cling to the old-fashioned strategy of giving an author a chance to explain his or her self.

Finally, some readers may find it peculiar that I do not approach postmodernism directly, as if "it" were something "real" to be explained. I do not regard as fruitful the efforts by Anthony Giddens (1990, 1992) to deny that postmodernity exists, and to invent a new phrase, "high modernity," to account for it. Such language games have not made the problems that concern contemporary intellectuals go away. Instead, I focus on postmodern *culture*, and analyze the contradictory characteristics of that culture. My reason for this strategy is that I hope to avoid reifying the concept of postmodernism, along with its attendant ideas, modernity, and progress. To enter the discordant debate whether postmodernity extends or undermines modernity is to assume the existence of Enlightenment narratives as ahistorical abstractions that postmodernism purports to rebel against. Such an approach embroils the intellectual in a tautology from which there is no exit. Hoping to avoid this trap, and following Durkheim's and Jung's lead, I regard postmodernism as being "real" on the level of culture only, as a set of collective representations that must be taken seriously, but that do not necessarily point to a universal, "hard" fact.

To my readers who possess a Jungian bent, I declare that I do, indeed, imply a Jungian reading of Durkheim throughout the text. Even my conclusions are implicitly Jungian: to reconcile opposites in the hopes of finding psychic and societal integration. Moreover, I refer those readers to Jung's many explicit references to the philosophy of Arthur Schopenhauer. The reason that these connections are not made explicit by me in this book is that the "real" connections among Jung, Durkheim, and Schopenhauer are impossible to prove. I hope to let the sleeping positivists lie. Still, I cite Henri Ellenberger's *The Discovery of the Unconscious* (1970) as an important study of the *cultural* connections among them.

Many colleagues helped me find the pieces that are synthesized in this book, even if I would not claim that they would endorse my final synthesis. I owe the discovery of Henry Adams and his essay, "The Dynamo and the Virgin," to Richard Koffler. I came across references to Bachofen in David Riesman's and Erich Fromm's writings. Additionally, Riesman's studies of Veblen, Tocqueville, and American social character, as well as his correspondence, were helpful. Susan Greenwood's (1990) exploration of linkages between Jung and Durkheim also led me to make further conceptual linkages. Chris Rojek's (1990) article on Baudrillard and Veblen, as well as his correspondence and critique of drafts of some chapters were very stimulating and helpful. David Cartwright's (1984) analysis of the idea of compassion in Kant, Nietzsche, and Schopenhauer was illuminating, and I am grateful to him for his correspondence with me concerning Schopenhauer. Deena and Michael Weinstein's translation of Simmel's *Schopenhauer and Nietzsche* ([1907] 1986), along with their other thoughts on postmodernism, were helpful to me. Other colleagues who engaged me in helpful critiques of various strands of the argument that I put forth here include Ben Aguirre, Alex McIntosh, Jim Parsons, Peter Manning, Eugene Rochberg-Halton, David Frisby, C. G. Schoenfeld, Eugen Schoenfeld, Barry Glassner, and Michael Kaern. A separate note of thanks goes to Geoffrey P. Alpert, Harry Alpert's son, for making available to me his father's unpublished notes on Durkheim. While I am grateful to these scholars for their help, I am solely responsible for the arguments put forth here. Finally, thanks to my wife, Amber, and my newborn daughter, Ivy Elizabeth, for putting up with my devotion to this project.

# Chapter 1

## *Postmodernism as a Cultural Problem*

Scholars cannot seem to agree on the meanings of the most recent academic buzzword, *postmodernism*. Does it imply the dramatic end to modernity, history, even communism—or merely their transformation into something new? Bauman claims that those who celebrate the collapse of communism, "celebrate the end of modernity actually, because what collapsed was the most decisive attempt to make modernity work; and it failed" (1991:222). If Bauman is correct, then one has no good reason to believe that the brand of modernity that took root on this side of the former Iron Curtain will fare any better, in the long run, than the communist version. Yet Fukuyama (1990) and others claim that recently humanity has witnessed the "end of history," by which he means the end of nationalism, totalitarianism, and wars for territory. For Fukuyama, liberal democracy has triumphed over socialism, while for Lyotard (1984) and other postmodernists, all systems based on the Enlightenment are oppressive (Rosenau 1992).

Some, like Anthony Giddens (1990, 1992), deny the existence of postmodernism, and opt for the term "high modernity" to capture the gist of some of the contradictions that this term signifies. Nevertheless, whatever "it" is, a growing consensus is emerging that the French philosopher, Jean Baudrillard, ought to be regarded as "the high priest" of postmodernism. Baudrillard follows Nietzsche in reducing everyone to gladiators in a world based on anomic, infinite consumption as well as the will to power.[1] He portrays a social world of circulating fictions in which nothing is real, true, or grounded in any sort of metaphysical permanence.[2]

Moreover, Baudrillard is merciless in his attitude toward women, minorities, and all the weak and helpless—all of them "must exit," Baudrillard writes in his *America*:

> But this easy life knows no pity. Its logic is a pitiless one. If utopia has already been achieved, then unhappiness does not exist, the poor are no

1

longer credible. If America is resuscitated, then the massacre of the Indians did not happen, Vietnam did not happen. . . . The have-nots will be
condemned to oblivion, to abandonment, to disappearance pure and simple. This is "must exist" logic: "poor people must exit." The ultimatum
issued in the name of wealth and efficiency wipes them off the map. And
rightly so, since they show such bad taste as to deviate from the general
consensus. (1986:111)

Douglas Kellner writes of Baudrillard's *fin de siècle* exhaustion, and
concludes that Baudrillard began his career as a Marxist liberal but is
ending it with a "capitulation to the hegemony of the Right and a secret
complicity with aristocratic conservatism" (1989:215). In *Baudrillard: Critical and Fatal Theory,* Mike Gane (1991) joins a growing list of critics who
find in Baudrillard as well as other postmodernists a proclivity toward
cruelty that stems from writing under the sign of Nietzsche (see also
Kroker and Cook 1986:171).[3] Like all other generalizations, this one
could be, and has been, criticized and debated by intellectuals who are
engaged in the postmodernist discourse, with nothing like a final resolution on the horizon.

For the sake of discussion, let us assume that Baudrillard can represent well the broad outlines of the postmodernist movement, and
that its overall impact includes a rejection of many truths previously
held as sacrosanct. These are consequences that one would expect from
taking Nietzsche seriously, and there is no doubt that Nietzsche is the
most frequently cited author by postmodernists. Where does one go
from here?

The present study is a fresh response to the movement that
Baudrillard represents. It is a response to the onesidedness and narrow
intellectual context exhibited by postmodernists as well as by the traditional rationalists.[4] Infinite consumption was not discovered by the
postmodernists. On the contrary, it was described as "conspicuous consumption" by the American, turn-of-the century philosopher, economist, and sociologist, Thorstein Veblen (1857–1929) in his 1899 classic,
*The Theory of the Leisure Class* ([1899] 1967). Similarly, it was foreshadowed by the first bona fide professor of sociology in the world,
Emile Durkheim (1858–1917) as the anomic "infinity of desires" in his
1897 book, *Suicide* ([1897] 1951), as well as by other sociologists who
wrote in the previous *fin de siècle.*

The German philosopher, Friedrich Nietzsche (1844–1900), who attacked the idea of compassion, and whose logic is the basis for the
pitiless logic promulgated by Baudrillard, was not the only star on the
intellectual horizon during the era in which sociology was born. Another German philosopher, Arthur Schopenhauer (1788–1860)—who
was Nietzsche's ([1874] 1965) self-acknowledged master for a time—had

reached the zenith of his philosophical fame in Europe in the 1880s. Nietzsche and Schopenhauer were the *two* philosophical superstars of the previous *fin de siècle,* and exerted diametrically opposed influences upon intellectuals. Nietzsche stood for the aristocratic hardness based on the will to power, which finds its way in Baudrillard's account of the postmodern, whereas Schopenhauer stood for compassion and justice, which tend to be neglected by intellectuals as phenomena worthy of study, but illuminate and explain the concerns with human rights in the present era.

Unlike Baudrillard, Durkheim and Veblen ground reality in habits, collective representations, and the collective consciousness, in a word, *culture.* Culture is the one concept that is missing in the modernist as well as the postmodernist discourses. For example, neither Bauman (1991) nor Brzezinski (1989) raises the cultural question, How and why did communism take root in the lands it ruled up to 1989? To take this question seriously is to seek the cultural antecedents of communism as a modernist system, as well as its possible transformations into a new form of totalitarianism. Similarly, scholars seem to assume routinely that modernity, Enlightenment, and the postmodern circulation of fictions are self-begotten, that they exist a priori, and that they are not rooted in any sort of cultural tradition. In fact, tradition and modernity are assumed to be opposites. This overly tidy, modernist view cannot explain the modern West's many relapses into traditional nationalism, totalitarianism, and imperialism (see Spengler [1926] 1961), nor the postmodern obsession with history, nostalgia, and sentiment.

Unlike Baudrillard, but in line with Schopenhauer, Durkheim thought of compassion as the "glue" that holds society together. Durkheim offers a "feminine" vision of society that contrasts sharply with Baudrillard's chauvinistic emphasis on power. Durkheim's contemporary, Thorstein Veblen, also opposed the pecuniary impulse with matriarchal self-abnegation, which he felt was essential for social life. Unadulterated will to power, force, duty, constraint, and other phenomena usually associated with social order are more likely to lead to the war of all against all than the desired consequence of social stability. Here is another important gap in the contemporary thinking about social systems as non-cultural phenomena.

The German philosopher-sociologist, Georg Simmel (1858–1918), who was Durkheim's contemporary and one of sociology's several cofounders, emphasized the importance of this distinction in his neglected study, *Schopenhauer and Nietzsche,* first published in 1907 but not translated into English until 1986. Nietzsche began his philosophical career as Schopenhauer's self-acknowledged disciple, but parted with Schopenhauer precisely on the issue of compassion versus the will to power. Schopenhauer taught that compassion or identification with suffering humanity was the right antidote to the egoism and lust for power that had been unleashed by modernity. But Nietzsche mocked compassion as the morality of the weak and powerless—as refracted in Christianity in particular. For the sake of objectivity, we shall stress Schopenhauer's feminine, compassionate philosophy and its impact on sociology, particularly Durkheim's sociology, because it has been almost completely obfuscated by the Nietzschean, masculine, power-hungry model of social relations.[5] By objectivity, we mean a concern with documenting the lacunae in contemporary analyses of the cultural and philosophical roots of sociology, with filling in gaps, with addressing issues that have been obfuscated due to the one-sided emphasis on Nietzsche.

Our approach is commensurate with the broad outlines of Riane Eisler's *The Chalice and the Blade* (1987), in which she distinguishes between the male, dominator model of history versus the female, partnership model. She argues that in prehistory, values symbolized by the chalice—to give and to nurture—reigned supreme, but were replaced by the values symbolized by the blade—violence and domination. Now that the dominator model is purported by many to be reaching its logical limits, she calls for the "transformation of a dominator to a partnership system" (p. xx). I agree overall, but wonder whether a one-sided emphasis on partnership might not be too much of a good thing and pathological in its own right, as is often the case with any excess. And how should one undertake such a transformation without deforming one's goals? To teach partnership systematically is to engage in domination, and to produce a tainted product, along the lines of Spengler's ([1926] 1961:361) remark that socialism's efforts to systematize compassion negate genuine compassion. A sophisticated sociological theory is required to move beyond the simplistic argument that underpins many feminist treatises, namely, that patriarchal power should be replaced with the power of women (Game 1991). Finally, what is the cultural bedrock for both "systems"?

My book seeks to bring Durkheim as one such sophisticated sociological theorist into a cultural discourse and a value system that almost never mentions him, and that overemphasizes Nietzsche as the cultural bedrock for the sociology he established. He has been absorbed into sociology on the false premises that he was a status quo functionalist and defender of modernity, a proponent of social order, consensus, and other masculine-sounding values. All this may be somewhat true, but it is only one side of Durkheim. For the sake of balance, I will emphasize the other side of Emile Durkheim, who conceived of society and culture as also feminine, as a vast partnership that promotes mutual sympathy, integration, and humanity. For example, consider the following description of society from Durkheim's *Moral Education*:

> On the one hand, it seems to us an authority that constrains us, fixes limits for us, blocks us when we would trespass, and to which we defer with a feeling of religious respect. *On the other hand, society is the benevolent and protecting power, the nourishing mother from which we gain the whole of our moral and intellectual substance and toward whom our wills turn in a spirit of love and gratitude.* ([1925] 1961:92; emphasis added)

The overall thrust of Durkheim's sociology is entirely consistent with Eisler's aims to transform modern society into an entity that is more humane than was and is the case with the onset of modernity. Durkheim's feminine side has been obfuscated almost completely by the neo-Parsonian and Mertonian functionalists. However, Durkheim's humanistic program was considerably more complex than replacing one model of social relations with another. His use of the concept *society* seems to overlap, in significant ways, with the concept of *culture*. The aim of the present study is to explicate Durkheim's complexity in this regard. We shall engage in a criticism of Durkheim's perceived image with an eye toward exposing the one-sidedness of the masculine version of sociology that holds him up as the prince of positivism and regards postmodernism with disdain. Speaking metaphorically, we shall balance the right-handed (left-brain) Durkheim with the neglected, left-handed (right-brain) Durkheim.[6] In Jungian terminology, Durkheim's "shadow" and *anima* shall be brought to conscious reflection. And the object shall not be a new understanding of Durkheim per se (as if that were possible), but to find an alternative to the nihilistic, right-handed conclusions reached by many postmodernists in their incomplete critiques of the Enlightenment.

Several points need to be clarified before we proceed further. First, Durkheim is certainly not unique relative to his contemporaries with regard to his feminine voice. Among his sociological colleagues, one can point to Ferdinand Tonnies, Georg Simmel, Sigmund Freud, George Herbert Mead, and Thorstein Veblen, who praised empathy, *Gemeinschaft*, and other derivatives of compassion at the same time that they wrote with considerable ambivalence about *Gesellschaft*, civilization, and modernity. The more important point is that this emotional, subjective, even feminine aspect to their sociologies was suppressed and distorted along the lines of Max Weber's "value-free" sociology as it became the basis for Talcott Parsons's (1937) modernist rereading of their works. Parsons claimed to transform the newly born discipline of sociology into a "detached" and "objective" study of progress and systems theory. Yet, contrary to Parsons, Durkheim was writing in a way that was typical of his *fin de siècle* culture, and reading him and most of his colleagues in their proper context challenges Parsons's modernist obfuscation of his import, as well as Parsons's pretense that he was being objective. Thus, we are not dogmatic about our choice of Durkheim, and shall not hesitate to compare and contrast him with his colleagues when the occasion warrants it. Durkheim is a convenient choice, and a strategic choice as well, for if we can convince the reader that Emile Durkheim, the alleged prince of positivism and functionalism, was actually a feminist of sorts, we will have achieved a significant coup.

Second, our attitude toward Durkheim should not be dismissed as loyalty or hero worship. No doubt, a "detached" reading of Durkheim would and often has yielded trenchant criticisms of his sociology. But one wonders whether any study or point of view can be truly detached, because even such a view presupposes attachment to the dogma of the value-free scientist who works in a pristine, ahistorical, and noncultural context that is difficult to imagine. C. Wright Mills (1959) and others have challenged these assumptions already. Moreover, plenty of such studies exist, and little purpose would be served by adding to the deconstruction of Durkheim. Deconstruction tears a text apart, but its intent is not to improve or offer a better version of a text or author. Far from being neutral, such studies contribute to cynicism, and the disparaging view that sociology has nothing to offer to contemporary times. Our overall aim is not to add to another noncontextual study of Durkheim, and certainly not to tear him down.[7] Rather, it is to fill the lacunae left by Durkheim's modernist interpreters, as well as Baudrillard and the nihilistic version of postmodernism.

Third, the decision not to offer a detached study is made deliberately. Detachment can easily degenerate into sadism, even among scholars, who rarely exhibit kindness or empathetic understanding when reviewing the works of their colleagues. This connection leads us back to the observations with which we began this book, that Baudrillard's detached critique of the Enlightenment has been criticized for turning into old-fashioned, pitiless cruelty. We are seeking a way out of this impasse by arguing for a need to reconcile masculine objectivity with feminine subjectivity (from Simmel), the barbaric temperament with matriarchal peaceable traits (from Veblen), egoism with altruism (from Durkheim), the mind with the heart (from Schopenhauer), and other versions of *homo duplex* that characterize Western history. Thus, what some readers might misconstrue as our lack of detachment is based on a self-conscious decision, and is in keeping with the previously stated objectives of the present study: to find a way to reconcile the feminine side of humanity with the masculine, to find a non-nihilistic alternative to the powerful critiques of the Enlightenment offered by postmodernists, and to demonstrate Durkheim's neglected relevance to these debates.

While we do not follow the method of detached observation—because we are not convinced that it is possible or desirable—this does not detract from the objectivity of our study. On the contrary, the detached observers are biased, because they refuse to consider as legitimate thinkers and theories from the Romantic era that they reject on a priori grounds. Thus, we balance the overwhelming and biased emphasis on Nietzsche's will to power with an emphasis on his teacher, Arthur Schopenhauer. This is a crucial step in accounting for the lacunae in the contemporary postmodernist discourse, which is dominated by Nietzsche's philosophy. Similarly, the Parsonian version of Durkheim shall be countered with the original, *fin de siècle* Durkheim. Durkheim against Baudrillard, the masculine versions of history and language against the appreciators of the feminine versions of history and language—such is our dialectical method. The objectivity stems from appreciating opposing facets of a given phenomenon, not from a sadistic, detached coolness taken toward one's subject matter. And of course, plenty of old-fashioned documentation shall be offered for the arguments that are put forth.

## THE PLAN OF THE PRESENT STUDY

The aim in the present book is to disengage Durkheim from the false images of him as a status quo functionalist and to portray him as a kind of critical theorist whose texts are typical of the cultural ambiance of the previous *fin de siècle*. Durkheim's ambitions, insights, and talents in demystification paralleled those of Thorstein Veblen, Henry Adams, Carl Gustav Jung, and Theodor Adorno—among many other critics of the modernist project, of course. These are among the thinkers who were chosen to act as foils to Durkheim's sociology in order to highlight Durkheim's relevance to the postmodernist debate. Of course, differences between them and Durkheim shall be cited as well, when appropriate.

Thorstein Veblen (1857–1929) is ranked among the most famous American classical founders of sociology, although he was trained in philosophy, and also passes for an economist. David Riesman has captured the gist of Veblen's daring, satirical contribution to sociology with the line that "modern society was, in its essential tone, only a latter-day barbarism" (1964:391). The German philosopher, Theodor Adorno (1903–1969), is regarded as one of the most important members of the

Frankfurt school of critical sociologists. Like Veblen, Adorno argued that the Enlightenment tradition upon which modernity is based can lead to widespread barbarism. Carl Gustav Jung (1875–1961) was Freud's most famous disciple. Jung was also concerned with the seemingly paradoxical place of barbarism within the modernist project, and wrote about the need to reconcile opposing psychic forces in order to achieve some modicum of mental balance. Finally, Henry Adams (1838–1918) was an American historian who was also profoundly suspicious and critical of modernity. All of these thinkers, including Veblen, were influenced by the German school of Romantic philosophy.

The choice of these particular intellectuals to serve as foils for Durkheim's sociology is somewhat arbitrary, of course, as all such choices must be. It is not meant to imply that other *fin de siècle* thinkers would not serve as adequate foils. On the contrary, in previous works I have compared and contrasted Durkheim with Freud, Simmel, Nietzsche, Baudelaire, and Tonnies (Meštrović 1988, 1991). And in this book, I shall not hesitate to invoke H. G. Wells, Bachofen, Bellamy, Spengler, Sorokin, or any other thinker who will help to throw Durkheim's thought into its historical and cultural context. Whichever *fin de siècle* thinker one chooses, it is helpful to follow this strategy in order to highlight the radical, critical, liberal aspects of Durkheim's social thought, because of the deeply engraved yet false image of him as a conservative thinker.

Nevertheless, these thinkers were chosen primarily because they share with Durkheim the context of German Romanticism.[8] This strategy, which flows from the insight that the world is will *and* idea, focuses on antinomies that preclude any simplistic resolution to the dilemmas that beset postmodern discourse: order versus chaos, discipline versus freedom, unity versus multiplicity, heart versus mind, altruism versus egoism, among many others.

The German Romantic philosophical tradition highlights Kant, Bachofen, Hegel, Schopenhauer, and Nietzsche, among others. All of them challenged the easy optimism found in Anglo-American theories of progress and utilitarianism. Kant argued that one could never know reality, only representations of it. Bachofen reversed the patriarchal view of history with a matriarchal view. Hegel laid the groundwork for sociology by suggesting that societies and history itself possess a sort of consciousness or hidden intent. And Nietzsche exposed the will to power that lurks beneath the appearances of democracy. Nevertheless, we shall emphasize Schopenhauer over all the others for the simple reason that he encapsulates the most extreme version of German Romanticism's rebellion against the Enlightenment: He reversed the Enlightenment understanding that the mind can rule the passions by claiming that the will or passions rule the mind. For this reason, the German sociologist-philosopher, Georg Simmel ([1907] 1986:53), regarded Schopenhauer as the philosopher who gave the previous *fin de siècle* its "signature," and we concur.

Obviously, German Romanticism poses a serious threat to the assumptions shared by many modernists. Durkheim and Schopenhauer are neglected in the postmodernist discourse probably because they pose the most serious threat to the doctrines of progress and social order that are the staple of Enlightenment narratives. For this reason, Durkheim was *assimilated* into mainstream sociology—with all the overtones of absorbing a dangerous, foreign substance discussed by Bauman (1990)—in a manner that is exactly opposite to his intentions, as the prince of positivism and defender of status quo functionalism. These accolades ensure his place of honor in introductory textbooks, but ensure also that most sociologists will not take seriously his moralism and criticisms of capitalism as well as socialism. Schopenhauer's disciple Nietzsche can be discussed because he went mad, after all, so that his criticisms of modernity need not be taken all that seriously. But Schopenhauer remained sane, and his influence extends from Durkheim to Henry Adams, to the many serious thinkers who observed degeneration and decadence alongside progress. For this reason, most contemporary writers skip from Kant to Hegel to Nietzsche as if Schopenhauer never existed. And if they refer to Durkheim, they depict him as the enemy of postmodern fragmentation, as one of those old-fashioned defenders of rational social order that they seek to deconstruct.

In fact, Durkheim and Schopenhauer rejected the high place ascribed to human rationality by the Enlightenment's defenders from Kant to Hegel. Durkheim established society as the ground and referent for Kantian, a priori rationality, and Schopenhauer taught that the will was the ground for reason. Durkheim and Schopenhauer both dethroned the Enlightenment's worship of reason with a capital R. For them, the social world is one's idea, a system of representations beneath which lies irrationality. Those who took them seriously realized that the intellectual's new task was not the discovery of order in the universe, but the decoding, deconstruction, and interpretation of human culture conceived as a human product. They were postmodern long before the term could be conceived.

But they were not nihilists. They pointed to a ground or referent that the postmodernists either deny or seek—the will to life. The will to life is the dynamic, organic, inexorable driving force beneath *culture* that also animates the entire universe. To claim that the will, *not* human rationality, is the ground for human existence is to change the tenor of the present discourse dramatically. Durkheim and Schopenhauer will find in the social world fragmentation *and* integration, progress *and* pessimism, harmony *and* flux—in sum, they will focus on dualisms and antinomies of many sorts that must be balanced and reconciled. Thus, their social order is not the sort that postmodernists rebel against, or even recognize. One cannot characterize them as liberal or conservative, just existential.

Thus, a number of Durkheimian concepts relate directly to major concerns expressed by writers on postmodernism, and I shall take them up here for brief review in the rough order that they shall be treated in subsequent chapters: Durkheim's concept of anomie stems from Schopenhauer's concept of the "infinity of desires," and relates to Daniel Bell's (1976) notion of an unfettered will, to Veblen's (1899) conspicuous waste and consumption, and to Adorno's (1991) claim that the modern person regresses to an infantile condition of infinite wants that are never satisfied. The cardinal point here is that anomie afflicts the core of society, not its deviant subcultures, as taught by the functionalists following Merton (1957). The psychological accompaniments to *anomie* relate to the long discussions on postmodern cynicism and blasé indifference that accompanies narcissism (see Sloterdijk 1987). But, while Durkheim sought to control anomie he also recognized that it is indispensable to social progress. His thought in this regard, as in others, is complex and profound.

Durkheim's notion of *collective representations* sheds new light on the discussion of "hyperreality," because Durkheim denied that any "reality" is "objective" in the positivistic sense; yet he also managed to avoid the extreme relativism that leads some into nihilism. He managed to find a ground and referent for representations, even if the ground is dynamic and in constant flux. This aspect of Durkheim's sociology relates directly to Adorno's (1991) notion of "the culture industry" as well as the "mass society" concept found in the works of other critical theorists. Additionally, Durkheim, Veblen, Henry Adams, and many of Durkheim's other contemporaries used the word *habit* frequently to denote the power of past representations to carry over into the modern present. They implied a dialectic between centripetal and centrifugal forces that renders all visions of unilateral progress as childishly simple.

The notion of collective representations also enabled Durkheim to discuss *culture* as a phenomenon that is relatively autonomous of its "material substratum," yet not free-floating, as in Baudrillard's scheme of things. Durkheim's notion of *homo duplex* or the dualism of human nature enabled him to trace the relationship of collective ideas and symbols to the underlying will (from Schopenhauer). He exposed a dialectic between will and idea that is every bit as complex as that of Adorno and other critical theorists, and that lends itself to more subtle analysis and application than are found in current discussions of the nonreferential circulation of ideas that is supposed to characterize postmodernism.

Durkheim's neglected writings on language throw into a new perspective the postmodernist discussions of epistemology, circulating fictions (from Baudrillard), and the efforts by Habermas and his followers to establish morality upon rational communication. Like Veblen and Adorno, Durkheim was mindful of the power of language to distort and obfuscate "reality" at the same time that language is a resume of the collective wisdom of the past, the ultimate seat of a culture's "habits of the heart" (from Tocqueville and Bellah) as well as "habits of the mind" (from Veblen). Durkheim's curious treatment of religion as a system of collective representations that does not need to refer to a male deity, dogma, or patriarchal subservience, and that is the *womb* that gave birth to all other social institutions, is radical. It allows one to reexamine Bellah's controversial usage of the concept of "civil religion" as well as the implicit chauvinism in most contemporary accounts of religion criticized by Veblen. Like Veblen and Henry Adams, Durkheim was advocating a religious system that would balance masculine and feminine elements, justice and mercy, Christian love and the emancipation of the individual.

Durkheim's discussion of suicide parallels Baudelaire's and Benjamin's focus on suicide as an inevitable aspect of modernity. Schopenhauer was the first major philosopher to declare that suicide is less the act of rational choice and more the unwitting result of excessive desires that exhaust the individual in a never-ending and futile chase for ultimate satisfaction and happiness. We see here, again, the foreshadowing of Veblen's searing critique of the pursuit of useless ornamentation, characteristic of the leisure class, which leads ultimately to moral fatigue. More importantly, Durkheim used suicide as a vehicle for discussing wide-ranging themes that pertain to the individual's morale in a modern society. Along with Simmel, Durkheim was among sociology's first existentialists.

Durkheim's notion of the "cult of the individual" can be related to some postmodernist themes of openness and the challenging of oppressive narratives from the Enlightenment. It betrays his moralist, liberal, utopian—even Christian—leanings, despite his high regard for tradition, in a manner that is similar to Veblen's, Adams's, and Adorno's seemingly contradictory humanism. Durkheim, Veblen, and Adorno sought efficiency and progress even as they longed for the restoration of altruism, sympathy, and morality, which they felt preceded the onset of "civilization"—and this apparently contradictory stance has bewildered their critics as well as their admirers.

Schopenhauer's philosophy was *the* philosophy of the previous *fin de siècle* according to Ellenberger (1970), Janik and Toulmin (1973), Magee (1983), Mann ([1939] 1955), Simmel ([1907] 1986), and many others. Schopenhauer was Kant's most formidable challenger, and introduced the concept of the will as the tyranny of the passions that breaks through the paltry barriers set up by the mind worshipped by the Enlightenment. In this sense, Schopenhauer foreshadowed the discoveries made by Durkheim, Veblen, Adorno, Adams, Jung, Freud, and many others of the hidden irrationalities that animate what is supposed to be efficient, modern, rational life. This is because Schopenhauer made the claim that the will is stronger than the mind and rationality the cornerstone of his philosophical system. He was the first to observe that suicide becomes a problem for modern humans not only despite their enlightenment and bourgeois comfort, but *because* of them. The will is infinite and insatiable such that the more objects of desire one attains, the more one desires, and one is left unhappy even if materially well-off. And it was Schopenhauer, not Kant, Nietzsche, Hegel, or the other philosophers typically cited by intellectuals engaged in the postmodernist discourse, who first proclaimed that "the world is my idea," a revolutionary statement that continues to affect how we conceptualize language, thought, religion, and other symbolic forms essential to communication.

I shall make no effort to demonstrate any sort of direct link between Schopenhauer's philosophy and the cultural criticisms made by Durkheim, Veblen, Adams, Adorno, Jung, and others that shall be discussed here. According to Ellenberger (1970), the *fin de siècle* spirit coincided with the incredible popularity of Schopenhauer's philosophy in Western Europe from the 1880s to the turn of the century, and is characterized by emphases upon the themes of pessimism, estheticism, eroticism, and mysticism. Thus, the intellectuals I shall be considering had to absorb Schopenhauer's legacy—along with Nietzsche—by virtue of their proximity. It is fruitful to compare and contrast the contemporary *fin de siècle* spirit with these themes. I shall imply throughout this book that postmodernism is a feeble attempt to regain and restore these irrational antidotes to the excessive belief in Enlightenment progress, optimism, efficiency, and rationality. And it would not be necessary to rebel against the Enlightenment project were it not the case that this project carries within it barbaric, violent, and other disturbing tendencies that lead to civilization and its discontents. Hence, postmodern estheticism frequently degenerates into *kitsch*; eroticism is lost in the tendency to blur the distinction between the sexes; mysticism is smuggled into mass consumption via New Age paraphernalia—among the many other contradictory and perhaps frightening aspects of postmodern culture. The unconscious reason why so many thinkers from the previous *fin de siècle* are invoked in contemporary discussions of postmodernism is that they fill the lacunae of today's dismally one-sided social theory.

## NOTES

1. Baudrillard writes, "Consumption is the virtual totality of all objects and messages presently constituted in a more or less coherent discourse" (1988:22).

2. Baudrillard writes that in Nietzsche's time, philosophers believed that there was a sense of things that lay beyond them, but "there is nothing like that today, things merely follow on in a flabby order that leads nowhere" (1986:72). America, in particular, is "the world center of the inauthentic" (p. 109).

3. According to Gane, "With Baudrillard, then, we are not in the presence of a romantic; quite the contrary. here we are faced with a theorist who seeks to find a provocative, cruel face of hyperrealism" (1991:62).

4. By this I mean that the notion of "endings" is taken from the natural sciences, which purport to treat inanimate phenomena in the cold language of causes and effects. By contrast, organic phenomena cannot "end," although they do "die," only to be reborn in another form. Spengler and Sorokin take such an organic approach to history and culture. The closest that Spengler comes to the equivalent of Baudrillard's "end" of history is the following: "Man is not only historyless before the birth of the Culture, but again becomes so as soon as a Civilization has worked itself out fully to the definitive form which betokens the end of the living development of the Culture and the exhaustion of the last potentialities of its significant existence" ([1928] 1961:48).

5. But of course, it is possible to read Nietzsche in a way that completely contradicts this reading. See Graybeal's (1990) *Language and the Feminine in Nietzsche and Heidegger*.

6. It is worth noting that except for Harry Alpert (1938), most of Durkheim's subsequent commentators have accused him of committing almost every error of scholarship that can be conceived. This negative, destructive attitude toward Durkheim deserves to be analyzed in its own right, and cannot be rationalized as being objective. It is one-sided, hence subjective and distorted.

7. See Dugger (984), Eff (1989), Kennedy (1987), Leathers (1986), Posnock (1987), Strenski (1987), and Waller (1988), among others.

8. See Leathers (1986), Mestrovic (1988), Partenheimer (1988), Riesman (1953, 1964).

Chapter 2

# Rediscovering the Romantic Origins of Feminism

The feminine voice is one of the most important voices that is missing in most Western accounts of culture, and feminism constitutes one of the most significant anti-Enlightenment narratives found in postmodernist discourse. Especially from the 1960s to the present, various feminist writers have exposed the hidden, patriarchal, authoritarian voice in what passes for Western rationality, justice, and culture (Eisler 1987; Gadon 1989; Game 1991). But not surprisingly, even the feminist movement betrays the contradictory characteristics of what is termed postmodernism. The most important point of contention is the extent to which femininity should be associated with women or with humans regardless of gender.

For example, women have made unprecedented gains in securing a legal status that is approaching equality with men, but Adorno (1991) is critical of this apparent gain on the grounds that "mass society" is all too willing to absorb women and minorities into its capitalist clutches. In the 1990s, postmodernist culture industry still portrays women as willing, mindless sex objects and trophies for men, and Baudrillard (1990) has reduced women to nothing more than seducers. But these are the same barbaric trends that Veblen exposed in 1899 in *The Theory of the Leisure Class* ([1899] 1967), which now apply to the vast middle class. For example, *Playboy* centerfolds frequently disclose the fact that they consider themselves feminists. Instead of humanizing and softening male machismo, the culture industry has been bombarding the present *fin de siècle* generation with images of tough women who are able to compete with men on their traditional and quite aggressive turf. Using Veblen (1948, 1973), one notices that postmodern culture communicates the entrance of women into the traditionally male, barbaric, social world that glorifies liquor and intoxicants, war, hunting, sports, and religion.

Consider the Virginia Slims cigarette advertisement slogan, "You've come a long way baby," from Veblen's perspective: It glorifies the self-destructive and prestigious act of smoking cigarettes, which used to be confined to the male leisure class. The fact that women are increasingly entering the military and sports professions means that they are adopting the predatory "habits of the fight" that he criticized with regard to males. He wanted men and women to become *productive* and peaceful— even Christian, in the "highest" sense of the term[1] (see Leathers 1986)— and did not encourage equality between the sexes on predatory grounds. Advertisements typically portray women as construction workers to indicate the gains that women have made relative to males, but it is rare to find an image of a male nurse or social worker, because postmodern culture still finds "female work" demeaning—and this, despite decades of feminist consciousness raising.

My aim in this book is to hark back to the origins of the feminist revolt against patriarchal culture that occurred in 1861 with J. J. Bachofen's book on mother-right ([1861] 1967), which influenced Veblen, Durkheim, Jung, Adams, and other intellectuals from the previous turn of the century. Like so many other contemporary phenomena, feminism's roots are typically distorted as having originated with the liberal and Enlightenment traditions, with little discussion of the Romantic tradition. One suspects that the true version must involve both sides of the heart-mind dualism. The logic of my strategy is this: If one is to take seriously postmodernist claims that it rebels against Eurocentric, patriarchal, Enlightenment narratives, then one must note that this rebellion is not new, but began in the previous century. A comparison and contrast of how the culture industry portrays feminism in the present *fin de siècle* with the previous *fin de siècle* gives one a fresh perspective and, hopefully, solutions to the many apparent contradictions and paradoxes that beset postmodernist discourse.

The central difference between then and now is that the locus of masculine versus feminine images has shifted dramatically: Bachofen and his disciples believed that men and women share equally in masculine and feminine traits, whereas the postmodernist culture industry uses feminism to uphold essentially masculine images and values. Another way to phrase this is that Bachofen wrote in the Romantic era, which sought to balance heart with mind, whereas our *fin de siècle* is still moving in a decidedly positivistic, barbaric direction toward a dominance of the mind and "habits of the fight" even as it pays lip service to postmodernist and feminist rebellions.

A good example of how the feminist movement of only a generation ago stalled is Carol Gilligan's (1982) search for an alternative to Lawrence Kohlberg's, Piaget's, Habermas's and others' masculine versions of morality based on rational deliberation, supposedly universal principles of distributive justice, and utilitarian calculation.[2] Gilligan and others have argued that the concept of caring, not rational justice, constitutes the core of feminine morality.[3] But other feminist writers criticized Gilligan and the notion of a caring feminine voice as a weak, even false, alternative to the masculine, Enlightenment voice. Recourse to a feminine mystique is perceived by many feminists as continuation of the suppression of females relative to the masculine culture that is criticized (Fraser and Nicholson 1988). Thus, feminists in the present *fin de siècle* are decidedly split on the issue whether women should emulate barbaric, male toughness, rationality, and worldly, public success based on Enlightenment narratives, or whether they should humanize and feminize the masculine narratives.

A relatively neglected path in the eventual resolution of this polemic is that masculinity and femininity exist independently of gender. Carl Gustav Jung, in particular, crystallized this approach by referring to masculine and feminine archetypes and psychic forces that must be reconciled in males as well as females. Similarly, Durkheim conceived of society in the masculine terms of duty and constraint as well as the feminine terms of sympathy and nurturance. Of course, this modest step forward still leaves intact the widespread bias against the feminine aspects of the psyche as well as society. But at least it allows one to avoid the war between the sexes.

## REEXAMINING BACHOFEN'S LEGACY

Scholars agree that in 1861 J. J. Bachofen fired the first salvo at the Europe-centered, patriarchal representation of history and anthropology found in the works of Fustel de Coulanges, Maine, Jhering, and other nineteenth-century philosophers. Bachofen ([1861] 1967) wrote in the German Romantic, counter-Enlightenment vein that inspired Schopenhauer, Nietzsche, Herder, Tonnies, Durkheim, Veblen, Adams, the critical theorists, and others who were suspicious of the triumph of the Apollonian over the Dionysian principle, and that sought a balance between these opposing forces. Bachofen championed empathy and the heart over rational deliberation and the mind, a cause that is typical of Romantic philosophers from Schopenhauer to Nietzsche. His influence ranges from Henry Adams's discovery of the power of the Virgin versus that of the dynamo, to Jung's forceful emphasis on self-conscious reconciliation with the Great Mother archetype that lurks in the collective unconscious of males and females equally. Bachofen concluded that matriarchy preceded patriarchy, and is superior to patriarchy on moral grounds. One detects the echo of Bachofen in Eisler's argument in *The Chalice and the Blade* (1987).

Adorno, Simmel, Veblen, Durkheim, and the critical theorists warn that mass society's culture industry is violently hostile toward any notion of tenderheartedness. In Adorno's words, "in spite of all sententious humanitarianism, the obedient adept [in mass society] becomes ever colder, harder and more pitiless" (1991:79). Similarly, Simmel observed that "perhaps the most neglected of all the great vital issues has been love—as though this were an incidental matter, a mere adventure of the subjective soul, unworthy of the seriousness and rigorous objectivity of philosophical endeavor" (1971:235). Even Veblen admitted, "Where life is largely a struggle between individuals within the group, the possession of the ancient peaceable traits in a marked degree would hamper an individual in the struggle for life" ([1899] 1967:223). More than these other theorists, Durkheim ardently and consistently raged against egoism and promoted altruism, empathy, and other qualities that promote social solidarity (see Durkheim [1925] 1961). Thus, it is not surprising that most contemporary scholars hardly ever mention Bachofen, and when they do, their reaction is hostile. Simmel's essay on Platonic versus modern Eros is typically ignored. Veblen, Adorno, and Durkheim are decidedly out of fashion today compared with theorists who promote egoistic "rational-choice theory" or some other variant of the will to power.

It is important to realize that the question whether matriarchy preceded patriarchy is absolutely insoluble on positivistic grounds: Scholars will never have sufficient access to prehistoric data to settle the matter. The question is important on the level of myth, collective imagery, and communication, not factual evidence. In this regard, it is significant that Bachofen's myth of the feminine origins of history dominated up to the previous *fin de siècle*, whereas our *fin de siècle* continues to be dominated by the patriarchal myth.

Thus, contemporary anthropologists who mention Bachofen conclude that he was incorrect in claiming that matriarchy is older than patriarchy *even though* they admit that the issue can never be resolved because it involves prehistory (Greisman 1981). Bachofen's more significant and completely unpositivistic claim—that matriarchy is morally superior to patriarchy—tends to be obscured, even though it is the more important point. According to Bachofen:

> How significant become all those examples of loyalty to mothers and sisters; of men inspired by the peril or death of a sister to undertake the gravest hardships; and, finally, of pairs of sisters who stand out as univer-

sal prototypes. Yet the love that arises from motherhood is not only more intense, but also more universal. . . . Whereas the paternal principle is inherently restrictive, the maternal principle is universal; the paternal principle implies limitation to definite groups, but the maternal principle, like the life of nature, knows no barriers. The idea of motherhood produces a sense of universal fraternity among all men, which dies with the development of paternity. The family based on father right is a closed individual organism, whereas the matriarchal family signifies the typically universal character that stands at the beginning of all development and distinguishes material life from higher spiritual life. Every mother's womb, the mortal image of the earth mother Demeter, will give brothers and sisters to the children of every other woman; the homeland will know only brothers and sisters until the day when the development of the paternal system dissolves the undifferentiated unity of the mass and introduces a principle of articulation. ([1861] 1967:80)

Positivistically inclined scholars conclude that if Bachofen's theory holds any merit, it is on the grounds that it constitutes a myth that some feminists and other writers have invoked—but the positivists use *myth* in a pejorative sense (see Cantarella 1982). Indeed, Bachofen's myth of a peaceful, utopian, matriarchal, egalitarian past was assumed, although never proved, by Veblen (see the discussion by Riesman 1953). It is implied by Durkheim's sociology, and was invoked briefly by some feminists in the 1960s in the United States, by the Green movement in Western Europe, by some Scandinavian feminist groups, and by some fringe elements of the contemporary postmodernist movement: ecofeminists, New Age healers, some Jungian feminists, and pagan Goddess worshippers in California (Gadon 1989). But overall, the feminist movement has not embraced the large-scale revival of Goddess worship, and Bachofen's legacy for the 1990s is ambiguous at best.

Some feminists have argued the obvious point that mothers influence children at their most impressionable age far more than fathers ever could, implying a universal, albeit limited matriarchy (Levy 1989). Yet, despite mountains of research data on other aspects of socialization, surprisingly little is known of what mothers actually teach their children compared with fathers.

The attitude toward Bachofen is curious. To dismiss his theory as mere myth—as opposed to positivistic fact—is hypocritical, given that the patriarchal story of the origins of humanity is equally impossible to prove, and equally mythical. After all, the same dearth of hard data from prehistory precludes an easy solution to the question whether humanity was originally promiscuous, matriarchal, or patriarchal. We are dealing here with Durkheimian *collective representations*, not hard facts. Postmodern writers challenge the Enlightenment narrative of history precisely on the issue that it is a myth like other myths.

The dismissal of Bachofen on positivistic grounds is unsatisfactory even on positivistic grounds. First, it assumes the kind of circular reasoning that Bachofen criticized in the first place, because it assumes a factual world order of positivistic truths, whereas Bachofen analyzed ancient religious art, myths, and other collective *representations* on the basis that they are "fictions."[4] Like many other Romantics, Bachofen was rebelling against patriarchal positivism. Second, even if Bachofen was wrong regarding one minute, positivist aspect of his theory—that matriarchy preceded patriarchy in the contemporary sense of these terms— or even several details, this does not affect the import of the remainder of his Romantically informed theory, that in *some* past historical epochs, women were perceived as sources of life and purity, whereas from Genesis to the present, women are defined in official Christian dogma as the cause of Adam's fall, and humanity's struggle with original sin (see Atkinson, Buchanan, and Miles 1985; Daly 1978; Turner 1987). The important point is that Bachofen's portrait of earth-centered, body-centered, sensual, egalitarian, Dionysian aspects of life has been abolished with the advent of modernist, taken-for-granted, collective representations that God is male, Apollonian, abstract, lives in the sky (as opposed to the earth), and creates out of nothing. To repeat, the question of the teleological origins of humanity with respect to matriarchy or patriarchy is impossible to prove. The same scholars who universally discredit Bachofen's theory also admit that evidence for the worship of female deities in the world is overwhelming—but that is the essential point of Bachofen's theory.

Third, and most important, the positivistic, neo-Enlightenment critiques of Bachofen dismiss the verifiable impact that Bachofen exhibited on important *fin de siècle* thinkers, social movements, and other collective representations.

For example, scholars agree that Bachofen influenced directly and strongly Marx, Engels, Nietzsche, Veblen, Frazer, Kropotkin, Wilhelm Reich, Erich Fromm, Lewis Morgan, Mary Daly, the expressionist O. Gross, and many feminists from the previous *fin de siècle*.[5] Freud and his followers, Jung, Rank, Fromm, and Suttie, as well as Durkheim, Malinowski, Simmel, Tonnies, and other important precursors of contemporary social science, were also influenced by Bachofen's thesis.[6]

For example, Marx's utopian vision of archaic family and social life as peaceful and egalitarian prior to the establishment of an organized division of labor is drawn from Bachofen (see Fluehr 1987). In *The Origin of the Family, Private Property and the State*, Friedrich Engels invokes Bachofen's "myth" to conclude that the transition from mother-right to patriarchy was one of the most decisive revolutions ever experienced by humanity, that "the overthrow of mother-right was the *world historical defeat of the female sex*" ([1884] 1972:14, emphasis in original).

Nietzsche's influential notion of Dionysian, feminine religion is drawn directly from Bachofen. In his neglected and misunderstood *Theory of the Leisure Class*, Thorstein Veblen ([1899] 1967) drew on Bachofen to assume that the leisure class is a throwback to the predatory habits of the barbarian stage in which women were perceived as trophies to be won through war and later displayed conspicuously as a sign of prowess. He assumed that women were equal in status with men prior to the barbarian stage and that society did not care who had fathered the children. Throughout his writings, Veblen (1948, 1973) assumes that men, not women, tend toward idleness, gossip, and conspicuous leisure.

Erich Fromm and Michael Maccoby (1970) praised Bachofen as part of their critique of Freud's male-centered psychoanalysis.[7] Fromm (1955, 1962, 1963) made the distinction between mother-centered and father-centered cultures a key aspect of his efforts to synthesize Freud and Marx, psychology and sociology.

The German expressionist O. Gross considered the psychology of the unconscious as essentially feminine and vitally important to the undermining of authoritarian patriarchy and the renewal of a matriarchal society (see Mitzman 1977). It is true that in *Totem and Taboo* ([1912] 1950), *The Future of an Illusion* ([1927] 1955), and his other writings on religion, Freud depicted totemism and Christianity as derivatives of unconscious patricidal fantasies—women seem irrelevant to his theory. Yet, despite Fromm's and Jung's differences with Freud on the centrality of patriarchy, Vitz (1988) has recently demonstrated the role of Freud's own Christian unconscious, including the influence of matriarchal, Roman Catholic culture even upon his decidedly patriarchal ideas on religion, which many of his followers rejected. The important point is that even Freud's dispute with his followers can be reappreciated in the context of Bachofen's legacy.

James Frazer's *The Golden Bough* ([1890] 1981) drew its inspiration from Bachofen, and was immensely influential upon Freud, Durkheim, Jung, and other *fin de siècle* social theorists of religion. Jung made the feminine archetype a universal element of his depth psychology. Durkheim ([1912] 1965) regarded religion itself as the "sacral womb" from which are derived all the other social institutions. Ellenberger (1970) has already suggested that the concept of the unconscious, which was important to most *fin de siècle* thinkers, is derived from the same Romantic, counter-Enlightenment worldview that led Bachofen to challenge the patriarchal version of a hyperrational, conscious, Enlightenment narrative. Pessimism, estheticism, eroticism, and mysticism, which Ellenberger regarded as the chief characteristics of the *fin de siècle* spirit, were related by scores of literary writers to the tension between masculine versus feminine archetypes.[8]

Ferdinand Tonnies ([1887] 1963) derived the entire philosophy of his notion of *Gemeinschaft* (community) from the mother-child relationship: The individual's relationship to *Gemeinschaft* is based on motherly love, as opposed to the abstract, emotionally cold social relationships found in *Gesellschaft* (society). Tonnies ([1921] 1974) also digested and commented upon Marx's own stand on the implicit matriarchy of precapitalist *Gemeinschaft*. In sum, Tonnies was echoing Bachofen in criticizing the onset of modern urbanism as the transition from feminine to masculine social forces. But who reads Tonnies anymore?

Emile Durkheim reviewed, commented upon, and responded to Tonnies, Marx, and their influence on Marianne Weber in his own scattered writings on matriarchy, the origins of the family, and the war between the sexes.[9] It is noteworthy that Durkheim seems to have accepted Bachofen's myth that humanity evolved from a promiscuous clan, to the establishment of the family on mother-centered principles, to patriarchy.

In general, the interconnections among towering intellectual figures from the previous *fin de siècle* regarding the influence of matriarchal thinking upon the rest of their social theories are intricate and extensive. It is certainly false to dismiss these thinkers as bourgeois chauvinists, even if it is reasonable to conclude that they were not feminist in their orientations by contemporary standards (see Kandal 1988). Compared with the one-sided dominance of contemporary positivism, they were at least aware of Romantic counterarguments to masculine, positivist narratives spun from the Enlightenment.[10]

These are among the issues and controversies that are exposed when the current of postmodern feminism is traced back to its most important recent source. Bachofen is disparaged even by feminists who repeat, unwittingly, the essential elements of his discovery. And the most important aspect of that discovery, for the purposes of the present discussion, is that the feminine aspects of culture, history, and society are older than and superior to the modern and, by implication, postmodern and masculine aspects of these same phenomena.


## THE DYNAMO AND THE VIRGIN REVISITED

One of the most interesting refractions of Bachofen is found in the work of the American novelist and historian, Henry Adams. In "The Dynamo and the Virgin," Henry Adams ([1900] 1983) used the Great

Exposition of 1900 to suggest that modernity is symbolized by the power of the dynamo, whereas medieval European culture derived its "power" from the Virgin. He points to representations of the Virgin at Chartres, Notre Dame, the Louvre, and other well-known landmarks to conclude that she was the highest energy ever known to man, the creator of four fifths of his noblest art, exercising vastly more attraction over the human mind than all the steam engines and dynamos ever dreamed of; and yet this energy was unknown to the American mind. An American Virgin would never dare command; an American Venus would never dare exist. He went so far as to conclude that because of their one-sided estimation of the dynamo, Americans do not really think (Adams [1900] 1983:1071).

In "The Education of Henry Adams in German Philosophy," David Partenheimer (1988) traces Adams's pessimism and passion for antinomies to German Romanticism, especially the works of Schopenhauer and von Hartmann. Adams's American contemporaries were smitten with the notions of progress and Social Darwinism (see Wells 1906), convinced that "Anglo-American civilization represented the highest point mankind had ever reached, that the reign of rationality could be painlessly achieved through the expansion of industrial capitalism, that material improvement meant moral advance as well" (Lears 1983:85).

But Adams was concerned with the questions: Is the universe ordered or chaotic? Is it spiritual or material? Is there progress or decline? I want to suggest that even if Durkheim and Adams never read each other, Durkheim was concerned with similar questions, because the European *fin de siècle* spirit pushed these questions—which are derived from Bachofen's discovery—into the forefront of intellectual discussion. Moreover, these and similar questions that touch on degeneration versus progress are implicit in the postmodernist discourse (see Moreland 1989). For example, the collapse of communism in Eastern Europe and the USSR in the midst of the postmodern debate has brought out the same unilateral optimism that capitalism "won" the race against socialism, and will save the world. Along these lines, Fukuyama (1990, 1992) has proclaimed the "end of history," by which he means that the capitalist, liberal ideology of Western societies will now become globalized. We need to remember Durkheim, Henry Adams, and other intellectuals from the previous *fin de siècle* to ensure any semblance of an objective, balanced appraisal of the current situation.

No serious scholar would challenge the claim that the Madonna with the infant Jesus constitutes *the* symbol of the Middle Ages in Western Europe. Bachofen, Adams, and Durkheim lived and wrote in an age that still derived its power from the Virgin Mother,[11] and in which the dynamo was only beginning to appear. Similarly, Durkheim, Veblen, Adams,

Schopenhauer, Jung, and the other *fin de siècle* thinkers we are using in the present discussion were able to discern more clearly than we can the dividing line between power based on the Virgin versus that based on the dynamo. Moreover, contemporary Eastern European culture is still dominated by the Virgin more than by the dynamo, through the Roman Catholic and various Orthodox churches, as well as the "habits of the heart" of the Slavic people, which are decidedly mother-centered. In general, the indigenous culture that survived communism is still essentially medieval. Far from witnessing signs of the end of history, formerly communist nations are stepping back into history. Meanwhile, contemporary Western Europe is increasingly becoming more like the dynamo-centered America that Henry Adams "discovered" in 1900. And the America of the coming *fin de siècle*—which fascinates Baudrillard (1986) and other postmodernists—is more dynamic and less mindful of the Virgin than ever. The question that begs an answer in postmodernist discourse is the following: Does postmodernist discourse derive its metaphorical, cultural power from the dynamo or the Virgin? The answer to this question makes all the difference in determining whether postmodernism constitutes a genuine rebellion against Enlightenment narratives, or is merely an extension of these same patriarchal narratives.

This contrast in cultural outlooks exposed by Bachofen and Henry Adams is stark and obvious, even if it is taken for granted and hardly ever mentioned in postmodern discourse. Foreshadowing Adams, Bachofen captures many of these aspects in this intriguing passage:

> The homogeneity of matriarchal ideas is confirmed by the favoring of the left over the right side. The left side belongs to the passive feminine principle, the right to the active masculine principle. The role played by the left hand of Isis in matriarchal Egypt suffices to make the connection clear. But a multitude of additional data prove its importance, universality, primordiality, and freedom from the influence of philosophical speculation. Customs and practices of civil and religious life, peculiarities of clothing and headdress, and certain linguistic usages reveal the same idea, the *major honos laevarum partrium* (greater honor of the left side) and its close connection with mother right. Another no less significant manifestation of the same basic law is the primacy of the night over the day which issued from its womb. The opposite relation would be in direct contradiction to matriarchal ideas. Already the ancients identified the primacy of the night with that of the left, and both of these with the primacy of the mother. And here, too, age-old customs, the reckoning of time according to nights, the choice of the night as a time for battle, for taking counsel, for meting out justice, and for practicing the cult rites, show that we are not dealing with abstract philosophical ideas of later origin, but with the reality of an original mode of life. Extension of the same idea permits us to recognize the religious preference given to the moon over the sun, of the conceiving earth over the fecundating sea, of the dark aspect of death over

the luminous aspect of growth, of the dead over the living, of mourning over rejoicing, as necessary characteristics of the predominantly matriarchal age. In the course of our investigation all these traits will appear many times over and take on an increasingly profound meaning. ([1861] 1967:77)

Durkheim's follower Robert Hertz ([1907–1909] 1960) was also concerned with the distinction between left and right as collective representations that signify unconscious aspects of culture struggling to find harmony and balance. Hertz argues that in patriarchal, modern cultures, linguistic, religious, and other cultural usages ascribe sanctity to the right, while the more primitive left is considered profane and is consequently mutilated. More specifically, the right in patriarchal cultures represents masculinity, honor, prerogative, activity, and the sacred, while the left signifies femininity, scorn, dependence, passivity, and the profane.[12]

Bachofen, Adams, and the Durkheimians suggest that this reversal of the more ancient linkage between the left and sanctity constitutes evidence for the occurrence of a drastic transition from mother to father centeredness in history. It exposes tremendous lacunae in the modern and postmodern view of culture, which is still right-handed and patriarchal, despite all the talk of equality. The remainder of this book is dedicated to exposing the repressed role of the left hand in postmodern culture and discourse.

## NOTES

1.  Veblen was against Christianity and religion in general as honorific enterprises sought merely for status and prestige. But he praised Christianity's focus on asceticism, peace, and self-restraint.
2.  For a fuller discussion, see Balbus (1981), Bocock (1979), and Blum (1988), among many others.
3.  See also Cortese (1984, 1989) and Cortese and Meštrović (1990). Spengler ([1926] 1961) also discusses the emphasis placed on caring in mother-centered cultures, which he believes tends to disappear in late civilizations such as ours.
4.  This is similar to Vaihinger's ([1924] 1935) "as-if" philosophy, discussed by Kaern (1985).
5.  See Cantarella (1982), Engels ([1884] 1972), Fluehr (1987), Greisman (1981), Mitzman (1977), Riesman (1953), Schlegel (1984), and Veblen ([1899] 1967), among others.
6.  See Burston (1986) and Kramer, Jell, and Werts (1985).
7.  See also Bocock (1979) and Burston (1986).
8.  Refer to the novels of Hesse, Tolstoi, Conrad, Mann, Zola, Hardy, Proust, and others, also discussed by Magee (1983).
9.  See especially the reviews that Durkheim wrote for L'Annee sociologique, some of which are translated in Nandan (1970).

10.   However, some refractions of Bachofen's original thesis are negative, even decidedly sinister. According to Hermand (1984), the Nazis used Bachofen to glorify their cause that mothers should produce a pure Aryan race. The Nazis bastardized many philosophies and doctrines, and this fact should not necessarily be used against Bachofen. Daniel Patrick Moynihan's infamous report on black matriarchy as the root cause of family instability and high crime rates is another negative refraction of Bachofen's thesis, and continues to be repudiated by scholars. Even Fromm concluded that excessive mother-centeredness may lead to apathy and sloth as opposed to the father-centered "productive character orientation." Ultimately, he called for a blending of father-centered and mother-centered cultural orientations. It could be the case that Bachofen's thesis has been neglected or criticized at least in part because of the reaction to Nazism, along with sensitivity to the issues of racism and ethnocentrism—but there is no evidence that Bachofen's intentions were racist or ethnocentric.

11.   This is a seemingly contradictory image that has given rise to many debates, but that can survive in the "no-sense" atmosphere of postmodernism—see Woodman (1985).

12.   See also De Wolf (1970), Garrett (1977), and Matarasso (1973).

Chapter 3

---

# The Romantic Antecedents of
# Postmodern Culture and Sociology

It is an easily verifiable historical fact that sociology was born in the "soft," Romantic era in which Comte's positivism was no longer the strong social force that it once had been. *Fin de siècle* sociology drew more heavily on the then dominant anti-intellectualist writings of Schopenhauer, Bachofen, Bergson, James, and Nietzsche than any Enlightenment narratives. Freud, Simmel, Weber, Durkheim, Tonnies, and other leading turn-of-the-century European social thinkers were decidedly leaning more toward the feminine heart championed by Romanticism than the mind glorified by the Enlightenment. Yet Auguste Comte is hailed as the father of sociology, and the strength of positivism in the previous century is exaggerated in most sociological texts in order to justify positivism's hold on sociology in the present century.

Jung (1959) understood the unconscious itself to be the feminine aspect found in males and females. The very notion of social integration that was vulgarized by functionalism into "normative consensus" meant Romantic totality and synthesis, and implied sympathetic attachment to others (Alpert 1941). Henry Adams ([1900] 1983) makes us aware that degeneration always accompanies progress. Finally, the Romantic emphasis upon compassion needs to be recovered from the modernist tendencies to ignore the role of compassion in moral development, and to conceive of morality as solely a cognitive process that involves principles of justice alone, devoid of mercy (as found in the writings of Piaget, Kohlberg, and their followers). These insights, in turn, will pave the way for the overall effort in this book to develop a feminine alternative to the patriarchal narratives of the Enlightenment that are of concern to postmodern writers.

It is necessary to repeat that my use of the word *feminine* does not imply that only women are or ought to be feminine. Rather, following

Bachofen and Jung, I use *feminine* as an archetype, a collective representation that is found in cultures and societies as well as all persons, male
and female. Similarly, I am not concerned with chauvinism in general
nor as found in some of the Romantic writers I shall address. For example, Arthur Schopenhauer wrote with pathos in favor of compassion and
against pure rationality, yet he seems to have been a misogynist. This
fact may be troubling for some feminists, but is irrelevant for the purposes of the present discussion. This book is not about men and women,
but about feminine and masculine voices in the narratives spun from
and counter to the Enlightenment.

No discussion of postmodernist culture is complete without contrast-
ing the contemporary debates with the legacy of the previous turn of the
century. For example, Baudrillard (1981, 1988) draws on Veblen in his
critiques of postmodern culture as geared toward consumerism and signification without language, a systematic manipulation of signs without
rhyme or reason. But Baudrillard fails to incorporate Veblen's (1943)
model of maternal, altruistic society as an antidote to this distressing
state of affairs. For all his criticisms of the capitalist, purportedly enlightened social order, Baudrillard never transcends the pitiless, machismo logic upon which it is built. And he is deaf and blind to Veblen's
soft side, a non-nihilistic call to embrace the kernel of Christian ethics.

Similarly, Daniel Bell's (1976) sour attitude toward the irrational "un-
leashing of the will" in the 1960s does not account for the fact that
Schopenhauer had uncovered the concept of the will as early as 1818,
and that Schopenhauer managed to find a benign aspect to this irrational explosion of will, namely compassion, as well as the anomic aspect
that is condemned by conservative defenders of the Enlightenment
project. Bell is a staunch, one-sided, neoconservative defender of the
Enlightenment.

Similarly, in his efforts to complete the Enlightenment project, Jurgen
Habermas (1987) merely assumes, but does not prove, that irrationality
is always dangerous. This assumption ignores the positive as well as
negative derivatives of Schopenhauer's "will to life" refracted in Simmel's (1971) writings on "life" as a force that opposes "forms"; Nietzsche's ([1901] 1968) high regard for Dionysian forces; Tonnies's ([1887]
1963) searing critique of the "rational will" of *Gesellschaft* in favor of the
"natural will" of *Gemeinschaft*; Bergson's ([1932] 1954, 1944) *l'èlan vital*;
and other complex analyses of social development found in writings
from the previous *fin de siècle*.

In this chapter, we shall place Durkheim's sociology in its proper,
cultural context as a typical fragment of social commentary from the
previous *fin de siècle*. We shall explore some of the affinities of this sociology with other intellectual movements of the previous *fin de siècle* and

contrast, sharply, this contextual reading of Durkheim's sociology with the ahistorical, vulgar misreading of Durkheim found in Parsonian functionalism. It is *not* my intention to add even remotely to the many existing critiques of Parsons, because none of these aim at restoring the Romantic, contextual reading of sociology's origins. Rather, the Parsonian narrative must be criticized because it is spun from the Enlightenment narratives that postmodernism purports to rebel against; because it is the most popular source of secondary analyses of Durkheim's social thought; and because it continues to inform contemporary sociological writings. No genuine progress can be achieved in the many postmodernist debates until this implicit tautology is resolved, that Enlightenment narratives continue to be criticized while critics cling to Enlightenment narratives that are used to explain and apprehend the origins of sociology in general and Durkheim's sociology in particular.

It is also important to repeat that I shall be treating Schopenhauer's philosophy as a cultural artifact, a symbol of the previous *fin de siècle* spirit. I am not concerned with proving or disproving Schopenhauer's direct influence on Durkheim or anyone else. The Durkheimian approach to Schopenhauer (or any philosopher) suggests that influential leaders in any field are successful less because of their individual talents and more because they ride on the currents of collective representations. I agree with Simmel ([1907] 1986) that Schopenhauer symbolized and articulated the *fin de siècle* spirit. His anti-Enlightenment phiphilosophy is an antecedent to the postmodernist rebellion against the Enlightenment.

## SCHOPENHAUER'S NEGLECTED INFLUENCE UPON THE ORIGINS OF THE SOCIAL SCIENCES

According to Magee, "by the turn of the century, Schopenhauer was an all-pervading cultural influence" (1983:264). Even if one wants to argue that Magee's assessment is extreme, it must be conceded that it is a noteworthy assessment. Yet in contemporary sociological theory, Schopenhauer has been almost completely overlooked in the studies of the cultural influences on sociology. In his *Influence de la philosophie de Schopenhauer en France (1860–1900)*, Baillot (1927) demonstrates that even though Schopenhauer's main work was published in 1818, it was not until the 1860s that he began to be influential, and that his influence reached its zenith in France and the rest of Western Europe in the 1880s. Durkheim began publishing in the 1880s, and his most influential writings were published in the 1890s. He could not have missed

Schopenhauer, because French translations of Schopenhauer were advertised on the back covers of the Durkheimian books published by Felix Alcan. Nevertheless, Durkheim's sociology, in particular, has been read predominantly in the context of the Enlightenment and utilitarian philosophies, which he criticized vigorously, and which are being criticized again by postmodernists.

Durkheim's teacher, Charles Renouvier (1892:5), draws sharp battle lines between, on the one hand, Schopenhauer and the Romantics, and on the other, Leibniz, the English school of utilitarianism, as well as Diderot, Turgot, Condorcet, Saint-Simon, Fourier, Hegel, Comte, Stuart-Mill, and Spencer. In general, Durkheim is highly critical of many thinkers on Renouvier's list, especially Spencer, the utilitarians, and Saint-Simon (see Durkheim [1893] 1933, [1928] 1958). Given Durkheim's highly polemical style, it is noteworthy that Durkheim never criticizes Schopenhauer directly nor by implication. For the purposes of the present discussion, it is significant that the list of Enlightenment and utilitarian philosophers criticized by Durkheim and Schopenhauer is part of the same "grand narrative of the Enlightenment" that postmodernist philosophy purports to rebel against. The strange contradiction in this purported rebellion is that it cannot be a genuine revolt so long as contemporary writers continue to draw on the Enlightenment and utilitarian traditions in order to reform the Enlightenment legacy—an important tautology missed by many writers—and continue to ignore Schopenhauer, who sought anti-Enlightenment solutions.

Durkheim's nephew and collaborator, Marcel Mauss, refers to Durkheim as "the pupil of [Wilhelm] Wundt and [Thèodule] Ribot" ([1950] 1979a:12), and adds that Ribot was a friend of Alfred Espinas and Pierre Janet. All of these important *fin de siècle* thinkers are discussed by Ellenberger (1970) in the context of the influence of Schopenhauer's philosophy upon the previous turn-of-the-century's thought. Ribot is widely regarded as the founder of French psychology, but Ribot also published *La Philosophie de Schopenhauer* in 1874. It was among the first introductions of Schopenhauer's thought to French intellectuals. Filloux (1977:18) believes that Ribot's book was probably Durkheim's introduction to Schopenhauer. Ribot (1874:155) concludes that Schopenhauer was certainly not a positivist, yet credits him for establishing empirical psychology—this, despite Schopenhauer's metaphysics. Ribot's (1896) psychology is similarly empirical, metaphysical, and nonpositivistic, and seems to have influenced Durkheim's sociology along similar lines. This is true especially with regard to Schopenhauer's focus on the indestructible "will" (see Ribot 1874:81), which was later refracted into Freud's concepts of Eros, id, instinct, and a host of other equivalents.

Thomas Mann ([1939] 1955) concurs with Ribot that Schopenhauer was the true father of empirical psychology.

Another of Durkheim's followers, Lucien Levy-Bruhl, captures the gist of Schopenhauer's influence on Ribot's psychology when he writes that:

> M. Ribot initiated the study of scientific psychology in France. He is not a Positivist, inasmuch as he does not, like Comte, regard metaphysical investigations as useless and even injurious; he has written an excellent little book on Schopenhauer, and wishes to leave all questions open. But his conception of psychology is in perfect conformity with the positivist spirit. (Levy-Bruhl 1899:462)

One is far more likely to encounter similar allusions to the "positivist spirit" in *fin de siècle* writings than outright praise for positivism.[1] Positivism was on the defensive at the turn of the previous century (Baillot 1927; Mill 1968). In fact, of all the Durkheimians, Levy-Bruhl was the most concerned with the history of philosophy up to his time, and especially the differences between German and French philosophy.[2]

Freud had to defend himself against the charge that he stole the concept of the unconscious—itself a refraction of Schopenhauer's concept of the will[3] from Janet (see Freud [1925] 1959:21). Whether this alleged impropriety is true or not will probably never be ascertained with any degree of finality and is not important for the purposes of the present discussion. The important point is that Schopenhauer's influence was so profound in the late 1880s that he could have influenced, indirectly yet simultaneously, various developments of the concept of the unconscious by Janet, Durkheim, Freud, Jung, Hartmann, and many other intellectuals (see Ellenberger 1970). And the unconscious is a feminine concept that represents desire, chaos, and everything that opposes the conscious, rational mind and its alleged powers.

Durkheim credits his teacher, Alfred Espinas, for helping to establish the groundwork for sociology (see Traugott 1978:93–95). In *Animal Societies*, Espinas ([1878] 1977) developed the Kantian and Schopenhauerian claim that society is a system of ideas (representations or symbols) long before George Herbert Mead arrived at a similar insight.[4] And unlike the utilitarians, who exclude the animal kingdom from the human domain of rational, symbolic activity, Espinas seems to have followed Schopenhauer's lead that humans and animals are directly linked by the "will to life." Here is another interesting, neglected contrast to the development of symbolic interactionism in the United States along the Enlightenment assumptions that humans are superior to and separate from the rest of Nature by virtue of rationality. Durkheim and his teachers seem to have followed in the wake of German Romanticism's high regard for the unity of Nature. Romanticism regarded human rationality as an accident, a mere tool in the struggle for existence, not an essential component of human nature.

Contrary to many depictions of Durkheim's alleged antipathy toward psychology, Mauss insists that Durkheim as well as his followers "have always been ready to accept the advances of psychology" (Mauss [1950] 1979a:12). But this was a predominantly Schopenhauerian, soft psychology during the previous *fin de siècle*. And the Durkheimians as well as German Romantics tended to find unity and synthesis among the social sciences, in sharp contrast to the contemporary compartmentalization of various disciplines.

Early in his career, Durkheim seems to have adopted many of Schopenhauer's starting points, which include pessimism and a reluctance to accept the unequivocal power of reason. Thus, following his study with Wilhelm Wundt in Germany, Durkheim makes an interesting observation about the times in which he lived by reproaching the German economist Alfred Schaeffle[5] for his excessive optimism:

> Schaeffle has a robust faith in reason and the future of humanity. Moreover, nothing troubles the calm and serenity of his analyses. In them we do not even sense those fears, those vague anxieties, which are so familiar to our age. Such optimism is rare today, even here in France. We begin to feel that everything is not so straightforward and that reason does not cure all ills. We have reasoned so much! *Moreover, was it not from Germany that we got the idea that unhappiness always increases with consciousness?* ([1885] 1978:114; my emphasis)

Durkheim's last sentence, especially, seems to be an indirect allusion to Schopenhauer, who made the extreme and disturbing claim that enlightenment always brings about unhappiness, one of the cornerstones of his philosophy.

Schopenhauer's influence could have reached Durkheim from any number of indirect sources. Magee (1983) has analyzed Schopenhauer's influence on Nietzsche, Wittgenstein, and William James in philosophy. Durkheim ([1955] 1983) writes on Nietzsche, James, and Romanticism in his neglected *Pragmatism and Sociology*. Magee also includes Freud, Wundt, Wagner, Tolstoy, Conrad, Proust, Zola, Maupassant, Hardy, and Thomas Mann in Schopenhauer's sphere of influence. Partenheimer (1988) adds Henry Adams to the long list of intellectuals influenced by Schopenhauer. Similarly, in *The Discovery of the Unconscious*, Henri Ellenberger (1970) adds to this list Henri Bergson, who was Durkheim's colleague at the Sorbonne; Carl Gustav Jung, who corresponded with Durkheim's disciple Lucien Levy-Bruhl; along with a host of other intellectuals who are less illustrious today than they were in the previous *fin de siècle*. Ellenberger (1970:356) also invokes Emile Durkheim briefly, though he does not investigate a direct link between Durkheim and Schopenhauer. In general, Ellenberger concludes, "It is difficult for us today to imagine the fascination that Schopenhauer's philosophy exerted upon the intellectual elite of that time" (1970:281).

According to Ellenberger (1970:280–311 passim), from 1880 to the turn of the century, writers in diverse fields were concerned with the Schopenhauerian themes of unmasking the surface, illusory aspects of phenomena; with decadence and degeneration relative to the "progress" of civilization; and of course, with the idea of the unconscious. Ellenberger writes: "In the last decades of the nineteenth century, the philosophical concept of the unconscious, as taught by Schopenhauer and Von Hartmann, was extremely popular, and most contemporary philosophers admitted the existence of an unconscious mental life" (p. 311). Yet, Durkheim's (1908) own concept of the unconscious remains among the most neglected aspects of his thought (Mestrovic 1988, 1991), and the concept of the unconscious in general has been practically obliterated from the social scientific vocabulary in this century.

To repeat: It is highly significant to note that for Carl Gustav Jung (1959), the unconscious is not only a repository of irrational forces, but is an aspect of the Great Mother archetype, and feminine archetypes in general, which exist in men as well as women. For Jung, coming to terms with the unconscious is a matter of harmonizing and balancing feminine and masculine functions within one's self, a theme taken up later by Erich Fromm (1964), and all but forgotten by subsequent positivists. The link to be drawn is that Emile Durkheim envisioned a similar balancing of opposing forces with regard to the collective psyche that is society.

Commenting on "Janet and Durkheim, Levy-Bruhl, and others among his contemporaries," Ellenberger is probably correct that

> It would be an impossible undertaking to try to ascertain the mutual influences these men had on one another. Seen from a distance, they appear like statues standing in majestic isolation; seen at close range, it becomes apparent that they were engaged in more or less intermittent dialogues. (1970:356)

Ellenberger concurs with Baillot (1927) and Magee (1983) that Schopenhauer's philosophy attained the status of a "fad" during the previous *fin de siècle*. Thomas Mann describes Schopenhauer's forgotten, diffused, yet powerful influence on turn-of-the-century thought as a whole with particular eloquence, worth quoting at some length:

Schopenhauer did something very bold, even scarcely permissible, though at the same time with deeply felt, almost compulsive conviction: he defined the *Ding an sich* [thing-in-itself], he called it by name, he asserted—though from Kant himself you would never have known—that he knew what it was. It was the Will. The will was the ultimate, irreducible, primeval principle of being, the source of all phenomena, the begetter present and active in every single one of them, the impelling force producing the whole visible world and all life—for it was the will to live. . . . All knowledge alike was foreign to the will; it was something independent of knowledge, it was entirely original and absolute, a blind urge, a fundamental, uncausated, utterly unmotivated impulse. . . . The will, then, this "in-itself-ness" of things, existing outside of time, space and causality, blind and causeless, greedily, wildly, ruthlessly demanded life, demanded *objectivation*. ([1939] 1955:vii)

Baillot (1927:306) at least mentions the link between Schopenhauer's pessimism and Durkheim's *Suicide*, although he does not elaborate upon this connection. The important connecting point, for the purposes of the present discussion, is that both Schopenhauer and Durkheim attribute modern, enlightened suicide to the exacerbation of the will to life: Civilization breeds discontent, not the utilitarian promise of average happiness. Baillot (1927) writes that Schopenhauer exerted an incontestable influence upon Von Hartmann, Renan, Fouillee, Guyau, Renouvier, Ribot, and Bergson, all of whom were searching for non-Enlightenment alternatives to the tyranny of progress. These alternatives included, but are not limited to, nationalism, the unconscious, *l'èlan vital*, irrationalism, "irreligion" (from Guyau [1885] 1907, [1887] 1909), and metaphysics. Is the situation that much different today, even if positivism seems to rule the universities, when one examines all the irrationalisms that postmodernism encourages (O'Keefe 1982), from New Age books to cults and astrology? Many of my university students disclose to me that they believe in the religious, creationist "theory" of the origins of the universe, and do not believe Darwin's theory, even if they know which answers to give in their examinations in order to pass their courses. In postmodernist culture, the crudest forms of metaphysics and antiscience coexist with stringent positivism. The major difference is that in the previous *fin de siècle*, highbrow intellectuals were openly critical of Enlightenment narratives, whereas today positivism remains as official dogma among intellectuals, a ceremonial badge of honor (from Veblen 1943).

Durkheim ([1887] 1976b) reviewed Guyau's *The Non-Religion of the Future* ([1887] 1909), a book that expresses clearly the *fin de siècle* spirit described by Ellenberger. Durkheim agreed with Guyau that future religions would become less dogmatic, but he did not believe that religion would disappear (as predicted by the Marxists and positivists). More than a century later, we sense that the postmodernist revolution against dogmatism is hardly new or original. In general, Baillot argues that in *fin de siècle* France, Comte's followers were on the defensive, that there existed disenchantment with positivism, and that Schopenhauer was in vogue. There is no good reason to suppose that Durkheim's sociology would have been immune from these cultural currents.

Most of Durkheim's followers were philosophers by training. Many of their works are still untranslated and almost never cited, but they used Schopenhauer's vocabulary. They referred to representations as their single, most important concept, and they used it in a Schopenhauerian manner of symbols that betray the hidden, unconscious workings of the social "will." The Durkheimian, *fin de siècle* understanding of representations refracts the influence of Schopenhauer's philosophy in positing a world to be interpreted, an unconscious aspect to symbolism to be reconciled, and an irrationality to be uncovered. In the context of Jung's Schopenhauerian psychology, the Durkheimians were stressing the feminine, anti-Enlightenment aspects of the representationalism that is used in communication, as opposed to the many Enlightenment-based theories of communication that have been dominant since then.

To return to one illustrious example out of many, Robert Hertz ([1907–1909] 1960) studied right- and left-handedness as collective representations that signified the sacred and profane, even the masculine and feminine, respectively, not just a convention that humans decided to construct. In addition, Durkheim's followers thought of sociology as a *synthesis* of the other social sciences and philosophies, and advocated a "total," holistic approach to the study of social phenomena, very much along the lines of Schopenhauer's focus on the unity of knowledge.

In *L'Annee sociologique*, the journal that Durkheim established, the Durkheimians reviewed works by authors—many are now almost completely forgotten—who were precursors of contemporary sociology. Many of these works were direct or indirect extensions of or replies to Schopenhauer. For example, Tonnies's *Community and Society* ([1887] 1963) was reviewed by Durkheim ([1889] 1978). Tonnies distinguishes between the natural will of *Gemeinschaft* versus the artificial, rational will of *Gesellschaft*, and Durkheim specifically cites Schopenhauer's influence on Tonnies's thesis. For the purposes of the present discussion, it is significant that Tonnies modeled his understanding of *Gemeinschaft* on the mother-child relationship: In premodernity, the individual's relationship to one's community is like the relationship to one's mother. What a fantastic example of Bachofen's and other Romantic influences on the crucial sociological distinction between community and society! For Tonnies, *Gesellschaft* is masculine, and consequently cold, heartless, and unsympathetic.

Consider also the refractions of Schopenhauer's concept of will in William James's ([1896] 1931) will to believe, Nietzsche's ([1901] 1968) will to power, Wundt's (1907) individual versus social will, and various versions of the irrational, desiring will to something or other in the writings of Freud, Simmel, Darwin, and many others in that generation. If one were to take contemporary postmodernists seriously in their claims to be rebelling at the grand narratives of the Enlightenment, one should be able to find a similar focus on the will as a force that opposes rationality in the contemporary intellectual landscape. Instead, even the writers who defend postmodernism draw upon vocabularies that focus on rationality, not the irrational will, and end up praising a fragmented social existence in which, following Kant, access to the will is still forbidden. This is part of the tautological trap from which we are attempting to escape.

## NIETZSCHE'S WILL TO POWER VERSUS
## SCHOPENHAUER'S COMPASSION

Georg Simmel's ([1907] 1986) *Schopenhauer and Nietzsche* deserves special mention. Simmel regarded himself as a philosopher even though twentieth-century sociology would eventually claim him as a sociologist (see Frisby 1984, 1986), minus his philosophical assumptions. Simmel was struck by the readiness of people in his *fin de siècle* to flock to Schopenhauer: "During the past several dozen years, the absolute preponderance of suffering over happiness in life is the definitive portrait of life's value that gave Schopenhauer's philosophy its general significance and signature" (Simmel [1907] 1986:53).

Simmel concluded that Schopenhauer was undoubtedly the superior philosopher compared with his disciple, Nietzsche. It is extremely telling that the contemporary writers on postmodernism cite Nietzsche frequently while they seem to have forgotten his master, Schopenhauer (Kroker and Cook 1986). If Schopenhauer truly gave the previous *fin de siècle* its signature as claimed by Simmel and so many of his colleagues, but contemporary intellectuals give this credit to Nietzsche and overlook Schopenhauer, this is bound to be a significant indicator of what went wrong at the previous turn of the century, and what is occurring in postmodernism.

Consider that Schopenhauer advocated compassion—but not charity or pity[6]—as the antidote to the existential dilemma posed by the will to life, while Nietzsche ([1901] 1968) attacked his self-acknowledged master on precisely this issue, and advocated power instead of compassion.

Note that charity and pity can be motivated by egoism, and can be dismissed as ceremonial hypocrisies practiced by the leisure class (from Veblen). Schopenhauer ([1841] 1965) thought of compassion as a genuine, albeit rare victory over egoism and as an identification with the suffering of others based on the insight that all creatures are one by virtue of the struggle for existence. One could conclude that whereas the previous turn of the century gave birth to socialism and doctrines of compassion, the present turn of the century is one of militant capitalism and incessant *wars*, real and metaphorical, on AIDS, cancer, ignorance, crime, the recession, and just about anything or anyone that is perceived as disturbing. War is a manifestation of what Veblen ([1899] 1967) called the manly habits of the fight, dominant in the business culture of contemporary capitalism, not Schopenhauer's insight that leads to co-suffering (the literal meaning of compassion). Nietzsche's power, not Schopenhauer's compassion, is the hallmark of the present *fin de siècle*. History has been rewritten conveniently by postmodernists to give Nietzsche more cultural importance than he objectively had during his lifetime, and to obfuscate the anti-Enlightenment impact of Schopenhauer.

The dividing line between Schopenhauer and his disciple Nietzsche concerns the existential response to the realization that the metaphysical essence of the world is the all-devouring will to life. For Schopenhauer, this realization leads to the conclusion that all the world's inhabitants are in the same predicament: Everyone is constantly struggling, and suffers from either desiring too many things because one is poor, or from boredom and ennui because one has obtained some of what one desired, and now desires more. For Schopenhauer, human desire is infinite and essentially insatiable. This insight should lead to compassion among humans, according to Schopenhauer, and this is the kernel he gleamed from all the world's major religions. But Nietzsche interpreted the same insight with a cynical twist, and concluded that because life is indeed struggle and nothing but struggle, only the weak and stupid adopt compassion and the religious doctrines based on love. Nietzsche twisted Schopenhauer's use of the word compassion into pity, a word that denotes condescending hostility toward those whom we assist (Cartwright 1984). Power, not love, is the ultimate goal in life for Nietzsche.

Based on his greater admiration for Schopenhauer over Nietzsche, Simmel (1971) wrote that the most serious and profound problem for modernity was love, but this aspect of his sociology tends to be obfuscated, and he is the least-known founding father of sociology. One can conclude that postmodernism's rebellion at the Enlightenment carries the Nietzschean twist of cynicism and hunger for power, as contrasted with the *fin de siècle* high regard for compassion. I would suggest also that Schopenhauer and Simmel wrote in an era that could still sense the power of mother-centered, Virgin-based culture (from Henry Adams) as exemplified by the cathedrals of medieval Europe, whereas Nietzsche ushered in the era of the mechanized, positivist dynamo in which power is perceived to be the ultimate goal in life. The frequent use of Nietzsche in the contemporary totemism of intellectuals betrays just how much so-called postmodernism is an extension of mechanical, cold, and hard modernity.

Similarly, Ellenberger (1970) argued that the Romantics and pre-Romantics prepared the field for Schopenhauer with their own focus on human suffering and on compassion as the appropriate response to that suffering.[7] It is important to repeat that Romantic and *fin de siècle* compassion is different from charity or pity, each of which presupposes an air of superiority on the part of the person who experiences it (see Mestrovic 1991:108-35). Schopenhauer's philosophy teaches that all of us should identify with humanity because we are all doomed to suffering due to the same infinitely striving will to life.

The link to Durkheim's sociology is that Durkheim constantly stresses the sympathy, commiseration, and identification that individuals must feel with each other for social integration to occur. Like Schopenhauer, Durkheim taught that "the more one has, the more wants, since satisfaction received only stimulates instead of fulfilling needs" ([1897] 1951:248). Thus, Durkheim could not follow the utilitarian program that sought the greatest good for the greatest number, because he noted that this program ends in anomie, the infinity of desires, which in turn leads to unhappiness for the greatest number. The main result of anomie is suffering that stems from the fact that one's desires are never satiated, and all desire is painful. Thus, for Durkheim, insight into the secret of anomie leads naturally to Schopenhauerian compassion.

The important point is that the role of Schopenhauer's thought in the genesis of the social sciences should not be ignored. And the fact that it has been ignored betrays the most important contradiction of postmodernist culture, that it is not a genuine rebellion against the narratives spun from the Enlightenment. By most historical accounts, including Simmel's ([1907] 1986) fascinating philosophical reading of the sociological enterprise, Schopenhauer gave the previous *fin de siècle* its distinctive signature.[8] Yet the connection between Schopenhauer and Durkheim has not been pursued in sociology textbooks, and Schopenhauer's influence upon the other precursors of the social sciences has never even touched, much less entered so-called mainstream thought and writing.

In the rest of this book, I propose to examine postmodernist culture from the perspective of Durkheim's sociology as it drew on Schopenhauer's philosophy. This is not meant to be a dogmatic choice of context, in the manner of the typical postmodernist choice of Nietzsche over Schopenhauer, for example. The reason is that I have pointed to a host of historical, philosophical, and other sources that suggest that Schopenhauer is really the primary *cultural* symbol for most *fin de siècle* intellectual movements—including sociology. Bachofen, Simmel, Freud, Tonnies, Adams, Veblen, James, Wundt, Herbart, Weber, Ribot, Bergson, Wittgenstein, Durkheim, Adorno, Horkheimer, Fromm, and a host of other precursors of the social sciences need to be reread relative to their interrelatedness and relationship to the *fin de siècle* spirit and culture exemplified by Schopenhauer's philosophy. This *fin de siècle* spirit, in turn, is the closest approximation to what contemporary postmodernist writers claim is their aim in rebelling against the grand narratives of the Enlightenment. Thus, our strategy has been to seek out what has been most repressed in contemporary discussions of this sort, namely Durkheim's sociology and Schopenhauer's philosophy, with the belief that the retrieval of this repressed material may be beneficial. This strategy is itself Freudian and Schopenhauerian.

## REREADING DURKHEIM IN THE CULTURAL CONTEXT OF SCHOPENHAUER'S PHILOSOPHY

Rereading Durkheim in the context of Schopenhauer leads to an almost complete reversal of how he is typically read, and makes him seem profoundly relevant to the discourse surrounding postmodernism. As Thomas Mann ([1939] 1955) suggested, Schopenhauer's lasting achievement was the uncovering of the will as a force that is stronger than human rationality. Simmel concurs, writing that:

> with some few exceptions, which amount really to a *quantitè nègligeable*, all philosophers prior to Schopenhauer conceived of man as a rational being [but that] Schopenhauer destroyed the dogma that rationality is the deep-seated and basic essence of man that lies beneath the other ripples of life. ([1907] 1986:27)

How could have Freud, Durkheim, Bachofen, Jung and other students of the irrational achieved their aims without the cultural edifice supplied by Schopenhauer's philosophy and the rest of the German Romantic movement? This new context for reading Durkheim challenges the representations of him as the prince of positivism, the heir to Auguste Comte and the Enlightenment, the alleged *sociologue*, realist, and neoconservative despiser of psychology. Above all, the Parsonian misreading of Durkheim as the theorist of rational social action is challenged. In other words, our aim is to uncover a Durkheim who is relevant to the seemingly contradictory debate that is a response to understanding postmodernism as rebellion against narratives spun from the Enlightenment.

Compare the vast fame that Freud enjoyed relative to Durkheim or, for that matter, the immense popularity of psychology versus the near extinction of sociology as the millennium approaches. As of this writing, psychology majors vastly outnumber sociology majors in American universities. In his autobiography, Freud confessed that to a large extent "psychoanalysis coincides with the philosophy of Schopenhauer—not only did he assert the dominance of the emotions and the supreme importance of sexuality, but he was even aware of the mechanism of repression" ([1925] 1959:59). All of these are important contributions to the exploration of nonrational aspects of being human that Enlightenment philosophers tended to overlook. To be more precise, and following Simmel ([1907] 1986), the Enlightenment philosophers admitted that nonrationality existed, but assumed that humans were nevertheless essentially rational, whereas Schopenhauer and Freud assumed that the human person is essentially irrational. This difference in starting points for analyzing human behavior makes all the difference in resolving the issue whether postmodernism truly rebels at the Enlightenment or merely extends it.

Ellenberger (1970) and Jones (1981) support Freud's list of the affinities between Freud and Schopenhauer: Both thinkers stressed the concept of the unconscious, focused on death as the problem that stands at the outset of every philosophy, uncovered the omnipotence of thoughts and representational reality, and arrived at the general proposition that one is *not* the "master of his own house"—among many others. Indeed, in the middle of one of his lectures, Freud paused and told his audience:

> You may perhaps shrug your shoulders and say: "That isn't natural science, it's Schopenhauer's philosophy!" But, Ladies and Gentlemen, why should not a bold thinker have guessed something that is afterwards confirmed by sober and painstaking detailed research? ([1933] 1965:107)

Freud's comment applies equally to Durkheim's work. Freud's and Durkheim's genius is *not* to be found in their positivistic propositions, which others have attempted to "falsify"—these falsifications continue to be debated and challenged in any case, with no resolution in sight—but in their insights, their focus on the Schopenhauerian will, which is the more important and stronger force in human affairs compared with paltry rationality. As Thomas Mann wrote regarding Schopenhauer (although it applies also to Durkheim and Freud): "Everyone realizes that when this great writer and commanding spirit speaks of the suffering of the world, he speaks of yours and mine; all of us feel what amounts to triumph at being thus avenged by the heroic word" ([1939] 1955:x). Durkheim covered many of the same topics as Freud, including the unconscious and sexuality. Both Freud and Durkheim avenge humanity in their choice of topics and their sensitive treatment—derived from pathos and identification with a suffering humanity—of those topics.

An important difference in the reception of Freud and Durkheim is that Freud was aligned with irrationalism from the outset while Durkheim had been misaligned with the Enlightenment, utilitarian, and positivistic narratives. With the passage of time, and especially as naive rationalism and positivism have come under attack even prior to the postmodernist movement, Freud's stature rose and Durkheim's fell. In the late twentieth century, it is almost impossible to defend the Enlightenment assumption that reason is in firm command over the tyrannical will, even if positivism controls academic social science.[9] Everyone has witnessed too many proofs to the contrary. Yet, incredibly, Durkheim continues to be aligned with dying systems of thought, even as sociology is gasping for survival.

Consider, for example, the "rational social action" paradigm instigated by Talcott Parsons (1937). It would never have captivated the imaginations of several generations of sociologists had it not fit the modernist collective representations that have dominated the present century. According to Parsons:

> Action is rational in so far as it pursues ends possible within the conditions of the situation, and by means which, among those available to the actor, are intrinsically best adapted to the end for reasons understandable and verifiable by positive empirical science. (1937:58)

Parsons aligns Durkheim, along with a number of other founding fathers of sociology (but not Simmel, who is omitted by Parsons), with this popular paradigm. According to Parsons, Durkheim's sociology is informed by utilitarian social philosophy, positivism, and British empiricism. Imagine a sophisticated *fin de siècle* thinker like Durkheim taking these doctrines seriously, when they were already dead or dying in his lifetime! Parsons's focus is on a rational, clear, and conscious relationship between goals and means. Parsons, Merton, and other functionalists assume that goals and means are able to exist in a rational relationship, and that persons can control their desires with regard to what society has mapped out as being worth desiring. But utilitarian, rationalistic assumptions represent the very systems of thought that Durkheim attempted to counter. They are also part of the Enlightenment narratives that postmodernism rebels against. And all of these systems presuppose the opposite of Schopenhauer's emphasis upon the primacy of the irrational will. They assume that reason is more powerful than the will.

Simmel makes us aware that Schopenhauer had already reversed the utilitarian assumptions that inform the writings of Parsons, and that Parsons seems strangely unaware of this fact. In *Schopenhauer and Nietzsche*, Simmel writes:

> It is a paradox that all higher cultures of our type are structured so that the more they evolve the more we are forced, in order to reach our goals, to proceed along increasingly long and difficult paths, filled with stops and curves. . . . The will of animals and of uncultured humans reaches its goal, if that will is successful, in, so to speak, a straight line, that is, by simply reaching out or by using a small number of simple devices: the order of means and ends is easily observable. This simple triad of desire-means-end is excluded by the increasing multiplicity and complexity of higher life. . . . Thus, our consciousness is bound up with the means, whereas the final goals which import sense and meaning into the intermediate steps are pushed toward our inner horizon and finally beyond it. ([1907] 1986:3)

Humans struggle with the question of the meaning of life precisely because the connection between ends and means is elusive in that this connection is veiled, obscured, or sometimes lost entirely. Bureaucracy and technology, the endless steps to achieving culturally prescribed goals, represent the cynical realities of modern, and postmodern, living. Riesman (1950) arrived at a similar conclusion when he traced the progress from tradition-directed to other-directed societies relative to goals and means. For the tradition-directed type, the goals are immediately accessible to the means. The inner-directed type sets his or her goals on a distant "star," although the relationship between goals and means is still maintained (1950:115). But for the other-directed forerunner of the postmodern type of person, the relationship between goals and means has been severed, replaced by "the Milky Way" of goals and means, and its attendant "uncertainty of life" (p. 137).

Thus, the kindest statement one can make concerning Parsons's goals-means scheme is that it is old-fashioned, and certainly irrelevant to the reality of everyday life in postmodern societies. It applies to traditional societies, and may have applied to the inner-directed era that nurtured Parsons to some extent, but it is completely inapplicable to contemporary societies. Quite apart from the inapplicability of Parsons's scheme, one can question his scholarship. How could Parsons have moved from the Enlightenment to the founding fathers of *fin de siècle* sociology without mentioning Schopenhauer, the Romantics, or other irrational movements of the previous turn of the century? Parsons dismisses all these historical facts as irrelevant and develops his theory on a deductive, a priori basis, the assumption that the social world is as mathematically elegant as his theory.

For example, Parsons transforms the most obvious exemplar of irrationality, the problem of social order or anomie, into Enlightenment terms. Parsons assumes that the world is essentially orderly, in contradistinction to the more postmodernist chaos theory, which assumes the very opposite. Thus, disorder occurs when various authorities fail to control individuals. Parsons begins this discussion with a reference to Hobbes:

> Hobbes' system of social theory is almost a pure case of utilitarianism, according to the definition of the preceding chapter. The basis of human action lies in the "passions." These are discrete, randomly variant ends of action. . . . In the pursuit of these ends men act rationally, choosing, within the limitations of the situation, the most efficient means. (1937:91)

As any educated person knows, Hobbes claimed that human rationality is a slave to the passions. And from Schopenhauer's perspective, the state of affairs depicted by Parsons is impossible. For Schopenhauer, the will "is a striving *without aim or end*" ([1818] 1977a:414; my emphasis). This is a key point for the purposes of the present discussion. One cannot derive rational goals and means from the existential portrait of human life uncovered by Schopenhauer and completed by *fin de siècle* sociologists, from Durkheim to Simmel, Freud, and Weber. The will simply wills, without any recourse to rationality. The reasons for the action are rationalized after the fact, even though humans delude themselves that they are the authors of their actions. In reality, they are driven by forces of which they are scarcely aware. For Schopenhauer, the will is blind, such that willing has no real end or purpose. Many writers on the postmodern condition find a similar situation in the blind, unceasing, and insatiable explosion of the will in contemporary times (see Baudrillard 1988; Bell 1976).

Finally, Parsons (1937) projects his own Enlightenment assumptions onto Durkheim, as part of the strategy summarized above. Parsons assumes that Durkheim began his career as a positivist and ended it as an idealist, but does not investigate, question, or support this assumption. When Parsons discovered that Durkheim did not adhere to positivism, he concluded that Durkheim "failed" to shake off positivism in his imaginary quest for "idealism:"

> From the beginning his early position was explicitly positivistic; this was, indeed, held to be a methodological requirement of science itself. . . . The breakdown of this synthesis, mentioned above, consisted essentially in a

breakdown of the entire positivistic framework itself. Certain of its features, however, he never completely shook off, and this fact largely accounts for his failure to achieve a new synthesis. (1937:306)


Parsons (1937:447) accuses Durkheim falsely of moving from empiricism to relativism and solipsism, "in short, a *reductio ad absurdum.*" Actually, it is not at all evident that Durkheim was explicitly or even implicitly
positivistic (see Mestrovic 1991), and Parsons fails to support his claims
with evidence. Durkheim specifically disavowed positivism and was
highly critical of its high priests, Auguste Comte and Henri de Saint-
Simon (see Durkheim [1895] 1982:33–34; [1928] 1958). In fact, Parsons is
working with the very Enlightenment narratives that postmodernists
purport to rebel against and that Durkheim's *fin de siècle* had already
shaken off.

Consider Merton's (1957) extension of the Parsonian felicity between
goals and means relative to the problem of anomie. Merton claims that
his intentions are to distance himself from the Freudian perspective, in
which social disorder is viewed as the result of the ungoverned id and
other biological tendencies. Merton's society is almost pure mind. But to
the extent that Merton ascribes his conceptualization of anomie to Durkheim, which he does at times, one must account for the fact that Durkheim's concept of anomie rests on *homo duplex*, which exhibits many
affinities with the Freudian, implicitly Schopenhauerian view that Merton rejects. It must, since Freud's thought is admitted to be, in large
measure, a refraction of Schopenhauer's philosophy, which also influenced Durkheim indirectly (see Ellenberger 1970; Jones 1981; Magee
1983). Merton, like Parsons before him, assumes that Durkheim was a
positivist, and treats anomie as normative confusion or "normlessness,"
a word that Durkheim never used or implied and that is impossible to
conceptualize or operationalize, despite all the positivistic rhetoric of
submitting concepts to hypothesis testing and falsification. Yet Merton
admits that for Durkheim, anomie is a state of ungoverned desires. The
question that begs an answer is, Where do the desires originate in the
positivist, hyperrationalist scheme of things? The answer is that Merton's theory cannot account for the idlike, desiring, "lower" pole of *homo
duplex*, which originates in the will, not the mental life of societies.

For Merton, society's goals and means are relatively fixed and deter-
mined. Society maps out "what is worth striving for" (1957:187). What
an old-fashioned, quaint portrait of modern life! For Durkheim as well as
realistic postmodernists, however, a single set of means can permit the
attainment of a multiplicity of goals. Humans routinely attempt to gain
as many different levels of benefits from a single act as possible. The
will, which originates in the individual, is infinite and tends toward

dispersion relative to goals. Merton assumes that society's goals and means are well-known to its members, as if individuals were a kind of offprint of society. But for those who are persuaded by Durkheim, diverse social currents, including goals and means, do not exercise a uniform action on all persons. Instead, there exists a gradation of knowledge and motives relative to these currents, which are all refracted through the individual's will. In short, Merton's normlessness minimizes the tension between individual will and collective representations. Contrary to Merton and the functionalists, and following Schopenhauer, Durkheim assumes that will and representation are by nature mutually antagonistic (see especially Durkheim [1914] 1973).

In sum, the tremendous popularity of the functionalist version of Durkheim's sociology espoused by Parsons, Merton, and their followers may be regarded as an instance of Veblen's cultural lag. The functionalists write as if they were living in the eighteenth century, when goals and means were less problematic than they are today. But they are out of touch with the postmodernist reality of everyday life in which goals and means are in flux, and individuals struggle to make sense of their complicated lives. And they miss completely Durkheim's genius in foreshadowing the existential problems that beset postmodern individuals.

## BAUDRILLARD VERSUS DURKHEIM ON SEDUCTION

In *Seduction*, Jean Baudrillard (1990) equates seduction with the feminine: With this bold connection, he links postmodern consumerism, concern with appearances, desire, and insatiability with the feminine principle. But he refuses to connect seduction with sex, sexuality, Nature, the unconscious, or culture—the very things that *fin de siècle* thinkers linked with the feminine. Thus, for Baudrillard, femininity holds a purely negative function: It seduces the masculine world of power, differentiation, and order. It does not contribute anything positive to human culture. Baudrillard has been criticized by feminists and others for his views in this regard (see Gane 1991:48–63; Kellner 1989:135–47).

But these criticisms amount to little more than the claim that Baudrillard is not politically correct. Baudrillard is right to point to infinite seduction and the explosion of desire as the hallmarks of postmodern culture. He should be faulted for his typically cynical and nihilistic conclusion that this is all that one can expect, for not bothering to explore the possibilities that the feminine principle might have a positive role, and that it might be reconciled with the masculine principle.

In the remainder of this chapter, I intend to link Durkheim's concept of anomie with Baudrillard's concept of seduction, and contrast it with the phallocentric image of anomie as mere disorder found in Parsonian functionalism. In other words, Durkheim foreshadowed Baudrillard's concept of seduction. But, unlike Baudrillard as well as the functionalists, Durkheim felt that the seductive power of anomie is benign as well as destructive, and could be reconciled with the masculine principle of asceticism. Either extreme—seduction or the ascetic principle—is harmful when excessive, and one must offset the other in a dialectic fashion.

Durkheim's description of anomie as a state of infinite desires that is exacerbated by enlightenment does *not* parallel the versions of anomie found in Parsons (1937), Merton (1957), or other functionalists. For Durkheim, as for Schopenhauer, human desires surpass and overpower the available means:

> But if nothing external can restrain this capacity [for feeling], it can only be a source of torment to itself. Unlimited desires are insatiable by definition and insatiability is rightly considered a sign of morbidity. Being unlimited, they constantly and infinitely surpass the means at their command; they cannot be quenched. *Inextinguishable thirst is constantly renewed torture.* ([1897] 1951:247; my emphasis)

I ask any unbiased reader to apply Durkheim's versus the functionalist reading of the relationship between goals and means to actual life in postmodernist culture. It seems evident that Durkheim has captured the *seductive* essence and complexity of contemporary life, even if he wrote about a hundred years ago. Everyone knows that without the inextinguishable thirst for novelty that Durkheim describes, Western capitalism would collapse. Despite all the technological innovations, useful appliances, and growth of science, industry, and the arts since Durkheim's time, postmodern humans are routinely dissatisfied with these fruits of the Enlightenment, and are still seeking new frontiers of status and prestige (from Veblen). *And seduction is torture, because the anticipation offers more pleasure than the actual conquest.* Thus, according to Durkheim, "to pursue a goal which is by definition unattainable is to condemn oneself to a state of perpetual unhappiness" (p. 248)—this was Schopenhauer's conclusion.

Moreover, like Schopenhauer, Durkheim assumes that the ends of desire can never satisfy the will. This is because, to repeat, the will does not strive after ends, but merely strives, blindly and unceasingly. Thus, according to Durkheim:

> Overweening ambition always exceeds the results obtained, great as they may be, since there is no warning to pause here. Nothing gives satisfaction and all this agitation is uninterruptedly maintained without appeasement. Above all, *since this race for an unattainable goal can give no other pleasure but*

*that of the race itself, if it is one, once it is interrupted the participants are left empty-handed.* At the same time the struggle grows more violent and painful, both from being less controlled and because competition is greater. . . . Effort grows, just when it becomes less productive. How could the desire to live not be weakened under such conditions? (p. 248; my emphasis)

At this point, Durkheim echoes Schopenhauer's famous summary that "just because the suicide cannot give up willing, he gives up living" ([1818] 1977a:414). Suffering stems from the fact that the will is infinite: The more one obtains through rational means, the more one desires. Education, civilization, and all the instruments of so-called progress only unleash the previously restrained will by expanding the horizon of desires. Durkheim ([1893] 1933:233–55) concluded that the progress of civilization and the division of labor have *not* increased human happiness.

Thus, if postmodernism constitutes a genuine rebellion against narratives spun from the Enlightenment, it should challenge the boosterish optimism that is still found in most social theory. But neither Baudrillard nor the other postmodernists write about suffering as the final end of seduction, and they do not express concern about seduction's consequences.

In *The Division of Labor in Society*, Durkheim asks, "but in fact, is it true that the happiness of the individual increases as man advances?" and answers, "Nothing is more doubtful" ([1893] 1933:241). Durkheim concludes that as civilization and the division of labor progress, "the general happiness of society is decreasing" (p. 249). To be sure, Durkheim, like Schopenhauer, grants that civilization *offers many pleasures* (seductions, and the possibilities of seduction), but ultimately both thinkers conclude that happiness is negative in the sense that it constitutes a lessening of factors that lead to direct unhappiness (compared to our ancestors), not a positive increase in the sum of pleasures. According to Schopenhauer, happiness "cannot be lasting, but merely delivers us from some pain or want which must be followed either by a new pain, or by languor, empty longing, and ennui" ([1818] 1977a:413). Seduction cannot lead to genuine happiness.

Schopenhauer's existential solution to the tyranny of the will imposed upon humans by their desiring bodies is the practice of self-conscious temperance and asceticism, a solution pursued by Durkheim in his sociology:

If the teaching of experience bears fruit in us, we soon give up the pursuit of pleasure and happiness, and think much more about making ourselves secure against the attacks of pain and suffering. . . . Accordingly *it is advisable to put very moderate limits upon our expectations of pleasure, posses-*

*sions, rank, honor, and so on; because it is just this striving and struggling to be happy, to dazzle the world, to lead a life full of pleasure, which entails great misfortune. . . .* It is extremely easy to be very unhappy; while to be very happy is not indeed difficult, but quite impossible. (Mann [1939] 1955:401; my emphasis)

Clearly, Veblen (1943) sought a similar, Schopenhauerian solution to the quest for prestige and status that used to characterize the leisure class in his day and that characterizes the postmodern middle class in our day. One will never attain that final amount of status and prestige that will be satisfying so long as one is being seduced by what Veblen called the barbaric regression to predatory self-interest. So long as postmodern social philosophy continues to adhere to the goals of increasing happiness, dazzling the world, and increasing the "fun" that Riesman had already uncovered in modern culture, it cannot claim legitimately to be rebelling at narratives spun from the Enlightenment.

## CONCLUSIONS

Baudrillard (1988) draws on Veblen in his portrait of the senseless striving after unattainable goals that he believes characterizes postmodernism. Similarly, Bauman (1989, 1990, 1991) draws on Adorno to criticize the ruthless intolerance that modernity exhibits in its quest for total assimilation and order. In this chapter, I have complemented Baudrillard's and Bauman's efforts by drawing on Durkheim and Schopenhauer. I have also compared and contrasted key components of Durkheim's sociology with the functionalist misreadings of his thought. Baudrillard's portrait of postmodern culture as senseless seduction is accurate, but does not point to a solution, and is nihilistic in its tone. Similarly, Bauman's critique of modernity and order is cogent, but perhaps excessive, because some order *is* necessary for social life. But it must be a just and humane order. Here again, the cynical postmodernists point out that justice and humanity have been used by all sorts of oppressive narratives, even regimes. Notwithstanding the objective reasons for this cynicism, I have turned to the Romantic era as the ground or referent for the postmodernist search for innocence. Durkheim, Veblen, Adams, Schopenhauer, and others from the previous century were apparently seeking, with complete sincerity, a nonoppressive basis for social order, one that would attempt to curtail human egoism and soften it with altruism. This program is a continuation of the Romantic discovery of the feminine voice in history that was addressed in the previous chapter. The remaining chapters in this book will flesh out the key components of the alternative that Durkheim was trying to find.

For example, Baudrillard argues that "consumption is the virtual totality of all objects and messages presently constituted in a more or less coherent discourse" (1988:22) in postmodern culture. Everything is fluid, geared toward the "fun-system," and trying new things (even "trying" Jesus). In their supreme egoism, everyone feels unique even as they conform and are manipulated by the media and the culture industry (from Adorno). Consumption becomes an active mode of relating (from Veblen). Many other authors who describe postmodernist culture echo Baudrillard's observations, and these contemporary writers are following the leads established by Durkheim, Veblen, Schopenhauer, and other writers from the previous *fin de siècle*, albeit often unwittingly and in a superficial manner.[10] Missing in the postmodernist scenario is a theoretical scaffolding that might ameliorate these anomic tendencies. It was important to disengage Durkheim's sociology from the lifeless perspectives of functionalism in order to pave the way for a new and serious appreciation of what Durkheim's sociology has to offer.

## NOTES

1. See Alpert (1937, 1938, 1939).
2. See Levy-Bruhl (1890, 1895, 1899, 1903a, 1903b).
3. As noted by Renouvier (1892:33), Ellenberger (1970), and many others.
4. Contrary to Stone and Farberman (1967), one could argue that Mead was moving toward the Durkheimian position, not the other way around.
5. Veblen also admired this German *fin de siècle* economist.
6. For more on this distinction, see Cartwright (1984, 1987, 1988a, 1988b).
7. See also Clark (1975), Crawford (1984), and Menand and Schwartz (1982).
8. One is tempted to ask what philosopher has given our *fin de siècle* its signature, and arrives at the answer that we are still harking back to the previous turn of the century.
9. This is not to deny that Fukuyama (1989) and others claim that postmodernists have witnessed the end of history, meaning the end of irrational social phenomena like nationalism, wars for territory, and totalitarianism.
10. Veblen has much more to offer to the postmodernist discourse than Baudrillard uses.

# Chapter 4

## *The Social World as Will and Idea*

Jean Baudrillard depicts a postmodern culture that is dominated by simulations, objects, and discourses that have no firm origin, referent, ground, or foundation. Culture is appearance, and only appearance. In contrast with the title of Schopenhauer's 1818 classic, *The World as Will and Idea*, Baudrillard and the postmodernists give us "the world as idea." To be sure, Baudrillard writes of human desire, but it is "a primary, visceral, unbounded vitality, springing not from rootedness, but from the lack of roots, a metabolic vitality, in sex and bodies, as well as in work and in buying and selling" (1986:7). "Image alone counts," Baudrillard adds (p. 109). Reagan becomes the penultimate postmodernist hero, and America becomes the world center of the inauthentic. In the postmodern depiction of culture, there is no "beneath" or "underneath," and certainly no dissidence or suspicion (p. 85). Everything is what it seems to be—but only for a moment, until it is replaced by another image.

In sharp contrast to Baudrillard, Schopenhauer depicts the representation or idea as the other side of the will. The will exists beneath the image, and it counts more than the image. Schopenhauer's doctrine of the will promotes the suspicion that everything that seems to be true is merely ideology (see Eagleton 1991). The meaning of the concept of *will* is notoriously difficult to capture in the English language, because it does not imply effort or conscious choice. On the contrary, in Schopenhauer's usage, it denotes the tyranny of passions imposed upon the human agent by virtue of being trapped in a body. But the will is also Kant's hitherto inaccessible thing-in-itself. It is the ground or referent for conscious knowledge, even though it is constantly changing. The purpose of this chapter is to portray Durkheim's sociology as one that followed the German Romantic lead to regard society as will *and* idea. As such, society involves the circulation of fictions that concerns postmodernists, but these fictions are rooted in the fluid social will.

Durkheim's conception of society implies this German *fin de siècle* idea that history is more than a series of events, and that society is more than a sum of individuals: There is a secret *intention* to history and society, a will that works itself out *through* individuals, whether or not they are aware of this hidden intention. This Romantic insight is found in thinkers as diverse as Hegel, Schopenhauer, Nietzsche, Veblen, Henry Adams, Adorno, Spengler, Toynbee, Freud, and of course, Durkheim (among many other *fin de siècle* thinkers). It is also almost completely alien to the postmodern American mind, and requires considerable explication. There can be no end to history in Romanticism. But according to Baudrillard, for Americans, "a face does not deceive, behaviour does not deceive, a scientific process does not deceive, nothing deceives, nothing is ambivalent (and at bottom this is true: nothing deceives, there are no lies, there is only simulation)" (1986:85).

Modernity took firm root in American social consciousness, as noted by Tocqueville long ago, because modernity tends to detach ideas from their context or anything else that might serve as a foundation for ideas. Postmodernism only exacerbates this process, which seems to come naturally to Americans. In his *Democracy in America*, Tocqueville wrote that Americans have little or no sense of history, that "no one cares for what occurred before his time," and that "in America society seems to live from hand to mouth, like an army in the field" ([1835] 1945:219). He adds that "if the United States were ever invaded by barbarians, it would be necessary to have recourse to the history of other nations in order to learn anything of the people who now inhabit them" (p. 219). What a perfect setting for accepting the "end of history" concept, the circulation of fictive forms, decentering, and hyperreality discussed by postmodernists.

Western Europe exhibits some of these same postmodernist trends, but not to the same extreme degree as the United States. After all, Disney World, Madison Avenue, and Hollywood, the grand centers of what Adorno (1991) called the culture industry, originated in the United States, and disseminate fictions for the entire world to consume. By contrast, Europeans are routinely exposed to architecture and landmarks that remind them of their Classical pasts.[1] Still, even the Europeans have been Americanized. Postmodernism shares many affinities with American social character: From Tocqueville's *Democracy in America* to Baudrillard's *America*, American culture continues to serve as a kind of shorthand for modernity, and to seduce the world.[2] Witness the fact that sociology was born a century ago in Europe during the Romantic era, but that European sociology has been eclipsed and continues to be dominated by American social theory that began with the modernist assumptions of the Chicago School. Durkheim, Freud, Weber, and the others—

they were all Americanized and modernized by Parsons and his followers. We shall attempt to search beneath and beyond the images of sociology that are extant in postmodern culture.

## THE PHILOSOPHICAL VOCABULARY SHARED BY SCHOPENHAUER AND DURKHEIM

Both of Schopenhauer's pivotal concepts, representation and will, were in common usage in Durkheim's time. The French term *reprèsentation*, which is translated into English as *idea* and into German as *Vorstellung*, were standard terms not only for the Durkheimians but also among the phenomenologists, Freudians, and most philosophers of the previous *fin de siècle* (Janik and Toulmin 1973). But in the present century, and up to these postmodern times, the term *representation* and its original philosophical context have been steadily eclipsed.[3] Instead of representations, contemporary social scientists refer to attitudes, opinions, stereotypes, and images that are formed through the very act of communicating (see Fraser and Gaskell 1990). The intent is found in the motives of human agents who communicate through symbols or after the fact, not in the will that lurks beneath the collective representations. Habermas (1987)—who began his career as a critical theorist, but might be regarded as one of Parsons's foremost disciples in contemporary Europe—places an almost magical twist on this postmodernist expectation that human communication will spontaneously and of its own accord create moral relationships among communicating human agents.[4] This supposed liberation from the structural restraints placed on representations that were recognized in the previous *fin de siècle* has also been criticized for producing anarchy.

It is interesting to contrast the postmodernist tendency to disengage representations from anything permanent and objective with the opposite tendency of thinkers from the previous *fin de siècle* to find a root and anchor for nearly everything. They were always mindful of the other side of representations. William James ([1896] 1931) rooted the changes he observed in the will to believe, an assumed human need for faith that withstands all representational shifts. Nietzsche ([1901] 1968) eventually hung his philosophy on the infamous will to power. Tonnies ([1887] 1963) centered his social analyses on the primacy of maternal natural will, the human longing for community. Many other thinkers from the previous turn of the century focused on a will to something permanent that would offset the ahistorical tendency uncovered by Tocqueville that Americans and modern persons in general seem to live from hand to mouth, like an army in the field. What postmodern thinker would argue that humans have an essential need for faith, power, community, or anything else? Instead, essentialism has been criticized as a barrier to human freedom. Postmodernism is purported to be an amorphous rebellion at all essences that paradoxically liberates one into nothingness. The previous *fin de siècle* thinkers may have been wiser, and continue to be relevant, because even postmodern humans contradict their Enlightenment tendencies with incredible revivals of nostalgia, blind faith, patriotism, religion, and all sorts of other efforts to anchor their representationalism in something permanent.

Schopenhauer begins his famous *The World as Will and Idea* with the bold claim that "The world is my idea." He continues:

> This is a truth which holds good for everything that lives and knows, though man alone can bring it into reflective and abstract consciousness. If he really does this, he has attained to philosophical wisdom. It then becomes clear and certain to him that what he knows is not a sun and an earth; that the world which surrounds him is there only as idea, i.e., only in relation to something else, the consciousness, which is himself. . . . No truth therefore is more certain, more independent of all others, and less in need of proof than this, that all that exists of knowledge, and therefore this whole world, is only object in relation to subject, perception of a perceiver, in a word, idea. ([1818] 1977a:1)

This was part of Schopenhauer's way of reconciling the object-subject distinction that Kant had exposed with great force. Its consequence is that the objective world can never be known as a thing-in-itself, but only in relation to a knowing subject, and that this knowledge is never objective, only an image that exists in relation to the human subject. Obviously, Schopenhauer had foreshadowed the decentering and cultural relativist themes that form the staple of most postmodernist discourse as well as critical theory. However, Schopenhauer did not stop with this insight, as most postmodernist discourse does. The world is not just one's idea. He went on to argue that the idea or representation is only one side—the surface side, easily accessible to consciousness—of the phenomenon, whose dark, hidden side shrouds the will. The mind can grasp the idea, but the heart, including sentiment and intuition, must be involved in order to grasp the will. Whereas Schopenhauer's existential vision involves the entire person, modernity, postmodernism, and the culture industry almost completely ignore the will, and focus entirely on conscious imagery, fiction, and hyperreality. Yet, in a Nietzschean sense, the will avenges itself in outbreaks of irrationality within the heart of modernity.

For Schopenhauer, the other side of the representation is the will. Though will and idea are a unity, they are an antagonistic, dialectical unity. In Schopenhauer's vocabulary, the will stands for what humanity is used to calling the heart, and the idea stands for the mind. The will encompasses dreams, impulses, affection, passions, and all that is obscure, unconscious, and emotional. It is interesting how Bachofen, Henry Adams, and Jung eventually came to associate these characteristics of the will with the archetypes of the Great Mother and femininity (but to repeat, not necessarily with women). The mind came to stand for masculine reflection, thought, abstraction, the impersonal, and all that controls or discounts the will (but not necessarily males). Thus, from Schopenhauer through Durkheim to Jung, the aim was to balance masculine with feminine archetypes, to reconcile the mind with the heart, and to restore the original unity of the will and idea. The careful scholar will observe that these thinkers were refracting the single-sex theory derived from Plato in which masculine and feminine were two aspects of the same thing (see Laquer 1990).

In stark contrast to this Schopenhauerian legacy (which Schopenhauer traced back to Plato), the postmodernist debate is framed in terms of mutually exclusive oppositions: Either rebel against the mind, or complete the Enlightenment project; either revel in emotional kitsch, or regard all emotionalism as dangerous. Even feminists disagree whether they should embrace postmodernism as liberation from oppressive narratives or regard it suspiciously. The bedrock cause of all this confusion seems to be a splintering of the will-idea, object-subject, heart-mind unity that Schopenhauer and Durkheim had rediscovered in the Platonic heritage of Western civilization.

## CONCEPTUALIZING THE SICK SOCIETY

Adorno (1991), Fromm (1955), Horkheimer (1947), Benjamin (1968), and other critical theorists make the point that societies, like individuals, can become sick, in opposition to the functionalist assumption that societies are by definition self-maintaining, integrative systems. Adorno's (1991) *The Culture Industry*, for example, refers to the narcissism, blasé sense of adjustment, and lack of spontaneity that modern societies seem to cause their individual members to feel. Partly as a result of Fromm's influence, Riesman (1980) has also bemoaned the excessive narcissism and egocentrism that seems to have resulted from a shift to other-directed character structure. Typically, these theorists of mass society have been criticized as being out of touch with the essential individualism of modern societies, especially by Daniel Bell in *The End of Ideology* (1988). If modernity leads to diversity and choice for individuals, how can it also lead to mass society (Bauman 1991)? If modernity leads to narcissism, how can it lead at the same time to mass society conformity? Critical theorists have never resolved these issues. Additionally, and as indicated previously, many commentators on postmodernist culture deny any possibility of judging healthy versus sick societies on the basis that this implies an essentialist or otherwise rigid standard that they seek to rebel against, as well as the basis that society is somehow an entity different from the individuals who comprise society.

Durkheim's neglected contribution to this discussion follows in the wake of Schopenhauer's philosophy: It *is* possible to conceive of society as a system of representations separate from its members, and these representations can become imbalanced relative to *homo duplex* or the dualism of human nature, such that the entire social system and consequently its individual members become sick and suffer. Society is sick when its members are unable to integrate adequately their conscious motives with society's hidden, unconscious will. Pathology results from other aspects of malintegration: History is severed from visions of the future, masculine values from feminine values, individualism from collective responsibility. In all these cases, narcissism, choice, and individual freedom revert into their opposites—mass conformity. This is the gist of the insight shared by Adorno, Jung, Veblen, Durkheim, and others whose arguments we are following in this book.

The analogy may be drawn that in the previous *fin de siècle*, the neurotic individual was sick when his or her conscious motives were unintegrated with his or her unconscious will due to repression and other mechanisms. Freud made the most of this insight, but it was anticipated by and erected upon the scaffolding established by the German Romantics. Durkheim's genius was to apply this typically *fin de siècle* insight to society conceived as a totality sui generis, a being with its own will that is something other than the sum of its parts. This is the full import of Durkheim's famous yet still misunderstood concept of the anomic society.

For Durkheim, anomie and narcissism, what he called egoism, exhibit an affinity for one another ([1897] 1951:325). He calls anomie the "disease of infiniteness" (p. 304), an echo of Schopenhauer's references to the "infinite" strivings of the will, which, if unrestrained, cause suffering. Durkheim refers to anomie also as a painful state of *dérèglement* (p. 281), a word loaded with medical connotations that essentially means derangement (see Mestrovic 1988). With tremendous pathos that rivals the writings of Adorno and other members of the Frankfurt school, Durkheim describes the manner in which the anomic state of society brings to its individual members psychological as well as physiological weariness, disillusionment, disappointment, psychic pain, and a tendency to grope at random, which in turn bring on still other crises, until life itself seems "intolerable" (pp. 250–57). This may seem like an extreme assessment of modernity, given that an upbeat spirit of optimism is an essential component of modern living, until one considers the dramatic increase in the objective and subjective uses of the stress concept in this century. Stress may very well be the postmodern representation for what Durkheim called anomie (discussed in Meštrovíc 1991).

But why would this painful state of psychic imbalance occur in modern and postmodern culture? Adorno (1991:166) touches on this question by referring to Schopenhauer's pessimistic assessment of the fruits of the enlightened will, but concludes that Schopenhauer's assessment applies only because of an advanced division of labor. This strange and incomplete analysis by Adorno begs the question of why the progress of the division of labor is inevitable and cannot be reversed, even if it does produce pathology. Schopenhauer's answer is this: The will produces the enlargement of the brain as a means of survival for the human animal, which is otherwise relatively defenseless. This in turn leads to enlightenment, whose end results include the division of labor and civilization. But the process is dialectical, such that an enlightened consciousness exacerbates the will by presenting the animal nature of humans with more things to desire compared with the limited consciousness of animals. Thus, for Schopenhauer, the logical conclusion is that an enlightened will must produce psychic pain, because all longing is painful, and the process is irreversible. There is no way to go back to a paradise lost.[5]

Furthermore, and harking back to the apparent contradiction between narcissism and mass society mentioned earlier, Durkheim's Schopenhauerian sociology allows one to resolve this apparent paradox as follows: The narcissistic, detached individual still maintains a nonrational need for social communion that emanates from his or her will. If this need cannot be met in a healthy fashion through altruism, sympathy, compassion, or other ways that balance one's egoism (for example, what Veblen called the parenting instinct), then it will be met in explosively irrational ways, from wars to lynch mobs, that contradict the liberal, enlightened tenets of civilization. The important point is that, for Durkheim, the human person is not only a representational animal, but has a willful side as well.[6]

In "The Dualism of Human Nature and Its Social Conditions," Durkheim ([1914] 1973) seems to have borrowed Schopenhauer's philosophical assumptions, even specific phrases, to conclude that everyone leads a "double existence" torn between will and idea. More importantly,

Durkheim (pp. 162–63) arrives at the same horrifying conclusion that the psychic tension that results from *homo duplex* will get progressively worse with the advancement of civilization.

Several important consequences follow for the purposes of the present discussion. The functionalist misreading of Durkheim focuses only on the social control of human passions (as if that were possible), but misses the Schopenhauerian context for Durkheim's remarks, which leads to an antifunctionalist conclusion: Modern societies are characterized by inevitable, ever-increasing disequilibrium and disquietude. This distressing conclusion, in turn, exposes the sorely uncomplicated, glib optimism concerning enlightenment in most postmodernist discourse. Those for and against postmodernism assume that only enlightenment is involved, as if the will did not matter, as if one *could* "rebel" at the Enlightenment and get away with it. Something similar applies to those who claim that history could end, as if the lower and disquieting pole of *homo duplex* that has plagued humanity in its history could be eliminated—the wars, nationalism, totalitarianisms, and other evils.

Durkheim's Schopenhauerian and extremely complex assessment of human development seems to apply still to our deceptively happy, but troubled, postmodern times obsessed with fun and fun-systems (from Baudrillard and Riesman). Schopenhauer had warned that even when the will is satisfied, the satiation is temporary and fleeting, for humans will suffer boredom until a new longing sets in. Similarly, Durkheim writes in *The Division of Labor in Society*:

> Assuredly, there is a host of pleasures open to us today that more simple natures knew nothing about. But, on the other hand, we are exposed to a host of sufferings spared them, and it is not at all certain that the balance is to our advantage. Thought, to be sure, is a source of joy which can be very intense, but, at the same time, how much joy does it trouble! For a solved problem, how many questions are raised without solution! For a cleared-up doubt, how many mysteries come to disconcert! Indeed, if the savage knows nothing of the pleasures of bustling life, in return, he is immune to boredom, that monster of cultivated minds . . . if we are open to more pleasures, we are also open to more pain. ([1893] 1933:242)

Even a newspaper as conservative and pragmatic as *The Wall Street Journal* has noted that boredom and a blase indifference are the most common response to the tremendous variety of representations offered by the media, especially in advertisements. The mental, representational life of humans may well possess certain limits for withstanding stimulation, beyond which pain, boredom, and pathology will result. Durkheim's sociology seems to advocate that while we cannot turn back the hands of time regarding progress, this progress is a double-edged sword. Humanity must learn to balance the opposing sides of *homo duplex*, and actively strive to maintain its collective mental health. But these goals are far from attainable given the state of chaos in postmodernist discourse, which routinely ignores the role of the will in the Enlightenment project.

## PERCEPTION AND THOUGHT IN DURKHEIM'S SOCIOLOGY

We have already emphasized the connection between Durkheim's typically *fin de siècle* focus on representational life and the postmodernist concern with hyperreality and the circulation of fictions. The contrast between the two positions has also been discussed, that postmodern representationalism lacks depth whereas the previous *fin de siècle* was mindful of the other side of the representation. But another level of complexity is added to this discussion when one considers that, for Durkheim, there exists a profound difference between the feminine nature of perception versus the masculine nature of conceptualization.[7]

For Schopenhauer, humans, animals, and even plants respond to stimuli, but a brain is required for stimuli to be transformed into perceptions. An advanced brain is capable of transforming perceptions into conceptions, and enlightenment renders the human agent capable of transforming conceptions into abstract hyperconceptions. This is another way of saying that humans are able to think about thinking. But instead of concluding, like the positivists, that this enlightened consciousness is superior to perception in all ways, Schopenhauer concluded instead that an exclusive focus on conscious, conceptual representationalism is limiting because it is deprived of depth:

> The abstract concepts of reason can only serve to handle what is immediately understood, but never to bring about understanding itself. Every force and law of nature . . . must first be known immediately by the understanding, must be intuitively apprehended, before it can pass into reflected consciousness. ([1818] 1977a:21)

Perceptions are associated with the will, which "has not wholly entered into the form of the representation" and "makes itself known in an immediate way in which subject and object are not quite clearly distinguished" (p. 109).

In general, for both Schopenhauer and Durkheim, perceptions are private, subjective, and pertain to the will, while conceptions are essentially representations, public, and social. A dialectic is implied, such that perception and conception depend upon each other. The limited brain and consciousness of animals means that most of their perceptions remain on the level of stimuli, because perceptions require some degree of enlightenment in order to be transformed into conceptions. But, through hyperenlightenment, it is possible for the conceptions to become reified, divorced, and detached from the perceptions that gave rise to them in the first place. This is the dangerous state of affairs that Horkheimer and Adorno warned against in *Dialectic of Enlightenment* (1972) and other writings.

Genuine insight is the ability to link the conceptions to the perceptions and stimuli that gave rise to them in the first place. According to Schopenhauer, enlightenment without intuition leads to the paradox in which "the ordinary European's gaze is often almost like the animal's, and he would never suspect the invisible in the visible, if he were not told about it by others" (1988:4). Enlightenment involves concepts, but when carried to its extreme, conceptualization actually works against insight, which stems from the will. This is because Schopenhauer distinguishes between two types of knowledge, one based on the concept and the other on the perception. Perceptive, intuitive knowledge aims at understanding "reality" while conceptual knowledge is rational and aims at grasping "truth." The first tries to break through illusion while the second merely attempts to avoid error. Schopenhauer treats both kinds of knowledge as a unity, in that the wise person will know how to move from perception to conception—but feels that perceptive knowledge, which is associated with the will, is superior to the other type, which merely avoids errors. Clearly, postmodern culture denies the possibility of grasping "reality," and has opted for the more limited, positivistic goal of avoiding errors. Yet, according to Schopenhauer:

> In all ages and countries the words understanding, *intellectus*, acumen, *perspicacia, sagacitas*, etc., had been used to denote the more intuitive faculty . . . and its results, which differ specifically from those of Reason here in question, have always been called intelligent, sagacious, clever etc. Intelligent and rational were accordingly always distinguished one from the other, as manifestations of two entirely and widely different mental faculties. ([1813] 1899:131)

It is ironic that in postmodern culture, rationality is considered a prerequisite for intelligence. For Schopenhauer, reason is nothing but form added to the content supplied by the will, so that reason "only conceives, but does not generate" (p. 137). Schopenhauer concludes that no lasting knowledge can ever be gained using rationality alone, which is why the perceptive, intuitive starting point of an analysis is its most important part. Thus, according to Schopenhauer:

> For proof by indicating the reason of knowledge only effects conviction, not knowledge. . . . This is why, in most cases, therefore, it leaves behind it that disagreeable feeling which is given by all want of insight . . . like the

feeling we have, when something has been conjured into or out of our pocket, and we cannot conceive how. (p. 159)

Schopenhauer's philosophy puts science in its place, so to speak. Reason without insight is incomplete. Hyperpositivistic reason results in mountains of research projects and hypotheses that have not curbed the human animal's propensity for wickedness and anarchy in this century, and that have yielded few insights (Sorokin 1948). Following Schopenhauer, Durkheim's classics were intended to yield insights, not just hypotheses to be tested, because science "does not entirely consist of some propositions which have been definitively proved" ([1893] 1933:362). But how many of Durkheim's critics have read any of his classics for their humanistic insights? The notion of insight is not even part of the positivistic vocabulary, and is not addressed by postmodernists either.

Schopenhauer's philosophy also offers an explanation for the strange tendency, exposed by Adorno and other critical theorists, of enlightened individuals to fall prey to propaganda and vicious lies of all sorts, despite their supposed intelligence and liberal worldviews. Rational intelligence stays on the surface of things, and cannot compare with the depth achieved by understanding. I agree with Adorno (1991) that one should not expect to find that the government or media wizards conspire actively and consciously to delude the masses. Rather, enlightenment itself falls victim to a strange dialectic of antienlightenment, and everyone—leaders and followers alike—is subjected to the same forces. Schopenhauer had foreshadowed Horkheimer and Adorno's *Dialectic of Enlightenment* (Horkheimer and Adorno 1972), but offers a different solution than that pursued by Habermas in response to Adorno: Instead of pursuing enlightenment exclusively, humanity should engage in balancing enlightenment with imagination, wit, judgment, and sagacity.

But for Schopenhauer, this does not imply an anti-intellectual relapse into some orgy of emotions and feelings (as implied by Lukacs 1980). Rather, the reflective, contemplative person must attain a state of pure will-lessness as far as he or she is able. Schopenhauer believed that geniuses are able to achieve this mystical state of pure perception more frequently than the average person, but that it is not a talent peculiar to genius. Even if Schopenhauer was critical of enlightenment, his aim was serene, deep, reflection. When one reflects authentically, one is able to "connect" a conception to its proper perception. Here, I shall not elaborate further on how this is to be achieved according to the tenets of Schopenhauer's philosophy. The important point is that postmodernists are overly concerned with the circulation of concepts and ideas, and insufficiently concerned with insight, serenity, and reflection.

Schopenhauer asserted that "reason is feminine in nature; it can give only after it has received" ([1818] 1977a:50) from the masculine will or perception. This was another way that Schopenhauer restated his belief that perception is the true generator of knowledge, whereas Enlightenment thinkers assumed that the mind, rationality, and conceptions generate knowledge. For the purposes of the present book, it is significant that in Schopenhauer's philosophy, feminine and masculine elements of thinking must be combined for authentic reflection and communication to occur.

Another consequence of Schopenhauer's thought on perceptions versus conceptions is that he felt that science must begin with inductive thinking and be completed in deductions whereas neopositivists have reversed this understanding. Similarly, Durkheim's (1895) sociological method is primarily inductive in its orientation: One must eradicate preconceptions to get at the objective social fact. Conceptions are drawn from perceptions, in opposition to the contemporary habit of drawing conceptions from conceptions.

## THE UNITY OF KNOWLEDGE

Few would deny that one of the more important neo-Kantian dilemmas that postmodern sociology has inherited has to do with various aspects of the object-subject distinction. Postmodernists claim to overcome this distinction by denying a privileged status to the object and by granting priority to the subjective interpretations of the world. Following this postmodern strategy, there is no correct way to apprehend Durkheim or any other great text. In fact, no text is objectively greater than another. Texts are merely voices that are apprehended according to one's subjective preference. How is this state of affairs, welcomed by many defenders of postmodernism, different from old-fashioned anomie? And why in the world would further fragmentation, disintegration, and splitting of the object from the subject be welcomed, given that modernity entails painful fragmentation of culture to begin with? Postmodernists aggravate the problems engendered by modernity more than they resolve them.

By contrast, the thrust of Schopenhauer's contribution to philosophy, in his own words, is that he "did not start either from the object or the subject, but from the idea, which contains and presupposes them both" ([1818] 1977a:32). For Schopenhauer, object and subject are a kind of unity, and his philosophy has been used as a rallying cry by some who have wished to criticize excessive positivism (Hamlyn 1980). Similarly,

Durkheim advocated a kind of synthesis of object and subject. Indeed, it seems that his followers understood his sociology in this holistic way— they did *not* see Durkheim as the prince of positivism and the heir to Comte. Moreover, the concepts of integration, totality, unity, solidarity, and other synonyms for these concepts are among the most important in Durkheim's vocabulary. Here again one can discern the feminine, erotic (in Plato's sense) element in Durkheim's sociology that was characteristic of his *fin de siècle*.

Marcel Mauss ([1950] 1979a, [1950] 1979b) insists that Durkheim advocated the study of the "total social fact," which assumes the simultaneous action of the social, psychological, physiological, and other dimensions of how a phenomenon may be studied. According to Mauss, Durkheimian sociology "presupposes the combined study of these three elements: body, mind and society" ([1950] 1979a:24). Mauss cites Durkheim's *Suicide* as an example of this total approach, as well as the works of several other Durkheimians. The important point of agreement with Schopenhauer is that Durkheim accounted for the other side of *homo duplex*, the will in its many manifestations.

Celestin Bougle is just as explicit about the goal of the Durkheimians. Bougle writes that Durkheimian "sociology appeared less as a separate discipline occupied exclusively with the formal side of groupings . . . than as a synthesis of particular social sciences" (1938:24). Bougle insisted that "the necessity of specialization must not make us lose sight of the ultimate ideal, which is to achieve a synthesis and to *renew* the various social sciences" (p. 22). Bougle dismissed as a "manifest exaggeration" the claim that "Durkheim wished to prepare this subthesis by eliminating all psychology, as tainted by subjectivism" (p. 22), and disagreed with Comte on precisely this issue. Bougle was careful in depicting Durkheim's intellectual indebtedness to Comte, writing of Durkheim that he was "positive in spirit, therefore, but no slave of the positivist system" (p. 22). Referring to Durkheim's epistemology specifically as a "renovated rationalism," Bougle called it a "rationalism *impregnated* with positivism" (p. 24; my emphasis; note the peculiarly sexual terminology).

As early as *The Division of Labor in Society,* Durkheim lamented the compartmentalization of science such that "science, carved up into a host of detached studies that have no link with one another, no longer forms a solid whole" ([1893] 1933:294). The compartmentalization that he witnessed in his *fin de siècle* has become much worse in our *fin de siècle*. The social sciences are out of touch with the natural sciences and the humanities. Within the social sciences, sociologists are continually at war with economists, psychologists, and others who are supposedly studying the same social reality. And even within sociology, the functionalists, conflict theorists, and symbolic interactionists act like warring nations. If the professors of these various disciplines are forced to interact with each other at a conference, the typical result is pathetic posturing and ceremonial seeking of prestige at the expense of other disciplines (see Riesman 1956; Veblen [1899] 1967). The totality of human knowledge has been lost. Postmodernist decentering from the object to the subject does not ameliorate this state of affairs.

Up to the times in which Durkheim wrote, philosophy served to unify the sciences. In fact, all of the sciences developed from philosophy, including psychology and sociology, among the last sciences to declare their independence from philosophy. Alas, Durkheim observed, contemporary philosophy is as subject to compartmentalization as the other disciplines, so that modern philosophy cannot fulfill the regulatory, unifying role it used to hold. The end result is what he called intellectual anomie:

> There are hardly any disciplines that harmonize the efforts of the different sciences toward a common goal. This is especially true of the moral and social sciences, for the mathematical, physical, chemical and even biological sciences do not seem to such an extent foreign to one another. But the jurist, the psychologist, the anthropologist, the economist, the statistician, the linguist, the historian—all these go about their investigations as if the various orders of facts that they are studying formed so many independent worlds. Yet in reality these facts interlock with one another at every point. . . . They afford the spectacle of an aggregate of disconnected parts that fail to co-operate with one another. If they therefore form a whole lacking in unity, it is not because there is no adequate view of their similarities, it is because they are not organized. . . . It is because they are in a state of *anomie*.([1893] 1933:368)

Durkheim proposed that sociology would take the place of philosophy as the intellectual foundation for science, even as the foundation of liberalism (see Logue and Bazon 1979; Logue 1983). His proposal calls forth an immediate defensive reaction from the other sciences (especially the social sciences), and must be elaborated. First, Durkheim's vision of sociology is a holistic, interdisciplinary, integrative one—he was *not* advocating sociological imperialism. Second, Durkheim's recommendation follows logically from the realization that philosophy could rule the sciences so long as the individual was perceived to be the humanistic center of the universe. The development of modernity entails a gradual realization that society is the most salient feature of all knowledge, even the knowledge generated by the so-called hard sciences. This is because no insight can be made practical without involving collective faith, effort, and representations. In Durkheim's defense, it should be noted that almost everyone today regards him- or herself as an amateur sociologist, even the media wizards and the gurus of the culture industry. Unfortunately, professional sociology has turned away from Durkheim's high vision and has been trying to emulate the methodology of the hard sciences, without realizing that hard facts exist only in relation to a cultural context.[9] Durkheim's vision is an alternative to intellectual anomie. For example, capitalism still tries to derive its strength from laissez-faire philosophy, which in Durkheim's view is unsuited to the complexity of modern life. His solidaristic individualism (only an apparent paradox) flows from the realization that individualism must be nurtured by society and protected by the state, and is no longer protected adequately by any philosophy that is derived from or oriented toward the egoistic individual.

The cynical reader might object that all this sounds like Kant's notion of totality that is indispensable for the act of judgment required in inductive reasoning. But Schopenhauer and Durkheim went beyond Kant in this regard. Kant never bothered to explain how the category of totality originates nor what props it up. Schopenhauer criticized Kant specifically in this regard, and argued that the will is the ground for the mental category *totality*. In *The Elementary Forms of the Religious Life*, Durkheim followed Schopenhauer's lead to proclaim that the concept of totality is the most important yet neglected of philosophical categories, and that its ground or referent is society:

> This idea of *all*, which is at the basis of the classifications which we have just cited, could not have come from the individual himself, who is only a part in relation to the whole and who never attains more than an infinitesimal fraction of reality. And yet there is perhaps no other category of greater importance; for as the role of the categories is to envelop all the other concepts, the category par excellence would seem to be this very concept of *totality*. The [neo-Kantian] theorists of knowledge ordinarily postulate it as if it came of itself, while it really surpasses the contents of each individual consciousness taken alone to an infinite degree. . . . *The concept of totality is only the abstract form of the concept of society: it is the whole which includes all things, the supreme class which embraces all other classes.* ([1912] 1965:489; my emphasis)

In a footnote, Durkheim adds that "at bottom, the concept of totality, that of society and that of divinity are very probably only different aspects of the same notion" (p. 490). The category of totality enables one to conceive society as an entity that is more than the sum of individuals. Against postmodern fragmentation and the circulation of fictions without referent, Durkheim points to society as the referent for the fictions, as well as for the category of totality. If concepts and categories are derived from the individual, then the so-called referent for society is subjective, which is not a referent at all, and one has succumbed to Baudrillard's nihilistic vision of society as a mess of circulating fictions.

Additionally, Durkheim's insight is relevant to postmodernist efforts to raise consciousness concerning the common fate of our planet and the ecosystem, the totality of the world and the universe. But how can these efforts succeed if they continue to draw on old-fashioned and defunct doctrines of rugged individualism and laissez-faire philosophy? Durkheim is the sociologist par excellence of the cosmopolitan unity of humankind, of international social solidarity.[10]

## IMPLICATIONS

We began this chapter with the observation that in American as well as postmodern social character, ideas are assumed to exist without will. Postmodern writers depict social life as a collection of rootless, endlessly circulating fictions that have no ultimate meaning. This dynamic state of affairs is described by some as liberating, and by others as a dangerous state of affairs that can lead to reification, nihilism, narcissism, and other evils. This postmodern state of ideas devoid of will was contrasted sharply with Schopenhauer's seminal idea that the world is will *and* idea. This fundamental opposition was refracted further into Durkheim's notion of *homo duplex* or the dualism of human nature, the tension between conceptions and perceptions, consciousness versus the unconscious, even *feminine* versus *masculine* principles of knowing and communicating (among many others). We ended with Durkheim's claim that society is the ground or referent for the most important mental concept or category of all: totality. In line with the previous chapters, this dualistic vision of social life influenced Freud, Durkheim, Simmel, Veblen, Jung, Nietzsche, and other intellectuals from the previous turn of the century.

The notion that the world can be both will and idea is alien to the postmodern mind. Thus far, my aim has been primarily one of exposition. Nevertheless, even at this stage of the discussion it is possible to discern how superficial and dangerous the postmodern version seems compared to the previous *fin de siècle* version. If the world is only my idea, then what shall restrain the fantastic generation of subjective ideas, opinions, and fictions? What shall prevent subjectivism from spilling over into totalitarian mind control? Adorno (1991), Horkheimer (1947), and the other critical theorists have described the end result of this narcissistic mass society: Truth is packaged and sold by public relations firms to the masses as if it were toothpaste.

# NOTES

1.   See Spengler's ([1928] 1961) discussion of architecture in Classical times versus modern civilization in volume 2 of *The Decline of the West*.

2.   Compare Tocqueville's line that "in America I saw more than America; I sought there the image of democracy itself" ([1835] 1945:15) with Baudrillard's claim that "[America] is a world completely rotten with wealth, power, senility, indifference, puritanism, and mental hygiene, power and waste, technological futility and aimless violence, and yet I cannot help but feel it has about it something of the dawning of the universe" (1986:23).

3.   With the minor exception of Farr and Moscovici's *Social Representations*, (1984)—where they self-consciously distance themselves from Durkheim's and other *fin de siècle* usages of this term.

4.   For a critique, see Cortese and Meštrovíc (1990).

5.   Perhaps this is an important point to contrast with my contemporary assessments of modern social problems. For example, Bellah et al. (1985), Bloom (1987), and Lasch (1991) are among the conservative thinkers who seek to revivify a lost tradition to offset modern narcissism.

6.   I agree with Collier (1991) in this regard, that the Victorians believed that hunmans are driven by passion, which must be restrained, whereas the new view became that human nature is completely malleable and controllable. Collier believes that is perhaps the most important change of mind in modern times.

7.   But Schopenhauer is hardly consistent on this point. If he associates the feminine with the feelings and desires of the will, he associates it also with passivity, and therefore with the mind, which he believed was a weak and passive power compared with the will. These contradictions in Schopenhauer's philosophy pose a serious obstacle to establishing a consistent account of his feelings toward masculinity versus feminity.

8.   On this point, see also Halbwachs ([1938] 1960:143).

9.   Spengler ([1926] 1961) is among the strongest proponents of this view. See, for example, his analysis of the differences in mathematics in Classical culture versus late civilization.

10.   It is significant that Veblen (1943:175–93) wrote an essay in 1884 entitled "Kant's Critique of Judgment," in which he presents an argument that parallels Durkheim's critique of Kant. Veblen wrote his doctoral dissertation on Kant's critique of judgment according to Riesman (1964).

# Chapter 5

## *Postmodern Language as a Social Fact*

Intellectuals who write on the postmodern consequences for linguistic communication claim some of the following: Semiotics, deconstruction, dedifferentiation, poststructuralism, and even "postlinguistics" supposedly challenge the modern, Western assumptions that language and communication are based on universal, objective, rational principles (Birch 1988; Ingram 1988; Lash 1986, 1988). Deconstruction purports to demystify, but has been criticized for reproducing the very fragmented, alienated, and nihilistic world it seeks to transcend. Postmodernism has been hailed as being liberating because it unchains the individual from the objectivity of the word, yet has been criticized for leading to relativism and nihilism, because it sweeps away all standards—even the ones that liberate the individual (Bauman 1991). Postmodernism allows many voices to be heard, whereas it is purported that rigid, reified, and evil modernity allowed only the exploitative or bourgeois voices to dominate. But with so many voices clamoring to be heard, it is more, not less difficult to be noticed: The voices are easily drowned out by the "noise" (Harvey 1989).

Our contribution to this aspect of the postmodern discourse shall be along the lines indicated previously. If the Enlightenment narratives pertaining to human communication are oppressive because they are excessively rational, it is not a satisfactory solution to follow Baudrillard and conclude that the world is fiction, or to follow Habermas and complete the Enlightenment project. We offer a third alternative, based on a reconciliation of the Romantics with the Enlightenment.

Jurgen Habermas (1984) is a voice that has broken through the confusing verdicts on postmodern communication. As noted previously, Habermas seeks to complete the Enlightenment project of modernity by establishing it on the postmodern theory of communication. His critics contend that the universal community of rational discourse that he seeks is negated by the intersubjective freedom of individuals that he espouses.[1] A universal discourse of rationality that leads to a new, post-modern morality is unlikely also because of the much discussed tendency toward cultural relativism. But we object to Habermas because he assumes that human culture is held together only by truth and rationality, and we contend that it is also held together by emotion and sentiment.

Another voice in the postmodern cacophony is that of Scott Lash (1986), who claims that humanity has entered the era of "postlanguage": Communication is less mediated by language, as it was in modernity, and is more mediated through figures, sounds, images, impulses, the body, and excess. Of course, Baudrillard (1981) has commented extensively on the fragmented, ever-changing sea of images that is supposed to constitute postmodern communication (for a critique, see Rojek 1990). The body has also been treated as the site of postmodern postlinguistic communication by Turner (1984), Glassner (1989), and others. If Lash and the postlinguists are correct, we cannot have Habermas's solution of a universal ground of rational discourse. If Habermas is correct, postlinguistics constitutes an anomic communication.

But given the claims made by writers concerning postmodernism, how can one determine who is correct regarding this or any other post-modern debate? To repeat, there does not exist anything like a unified postmodern theory or even position on language and communication (Kellner 1988). Thus, there does not exist a clear intellectual target to comprehend or criticize. Instead, there exist many voices, books, articles, and opinions even on the topic of dedifferentiation, the claim that the distinction between signifier, signified, and referent melts into the freedom of new voices.

What voices are not heard in the discourse of postlinguistics carried on by Derrida, Foucault, Lash, Habermas, Lyotard, Baudrillard, and other participants? These thinkers invoke Wittgenstein, Saussure, Peirce, and other linguists, but not Durkheim and Schopenhauer. Yet Janik and Toulmin (1973) as well as Magee (1983) demonstrate convincingly that Wittgenstein ought to be regarded as a disciple of Schopenhauer, and Saussure clearly built his linguistics on the Romantic edifice that had already been established by *Volkerpsychologie*, Wundt, and the Durkheimians (Harris 1985).[2] Durkheim's sociology is capable of sustaining the simultaneous need for community and the intersubjective freedom of individuals that these other sociologies and philosophies cannot. Language is a fertile ground for applying the notion that society is will and idea.

The claim that thought exists in a primordial state of flux prior to being fixed in language is essential to understanding Durkheim's and other *fin de siècle* conceptions of language. For example, Schopenhauer writes:

> Words and speech are thus the indispensable means of distinct thought.
> But as every means, every machine, at once burdens and hinders, so also
> does language; for it forces the fluid and modifiable thoughts, with their
> infinitely fine distinctions of difference, into certain rigid, permanent
> forms, and thus in fixing also fetters them. ([1818] 1977c:238)

Similarly, Durkheim described language as violence being performed
on thought, as the constraint imposed on thought considered as perpetual flux. Whereas Saussurean linguistics assumes a homogeneous
language, uniformly used by all members of the community, a Durkheimian linguistics assumes a dynamic state of flux before *and after*
thoughts are crystallized into language.

The deconstructionists argue that language ought to be subject centered, and open to interpretation. Critics argue that when this argument
is carried to its extreme, it leads to the unwelcome conclusion that language does not refer to anything objectively real. This is an intellectual
dead end that stems from assuming that language must be either objective or subjective, whereas thinkers from the previous *fin de siècle* assumed that object and subject are an antagonistic unity. On the other
hand, the postpositivists have sought to make language almost mathematical in its precision and objectivity. Critics of this position have argued that objective reality cannot exist without the human agent and,
further, that limiting ourselves to that part of reality that can be expressed with positivistic precision robs us of the rich reality that is ignored. Neither extreme is philosophically or sociologically welcome,
because each is subject to the criticism that it is one-sided.

We shall point to a resolution in which language is both object and
subject, will and idea. The portrait of monolithic objective modernity
versus liberating, subjective postmodernism is not only problematic for
contemporary discourse, it is not an accurate rendition of the birth of
linguistics as a science during the previous *fin de siècle*.

## RECOVERING THE GERMAN ROMANTIC CONTEXT
## OF THE BIRTH OF LINGUISTICS

That something new can be learned in this crowded field of postmodernist pronouncements on linguistics is attested by the observation that
contemporary sociologists typically invoke Durkheim's analyses of suicide, crime, and religion in discussions concerning social facts, but tend
to omit language as a social fact. And nonsociologists tend to downplay
the sociological dimensions of linguistics. True, Ferdinand Saussure
(1916) did assert that language is a social fact, but neither linguists nor

sociologists are sure what Saussure might have meant by this claim (Harris 1985). For one thing, contemporary sociologists are still debating what Durkheim meant by the concept of social fact. Durkheim's nephew and collaborator, Marcel Mauss ([1920] 1969:308–12), regarded language as the social fact par excellence, because it is simultaneously "psychic" and therefore psychological and subjective, yet it imposes itself with force and constraint upon the human will, and is therefore social and objective.[3] The celebrated linguist in Durkheim's group, Antoine Meillet (1906), who began his career as Saussure's disciple, agreed with Mauss (see also Mounin 1975:42). Nevertheless, it is Saussure, not Durkheim, who is frequently credited with establishing modern linguistics.

Consider that when Saussure asserted that "language [langage] is a social fact" ([1916] 1959:6), he did not have to explain to his audience what he meant by a social fact. Durkheim had done that long before Saussure arrived on the academic scene. However, Saussure did not elaborate on the notion that language might be a social fact in the dualistic sense we have been following—object and subject simultaneously, will and idea, masculine and feminine. And postmodern audiences are not clear as to what might be meant by the phrase *social fact*, in general nor with regard to language as a social fact.

Doroszewski (1932:90) suggests that Saussure was influenced by Durkheim in his claim that language is a social fact.[4] While it is true, as Leroy put the matter, that "the French school of linguistics incontestably bore the impact of the sociological spirit, and its promulgators did not fail to pay homage more than once to Durkheim's teachings" (1965:170), it is also true that postmodern sociologists and linguists have expressed little interest in the philosophical import of the claim that language is a social fact.

Doroszewski (1932) demonstrates convincingly, and in great detail, the parallels between Durkheim's treatment of a social fact in *The Rules of Sociological Method* ([1895] 1982) and Saussure's ([1916] 1959) treatment of language. He believes that Saussure's claim that language is a social fact may be understood as a reconciliation of the debate between Durkheim and Tarde (1969): the collective aspect of language is the concession to Durkheim, and the more individual speech is the concession to Tarde. Perhaps Doroszewski is correct, but it is also possible that the polemic between Durkheim and Tarde is a refraction of the object-subject debate that has been part of the Western narrative of history for many centuries now, and that received a great deal of attention from intellectuals during the previous *fin de siècle*. Without the concession to Tarde, Durkheim's sociology is still able to reconcile object and subject, will and idea.[5]

Dinneen elaborates: "Language can be considered a thing [social fact] separate from our use of it as individuals, because it is inherited entirely from the other speakers who teach it to us and is not our product" (1967:194). Wilhelm Wundt (1907), considered the founding father of German psychology, foreshadowed both Durkheim's and Saussure's moves with regard to language.[6] Durkheim was "Wundt's pupil," in the words of Marcel Mauss ([1950] 1979a:12), and Wundt's *Ethics* devotes almost a third of its text to the social study of language. And of course, Wundt was influenced by Schopenhauer and the founders of *Volkerpsychologie*, Lazarus and Steinthal, who were also influenced by Schopenhauer (see Kaern, Phillips, and Cohen 1990). Durkheim frequently praised *Volkerpsychologie* as a forerunner of his own distinctive version of sociology.

Consistent with the overall argument, we are not claiming that Schopenhauer influenced Durkheim's, Wundt's, or Saussure's linguistics directly. Rather, we are claiming that the role of Romantic German intellectual culture in the development of modern and postmodern linguistics needs to be acknowledged.

## LANGUAGE AS A SOCIAL FACT

Durkheim thought of language as a system of collective representations that can be treated as social facts. He argued consistently for the interaction of individual and society, object and subject. Let us begin with his analysis of language found in *The Elementary Forms of the Religious Life*:

> Now it is unquestionable that language and consequently the system of concepts which it translates, is the product of a collective elaboration. What it expresses is the manner in which society as a whole represents the facts of experience. The ideas which correspond to the diverse elements of language are thus collective representations. ([1912] 1965:482)

Durkheim regards the other varieties of social facts, from religion to suicide, as similar representations of social reality. In other words, language, religious beliefs, and suicidal tendencies (among other kinds of social facts) indicate aspects of social reality that otherwise lie hidden from the investigator as well as from the members of society. Durkheim's understanding is almost psychoanalytic, and close to Erich Fromm's (1962) interpretation of Freud's contribution to science: Society is the patient, the sociologist is the analyst, and language constitutes part of the symptomatology, the hieroglyphics that must be interpreted by the analyst. Suicide and religion are also social facts in this linguistic, psychoanalytic sense: They are *symbols*, representations of a veiled, underlying reality that must be deciphered and interpreted, *not* regarded as hard facts.

Durkheim understood representations to be symbols that are not mere mirrors of social reality, but also objects constitutive of it.[7] The mark of Schopenhauer in Durkheim's treatment of language in the above passage is found in Durkheim's belief that language expresses concepts. For Schopenhauer, concepts are general and communicable, but they never capture the full meaning of the particular object which they seek to represent. The antithesis between individual, private perception versus objective, collective conception is a hallmark of Schopenhauer's philosophy, and it found its way into Durkheim's linguistics.

For example, as early as 1885, Durkheim expresses how he had been influenced by German thinkers with regard to the study of language:

> Each of us speaks a language which he has not himself created: we find it ready-made. Language is, no doubt, like the clothing in which thought is dressed up. It is not, however, everyday clothing, not flattering to everyone's figure, and not the sort that anyone can wear to advantage. (Durkheim [1885] 1978:102)

This passage is partly metaphorical, but expresses Durkheim's sensitivity to the distinction between language as an objective representation (the clothing) and thought, which in itself represents reality. Thus, for Durkheim, language, religion, and other social facts are not invented by individual human actors, but are the objective work of the community even though individuals created the perceptions that gave rise to the social facts in the first place, and individuals subsequently comprehend these social products in their own private ways.

In 1903, Durkheim and Fauconnet again gave credit to German thinkers for the germ of the idea that language may be comprehended as a collective representation. Note their focus on language as the objectification of thought or will:

> *Volkerpsychologie* is a study whose subject matter is definite: it aims to investigate the laws of collective thought through its objective manifestations, in particular mythology and language.([1903] 1982:208)

The ideas that thought exists in a primordial state of flux prior to language; that language represents the collective will of a people; and that language may serve as an objective indicator of that will, are distinctly German Romantic insights.

Durkheim expressed clearly his belief that "linguistic sociology" was an integral part of sociology as conceived by him:

There are, in reality, as many branches of sociology, as many individual social sciences, as there are different types of social facts. . . . Language, which in certain respects depends on organic conditions, is nevertheless a social phenomenon, for it is also the product of a group and bears its stamp. Even language is, in general, one of the characteristic elements of the physiognomy of societies, and it is not without reason that the relatedness of languages is often used as a means of establishing the relatedness of peoples. There is, therefore, subject matter for a sociological study of language, which has, moreover, already begun. ([1885] 1978:101)

In a footnote, Durkheim cites Meillet's (1906) paper as an example. Other examples readily spring to mind: Durkheim's follower, Henri Hubert took it as a given that "language is one of the clearest and truest characteristics of societies" ([1925] 1934:33). He used language to reconstruct the history of the Celts. Similarly, Hertz ([1907–1909] 1960) applied Durkheim's sociological linguistics to understand the significance of the concept *left* versus *right*. Hertz eventually arrived at the conclusion that the right-left dualism corresponds to the sacred-profane dualism in all the languages that he considered—that it was another objectification of *homo duplex*.

For Durkheim, the words that constitute language carry within them a "resume" of the "wisdom and science which the group has accumulated in the course of centuries" ([1912] 1965:484). It is not a universal, positivistic wisdom, but it is objective in the sense that it emanates from the group, and is not created by the individual. In his conclusion to *The Elementary Forms* Durkheim claims that "a concept is not my concept; I hold it in common with other men; it is the work of the community" (p. 481). Schopenhauer expressed a similar dualistic view concerning the opposition between conceptions (or ideas) and perceptions (based on the will). To regard the word as a concept, a social fact, is to regard it as "relatively immutable," universal relative to one's group, and as an "impersonal representation; it is through it that human intelligences communicate" (p. 482).

Like other social facts, language exerts constraint, is general relative to one's group, and exists relatively independent of its individual manifestations in private speech (Durkheim [1895] 1982:59). According to Durkheim, language is *not* merely "the average of the corresponding individual representations" but is a phenomenon sui generis:

There are scarcely any words among those which we usually employ whose meaning does not pass, to a greater or less extent, the limits of our personal experience. . . . Thus there is a great deal of knowledge condensed in the word which I never collected, and which is not individual; it even surpasses me to such an extent that I cannot even completely appropriate all its results. ([1912] 1965:483)

Language makes communication possible in several ways. It provides a vocabulary with which one is able to think: "The system of concepts with which we think in everyday life is that expressed by the vocabulary of our *mother* tongue; for every word translates a concept" (p. 481; my emphasis on *mother*, to suggest another strand of Bachofen's influence, and to suggest that we are all constrained from referring to "father tongue"). According to Durkheim, prior to language, "sensual representations are in a perpetual flux; they come after each other like the waves of a river, and even during the time that they last, they do not remain the same thing" (p. 481). Writers on postmodernism have reversed Durkheim's understanding, albeit unwittingly: the perpetual flux is purported to come after the formation of concepts, and is often cited as a hallmark of postmodernism. From Durkheim's perspective, this postmodernist contradiction is impossible. This is because

> Thinking by concepts is not merely throwing a light upon the sensation which illuminates it, penetrates it, and transforms it. Conceiving something is both learning its essential elements better and also locating it in its place; for each civilization has its organized system of concepts which characterizes it. Before this scheme of ideas, the individual is in the same situation as the *nous* [soul] of Plato before the world of Ideas. He must assimilate them to himself, for he must have them to hold intercourse with others; but the assimilation is always imperfect. Each of us sees them after his own fashion. There are even a great many which we pervert in holding, for as they are collective by nature, they cannot become individualized without being retouched, modified, and consequently falsified. Hence comes the great trouble we have in understanding each other. . . . We all use the same words without giving them the same meaning. . . . We are now able see what the part of society in the genesis of logical thought is. (p. 484)

Note that contrary to the postmodernists, Durkheim does not posit an absolute opposition between universalist, objective modernity and subjectivist, dedifferentiated freedom following modernity. Rather, object and subject, conception and perception, are *always* opposed to each other. Durkheim never thought of modernity as being the objective, reified narrative whose oppression postmodernists exaggerate. This is because all objective realities exist in a state of flux prior to being crystallized in language, and return to a relative state of flux as each of us tries to apprehend language privately. This is a human process that is essentially the same in premodernity, postmodernity, and modernity.

Durkheim's conclusion in *The Evolution of Educational Thought* also addresses a Schopenhauerian opposition between thought as a bundle of will versus representationalism. According to Durkheim, collective representations strike one initially as a confused mass of ideas:

This vagueness reaches maximum intensity in the child, who cannot distinguish sensations from one another, who cannot even locate them at specific points in space. Because this confusion is fundamental it permanently inheres in the natural movement of thought. When we reflect on a subject or a question, what we notice first of all are vast blocks of vague ideas, of representations which are synthetic and consequently confused. . . . Between the point of departure and the point of arrival, between spontaneous thought in the state of nature and logical thought which is reflective, self-disciplined and self-conscious, there is thus a great gulf fixed. How has man been able to bridge it? ([1938] 1977:343)

Durkheim depicts the ability to communicate as a drama in which mind and reason must battle the overpowering will. He makes us appreciate communication as an exquisite achievement, and to consider the many possibilities for miscommunication due to the interaction of will and idea before, during, and after the leap from thought to words. Much of postlinguistics could be summarized as being trapped in what Durkheim considers to be the point of departure for linguistic communication.

Despite the fact that communication is a drama and a battle that each of us fights every day, Durkheim insists that it is "by means of language" that we are able to communicate, however imperfectly:

It is words that introduce distinctions into the thread of our thinking. For the word is a discrete entity; it has a definite individuality and sharply-definite limits. . . . In a sense, language does violence to thought; it denatures it and mutilates it since it expresses in discontinuous terms what is essentially continuous. (p. 344)

Without language, thought would return to its original state of confusion. It would revert to and remain will. Thus, according to Durkheim, "we owe to language the introduction into our mind of distinctness and logical organization" (p. 345). Durkheim emphasizes the tremendous importance of learning the etymology of words, and of instituting such a discipline into education—these exercises enable the child to distinguish and organize ideas logically:

For stylistic training should be understood, first and foremost, not as a means of teaching children to write elegantly and eloquently, but as a more complex exercise in analysis and logical synthesis. (p. 347)

This is why the study of style, grammar, and language used to constitute the common basis of all education.[8] Postmodern postlinguistics has liberated some children from the oppression of grammar at the price of diminishing their ability to reflect authentically—at least in Durkheim's opinion. In sum, the words of language, considered as social facts, carry within them impersonal meanings and thereby oppose the lower, ego-tistical, private part of *homo duplex* that we all carry within us. Without the interaction of these two poles of human nature, postmodernists shall not be more liberated compared to their ancestors, but merely more anomic and undisciplined. Indeed, the public reaction to postmodern developments in education has been an almost hysterical, conservative reaction to go back to emphasizing the basics of reading, writing, and arithmetic (Bloom 1987).

Durkheim's discussion of teaching children the etymology of words, found in his neglected *The Evolution of Educational Thought* ([1938] 1977), is akin to his discussion of teaching children the basis of morality in his *Moral Education* ([1925] 1961). The reason for the similarity becomes ap-parent when one considers that in both cases, the child learns essentially discipline, which is the basis for genuine human freedom (a point stressed also by Erich Fromm and other critical theorists). For Durkheim, as for many other *fin de siècle* intellectuals, license is not freedom. Post-modernist writers hardly take notice of this important distinction.

The rest of Durkheim's writings on language touch on truth, scientific reasoning, the epistemology of representationalism, and other im-portant aspects of what has come to be known as the sociology of knowl-edge. It is beyond the scope of this chapter or book as a whole to delve into all or even most of these issues. My aim has been to show that all of these important discussions rest on the assertion that language is a social fact, which makes it possible for the human agent to use logic and reason. Reason is not a private, a priori faculty as it was for the Enlight-enment thinkers and continues to be for many defenders of postmod-ernism, as if mere rebellion against all structures will liberate the human spirit. Rather, reason is a social faculty. Durkheim's understanding of language as a social fact rests squarely on the Schopenhauerian and other subsequent *fin de siècle* depictions of the antagonistic unity that is will and idea.

## WHAT IS A SOCIAL FACT?

Consider Durkheim's famous yet terribly controversial definition of a social fact in *The Rules of Sociological Method*:

> A social fact is any way of acting, whether fixed or not, capable of exerting over the individual an external constraint; or: which is general over the whole of a given society whilst having an existence of its own, indepen-dent of its individual manifestations. ([1895] 1982:59)

Durkheim's definition does *not* refer to any universal, rational categories that are criticized by postmodernists, but to one's society. But just because each society has its own language and other social facts unique to it does not mean that social meanings have been lost in the sea of cultural relativism. Constraint is still possible, even desirable, relative to one's society. The writers on postmodernism who end up with their terrible dilemmas of structure versus chaos really ought to consider other alternatives.

I agree with Willer (1968) that part of the controversy that surrounds Durkheim's definition of the social fact has to do with the problematic of translating the French *fait* into the English fact. A much more common meaning of *fait* is "act," such that:

> Reading into *The Rules of Sociological Method* "act" instead of fact leads to a startling new viewpoint toward Durkheim's thought. Consider the new and more dynamic message that the following translation produces when "acts" are substituted for "facts": "A social act is every way of action, fixed or not, capable of exercising on the individual an external constraint, or again, every way of acting which is general throughout a given society, while at the same time existing in its own right independent of its individual manifestations. (Willer 1968:180)

Note that in this new reading, Durkheim's definition of the social fact sounds very much like the common sociological understanding of culture. Indeed, Durkheim stressed in *Rules* that social facts must always be approached in the context of their social milieu, and should not be treated as if they were detached, positivistic, hard facts. Durkheim was a radical cultural relativist long before Oswald Spengler ([1926] 1961) and other intellectuals made relativism seem fashionable. Because even his contemporaries often missed his message, he repeated it many years later in *The Elementary Forms of the Religious Life*: "For the sociologist as for the historian, social facts vary with the social system of which they form a part; they cannot be understood when detached from it" (Durkheim [1912] 1965:113).

Nevertheless, Lukes (1982:4) has accused Durkheim unfairly of using the concept of constraint ambiguously and of "reifying" society in his definition of the social fact. But constraint is used very unambiguously by Durkheim, as I shall demonstrate below. As for reification, a sensitive and contextual reading of Durkheim suggests that his humanistic aspirations are in line with the antireification aims of Adorno and the Frankfurt school, something that I have been indicating throughout this book. From the perspective of Schopenhauer's philosophy used as context, Durkheim's definition is comprehensible: Collective representations constrain the imperious, tyrannical will even though the will gave rise to them in the first place. And the will is in constant flux. A delicate dialectic is involved here, such that in pathological manifestations, the representations can fail to restrain the will, which produces anomie, or the representations can become detached from the will, which produces a state analogous to the fragmented culture industry depicted by Adorno. The essential point is that Durkheim's sociology is every bit as complicated as Horkheimer and Adorno's *The Dialectic of Enlightenment* (1972).

Similarly, Talcott Parsons (1937:347)—who also completely overlooks the importance of Schopenhauer's philosophy to the *fin de siècle* spirit that nurtured Durkheim's sociology—misunderstands Durkheim's use of constraint as mere social control, the maintenance of an abstract social order. But Durkheim distinguished sharply between just versus unjust social order (see Schoenfeld and Meštrović 1989), a sentiment shared by the critical theorists. Again, as with Lukes's misunderstanding, there is no good reason for deriving these strange misconceptions from Durkheim's straightforward definition.

According to Parsons, Durkheim "set over against utilitarian teleology a positivistic determinism of the traditional sort" (1937:462). This Parsonian misunderstanding proved to be very influential, such that one commonly finds the expression in introductory sociology texts that social facts can and do constrain individuals, that is, restrict their freedom so that they are forced to choose rational goals. In general, constraint tends to be depicted in American sociology as a power or ability to produce some effect such as obligation, guilt, sanction, or other predictable behavior—as a kind of social control. These are all utilitarian, Enlightenment, overly rationalist understandings of constraint, loaded with implications that are inimical to Durkheim's thought. They make it easy for the postmodernists to criticize the authoritarianism of the grand narrative of modernity. The French, Latin, or other classical meanings of *contrainte* are not invoked as a clue to what Durkheim might have meant—this, despite the fact that Durkheim consistently insists that every social analysis must begin with an etymological analysis of definitions (Isambert 1982). Furthermore, given Durkheim's sensitivity to words and the importance of language, a linguistic analysis of Durkheim's problematic definition seems appropriate.

According to the *Littre* (Littre 1963), a highly respected French dictionary edited by a disciple of Comte, as well as the *Oxford English Dictionary*, constraint and *contrainte* are derived from the Latin *constringere*, which meant "to exercise violence." But this is not organized, bureaucratic violence affiliated with the Enlightenment and criticized by postmodernists (Bauman 1991). Other synonyms include coercion, force, captivity, and oppression, but in general, to constrain is to oppose the will, not the individual, with violence.

Recall that Durkheim asserts repeatedly that language and conceptualization perform *violence* upon thought. In this regard, Durkheim's discourse on language is commensurate with many of his *fin de siècle* contemporaries: William James asserted that prior to conceptualization, thought is a "stream of consciousness." Max Muller ([1879] 1965) depicted all translation and use of language as violence against thought, and Durkheim cited Muller frequently in *Elementary Forms* ([1912] 1965:89–102). In addition, the frequent use of the words *contrainte, coercition,* and *pression* in *Les Regles* (1895:4–11) reminds one of Durkheim's other claims that society is possible only at the price of "constantly doing violence to our natural appetites" ([1912] 1965:356).[9] This idea of violent restraint *of human egoism* (but not the individual) as a result of the social pole of *homo duplex* is integral to Durkheim's thought, and is a refraction of Schopenhauer's opposition between the will and idea.[10]

If social facts were not external to the individual, they would be equivalent to the individual's private sensations. That would lead to the postmodernist dilemma of not being able to communicate despite the purported freedom of the individual. With Schopenhauer as with Durkheim, only concepts are general and capable of being communicated.

Furthermore, Durkheim's claim that the constraint *of the will*—but again, not necessarily the individual—is violent is in line with Freud's, Pareto's, and other *fin de siècle* claims that one must pay a price for civilization, namely the discontent that results from restraint. Durkheim's use of *violence* does *not* mean aggression directed toward individuals in the manner suggested by Girard (1972, 1987a, 1987b) and others who have misinterpreted Durkheim's intentions. Indeed, Adorno and other critical theorists suggest that such other-directed violence in enlightened societies results from a childish, narcissistic regression in which the individual's desires are coddled and inflamed, not restrained, by the culture industry. In line with Schopenhauer's philosophy, Durkheim's classically correct use of *violence* implies asceticism, and asceticism precludes the relapse into fascism and mass society that have been analyzed by critical theorists.

Thus, when Durkheim elaborates that the sociologist ought "to consider social facts as things" ([1895] 1982:60), he is merely extending a classical, philosophical approach to social facts. Critics have accused him of social realism, materialism, contradiction, reification, and other alleged faults for this move, including the fantastic charge that his sociology can serve as the basis for fascism (see Lukes 1982, 1985; Ranulf

1939), a blind repetition of charges leveled at Durkheim in his lifetime that he had already expressly denied. One must repeat that for the critical theorists, fascism is never built on doctrines that take reality seriously, but on fantasies that become synthetically attached to idlike forces.

In addition, Schopenhauer's philosophy adds context for Durkheim's insistence as to why social facts ought to be regarded as things. Durkheim asserts that "as soon as we consider social facts *per se*, when we undertake to make a science of them, they are of necessity unknowns to us, *things* of which we are ignorant, for the representations that we have been able to make of them in the course of our lives, since they have been made without method and uncritically, lack any scientific value and must be discarded" ([1895] 1982:36; my emphasis). Schopenhauer wrote prior to Durkheim that our will contaminates our ability to conceptualize and hence communicate with each other. In this Schopenhauerian spirit, Durkheim elaborates:

> We believe ourselves disinterested, whereas our actions are egoistic; we think that we are commanded by hatred whereas we are giving way to love, *that we are obedient to reason whereas we are the slaves of irrational prejudices*, etc. How therefore could we possess the ability to discern more clearly the causes, of a different order of complexity, which inspire the measures taken by the collectivity? For at the very least each individual shares in only an infinitesimally small part of them; we have a host of fellow-fashioners, and what is occurring in their different consciousness eludes us. (p. 37; my emphasis)

Durkheim's elaboration is still relevant to postmodernist debates and to the legacy of the Frankfurt school, which was concerned greatly with irrational prejudices that thrive within the heart of liberal, enlightened society. Most contemporary writers ignore the possibility that enlightened individuals might be swayed by unconscious motives of which they are scarcely aware, whereas Durkheim was not only aware of this possibility, but held that in its focus on social facts as things, sociology might be able to ameliorate this dangerous tendency. And he foreshadowed the contemporary dilemma in which the enlightened, liberated individual would not be able to communicate with fellow-fashioners of meaning because each individual would be trapped in his or her private world of meanings.

For Durkheim, scientific conceptualization is *not* based on some positivistic, idiosyncratic grasp of predetermined hard facts that might be understood by only a small coterie of colleagues. Rather, language is the filter for reality, and language must be the starting point for ordinary as well as scientific conceptualization. It should be noted that as a rule, contemporary scientists (in the social as well as the natural sciences) are trained to develop their own specialized language, which is deliberately incomprehensible to the general public. The frequent end result is that scientific research results become irrelevant to society as a whole, even though the research was usually conducted in the positivistic spirit of seeking universal laws. And despite these lofty goals of universalism, scientists frequently disagree with each other regarding the language that they use. Here is another postmodern contradiction that Durkheim's sociology helps one avoid.

## LEFT VERSUS RIGHT AS COLLECTIVE REPRESENTATIONS

We have referred several times in this book to Robert Hertz's essay entitled "The Pre-eminence of the Right Hand: A Study in Religious Polarity." Regarded by Mauss as Durkheim's most brilliant follower, Hertz offers a fascinating sociological account of right- versus left-handedness that integrates many of the themes that we have been discussing in this chapter and this book. Briefly put, Hertz argues that in modern societies the left is associated with the profane, *feminine*, and weak, whereas the right is associated with the sacred, *masculine*, and strong. According to Hertz:

> To the right hand go honors, flattering designations, prerogatives: it acts, orders, and *takes*. The left hand, on the contrary, is despised and reduced to the role of a humble auxiliary: by itself it can do nothing; it helps, it supports, it *holds*. The right hand is the symbol and model of all aristocracy, the left hand of all common people. ([1907–1909] 1960:89)

Recall that according to Bachofen and scores of contemporary feminist writers, the state of affairs described by Hertz is a reversal of the preeminence of the left hand in ancient societies. For example, the ancient goddess Isis typically holds up her left hand as the sign of her power. If feminist writers are correct that the story of Adam and Eve and other Biblical stories were deliberately rewritten to make women seem wicked, weak, and profane,[11] then part of that transformation is surely reflected in language. Hertz's brilliant study sensitizes us to the role of language in reflecting and reifying this transformation from Bachofen's mythical state to present-day patriarchy. The overall aim of his essay is to call for a restoration of left-handed culture to complement and balance right-handed, modernist culture.[12]

Hertz refuses to explain the modern left-right distinction anatomically. He knows that the left brain is related to right-handedness, but concludes that since animals are ambidextrous, this connection should be explained socially. He turns to linguistic and religious collective representations for evidence. In order to follow Hertz's reasoning, I encourage the reader to look up right and left in the *Oxford English Dictionary* or its equivalent in any other language. The left is typically associated with phrases, proverbs, sayings, and meanings that denote something sinister, wicked, evil, weak, or otherwise profane. For example, to "have a baby by the left" meant giving birth to an illegitimate child in Shakespeare's time. The French *gauche* and the Italian *sinistro* capture these negative dimensions of left more directly than English.

But the right typically denotes honor, sanctity, goodness, and strength. Thus, one refers to one's "right-hand man." The right hand is used to bless, greet, console, perform religious functions, salute, even to marry. Hertz goes so far as to suggest that the wedding ring is worn on the left hand because that is the side that is tempted (p. 101). Hertz (p. 99) analyzes the meanings of the right as expressing good judgment, uprightness, moral integrity, good fortune or beauty, and juridical norm.

Thus, according to Hertz,

> It is not by chance that in pictures of the Last Judgement it is the Lord's raised right hand that indicates their sublime abode to the elect, while his lowered left hand shows the damned the gaping jaws of Hell. (p. 101)

Postmodernism has not shattered the linguistic structure uncovered by Hertz. For example, the general rule for contemporary males who choose to wear earrings may be summarized as, Right is wrong, and left is right. Because the earring came to be associated with females and the left, its use by males represents the new sensitivity exhibited by the postmodern male. Wearing it on the left seems to signify an identification with femininity. But when a male wears an earring on the right ear, it is no longer a fashion statement, but a signal that he is homosexual. A myriad of other contemporary uses of the right-left dichotomy lead to the conclusion that Baudrillard is quite wrong to depict postmodern culture as a mass of circulating, random fictions: Structure persists.

Although he does not mention Bachofen directly, Hertz confronts directly an issue that Bachofen uncovered in his study of ancient religions:

> In general, man is sacred, woman is profane: excluded from ceremonies, she is admitted to them only for a function characteristic of her status, when a taboo is to be lifted, i.e. to bring about an intended profanation. But if woman is powerless and passive in the religious order, she has her revenge in the domain of magic: she is particularly fitted for works of sorcery. "All evils, misery, and death," says a Maori proverb, "come from the female element." Thus the two sexes correspond to the sacred and to

the profane (or impure), to life and to death. An abyss separates them, and a rigorous division of labour apportions activities between men and women in such a way that there can never be mixing or confusion. ([1907–1909] 1960:97)

Hertz even adds that "Undoubtedly God took one of Adam's left ribs to create Eve, for one and the same essence characterizes woman and the left side of the body" (p. 103). Interestingly, this is Milton's version of the creation of woman in *Paradise Lost*, although the Bible is not specific on this point. It is important also to link Hertz's passage with Durkheim's depiction of the *religious* character of the war between the sexes such that "the male has functions which are forbidden to the female, even though she might be well suited to fulfill them" and "in our daily relationship with women, the men have adopted a special language, special mannerisms" ([1897] 1963:113). It would be important to analyze Durkheim's many references to male versus female totems in his *Elementary Forms* in light of the preceding. But in general, Hertz seems to illustrate the power of Durkheimian methodology when he concludes that based on language and religion, "Sacred power, source of life, truth, beauty, virtue, the rising sun, the male sex, and—I can add—the right side; all these terms are interchangeable, as are their contraries" ([1907–1909] 1960:103).

In his conclusion, Hertz reserved the right to explain the causes and meaning of the right-left polarity in a future work, although he adds that "this is one of the profoundest questions which the science of comparative religion and sociology in general have to solve" (p. 112). He never got the chance to return to this problem, because he died in World War I. But in his concluding paragraph, he clearly calls for an enlightened alternative to the masculine, right-side, mutilation of the feminine, left-side element of social life:

> If the constraint of a mystical ideal has for centuries been able to make man a unilateral being, physiologically mutilated, a liberated and foresighted community will strive to develop better the energies dormant in our left side and in our right cerebral hemisphere, and to assure by an appropriate training a more harmonious development of the organism. (p. 113)

And so Hertz ends his essay. We supposedly more enlightened and liberated postmodern individuals must confront the question his essay raises: Have the dormant energies of the right brain and the left side—specifically, feminine forces that exist independently of gender—been allowed to develop since Hertz published this essay in 1909? One wants to answer in the affirmative, to point to women's liberation and the equality between the sexes. But one could counter that equality between the sexes has meant that women have been assimilated into a cultural world erected primarily on masculine, right-side, left-brain characteristics, a tendency that belies the persistence of the inherent hostility toward the left-side, right-brain functions. Furthermore, the issue is not about men versus women, but about feminine versus masculine forces that affect both men and women.

The Durkheimian tradition teaches that reality is veiled beneath the collective representations of language and religion. Beneath the surface rhetoric of freedom, justice, and equality, there lurks the right-handed, masculine world of the will to power. In the present century, left-side, right-brain functions are not valued any more than they were in the previous century, or the centuries that preceded it (since the mythical break posited by Bachofen and Veblen). Rather, postmodern society continues to value and encourage success, strength, acting, ordering, and *taking*. The left side's functions of helping, supporting, and *holding* continue to be devalued.

## IMPLICATIONS

Durkheim regarded language as a social fact that should serve as the launching point and limiting border or constraint for conceptualization, general and scientific. Language is simultaneously will and idea, perception and conception, a constraint on thought as stream of consciousness *and* the privatization of all concepts. These insights by Durkheim, informed as they were by Schopenhauer's philosophy, are at least as momentous as Saussure's contribution to linguistics, because they enable one to be objective without succumbing to naive or dogmatic realism, and without making one vulnerable to the kinds of positions that postmodernists criticize. In fact, as we have noted, Doroszewski felt that Saussure could not have launched modern linguistics without Durkheim's philosophical sociology. Without Durkheim's assumption that language is a social fact, linguistics is subject to a kind of intellectual anomie, the promulgation of subjective, relativist, postlinguistic meanings that cannot be communicated or verified. Conceptualization becomes a complex social activity, as it is for Durkheim, but is not the quest for any sort of objective truth. But for Durkheim, thought is the will, which objectifies itself through representations or concepts. Thus, truth is simultaneously relative, regarding the collectivity that refracts our representations, yet objective in the sense of being external to the individual. This apparently paradoxical position is consistent with Schopenhauer's philosophy, and avoids the negative consequences of the postmodernist critique of modernity, namely nihilism, subjectivism, and postlinguistics.

Does cultural relativism necessarily lead to the position that we are all immersed in our own societies and must inevitably judge other societies in terms of our own? Are all views ethnocentric and parochial, merely assuming the concepts of the social group in which they originated? These pessimistic conclusions, found in much of the contemporary literature on the philosophy of science, assume that one's social group will not find points of contact with other social groups, and that one *must* conclude that one's conceptions are superior to those of other societies. These are static, excessively rational assumptions that ignore the role of the feminine, of sympathy and desire.

Durkheim argues that many collective representations eventually spill over the borders of one's society, and become gradually internationalized. Eventually, the concepts that characterize various collective representations, including language, can serve as the basis for greater and wider understanding, tolerance, and *sympathy* among the world's populations. A particularistic, parochial collective conscience is gradually transformed into a cosmopolitan, far-reaching collective conscience that will eventually embrace all of humanity. But this "cult of humanity" is based upon the feminine force of mutual sympathy. There is no good reason to suppose that only an oppressive, universal ideology, language, or other system of concepts based upon the will to power can guarantee harmony. In fact, such reasoning is decidedly chauvinist, right side, and derived from the left brain. The Durkheimians would have one balance our left-brain ethnocentrism with our mutilated right-brain sympathy and understanding for other people and other views.

Schopenhauer concluded that the realization of *homo duplex* should lead to compassion and sympathy for the profound reason that we understand within ourselves that everyone else is as trapped by the antinomy between concept and perception as we are. Why have postmodern writers completely ignored this option, and concluded that the breakdown of the grand narrative of modernity must lead to either chaos or instant liberation? In keeping with Schopenhauer's philosophy, the Durkheimian attitude toward language is far removed from naive realism and positivistic ideology, which are being increasingly criticized as stumbling blocks to a genuinely scientific sociology. Durkheim is clearly aware that reality does not and cannot speak for itself, and that prior to conceptualization, nature is in flux, chaos. Language imposes relative order on this chaos, making thought and communication possible, but the apparent order is again individualized. And Durkheim envisioned society itself as a system of representations. But these collective representations, these symbols of reality that constitute language, are a kind of reality in their own right. Durkheim's position enables one to criticize the naive separation found in much of the contemporary literature that reality is presumed to be objective, whereas symbols are presumed to be subjective.

For Durkheim, the collective representations and symbols that constitute language are objective only to a degree, because they must be privatized and individualized by persons in social interaction. Yet each private, subjective motive and thought must necessarily partake of the objective, because we cannot really communicate without concepts. Even the figures, sounds, images, impulses, and the body that Lash (1986) feels constitute postlanguage must strike collective chords of common understanding to be effective, or they will be dismissed as psychotic or be otherwise ignored. Similarly, Baudrillard (1988) exaggerates the nonreferential quality of circulating fictions in postmodern culture. Using Hertz's analysis of right-handedness, one can conclude that Baudrillard's fictions testify to the postmodernist continuation of the modern quest for prestige, status, and power that led some to characterize the 1980s as the greedy "me" generation, and that Veblen ([1899] 1967) had already uncovered in his studies of the barbaric temperament in modernity.

Communication is a drama that involves *homo duplex* in all its aspects at all times—and that means sacred and profane, masculine and feminine aspects of thinking, right and left. From Durkheim's Schopenhauerian perspective, the kind of liberation from the oppressive narrative of modernity that some deconstructionist postmodernists envision is impossible. These purportedly liberated individuals could not communicate with each other. And the dark portrait of oppressive modernity is equally improbable, because a system of concepts that rigid could not be used by individuals to express their subjective needs and interests, and would have died out long ago. Durkheim's call for balance, harmony, and the integration of opposing aspects of the human condition, including the left and right, seems eminently sane and reasonable.

## NOTES

1.   Among the most recent critical readings of Habermas, see especially Jane Braaten (1991) and Robert C. Holub (1991).

2.   However, I contend that Saussure vulgarized Durkheim much like Parsons vulgarized all the classical founding fathers of sociology. Saussure presents an overly rational, neat, and tidy picture of language.

3.   This is precisely the scaffolding that Habermas needs for his aims of establishing morality on rational, intersubjective communication.

4. Although Harris (1985) reports that many linguists disagree with Doroszewski.

5. And Saussure's distinction between the written word and speech does not necessarily carry the dimensions of the world as will and idea that we have been following. It is a weak, rational refraction of *homo duplex*.

6. Durkheim ([1885] 1978:102; [1887] 1976a:304) acknowledged his debt to Wundt. In stark contrast with Durkheim's repeated gratitude to the Germans, Saussure conspicuously omits any references to Wilhelm Wundt's *Volkerpsychologie*.

7. This is a move that resembles Ernst Cassirer's (1946, 1972) philosophical response to the dualisms inherited from Kant and Schopenhauer.

8. Albeit, this practice was criticized by Veblen ([1899] 1967) as being archaic and useless. Compare also with Bloom's (1987) and other contemporary calls to reinstate the traditional teachings of reading, writing, and arithmetic.

9. See also Durkheim ([1914] 1973:163), discussed in Mestrovic (1988).

10. See Durkheim ([1893] 1967:377, [1950] 1983:242, [1955] 1983:8).

11. See especially Condren (1989), Gadon (1989), Goodrich (1989), and Eisler (1987), among many other feminist analysts.

12. Note also Veblen's ([1899] 1967) relevance to the linkage between the right and aristocracy or the leisure class, and his own references to an archaic past in which this association was the reverse of what it is today.

Chapter 6

---

## *Postmodernism and Religion*

The postmodern discourse adopts an ambivalent stance toward religion. To the extent that postmodern means that humanity is today in a state that follows modernity, religion is perceived in the typically pejorative way, as something traditional, to be outgrown and abandoned. One does not find Baudrillard, Giddens, or most contemporary theorists seriously engaged with religion as a cultural phenomenon that might persist despite modernity. On the other hand, to the extent that postmodernism is interpreted as any sort of nostalgic revival of tradition, one encounters a limited treatment of religious fundamentalism, but again in pejorative terms.

In this chapter, we shall offer a new perspective that flows from Durkheim's sociology: Religion is a kind of language, a cultural phenomenon that enables society to communicate its hidden state of being to itself and to its members. As such, it can never be outgrown or out of fashion. Moreover, throughout history, religion has had its male as well as female deities who correspond to the needs of the mind versus the heart, respectively. This is not meant to imply the traditional stereotypes of male versus female behavior. Rather, we are applying a Jungian sort of interpretation of male and female as two archetypes that exist in all persons regardless of gender, only we are applying this scheme to Durkheim's sociology of culture. Nor is this unusual, given that Durkheim and Jung wrote in the same *fin de siècle* milieu. The gist of our critique of modernity shall be that it perpetuates a one-sided, masculine view of culture, and ought to seek a balance between cultural forces that, for the sake of convenience, may be termed masculine and feminine.[1] For example, consider Jean Baudrillard's reactionary and highly sexist claim in *Seduction* that "Freud was right: there is but one sexuality, one libido—and it is masculine" (1990:6).[2] It is not even clear that this is what Freud really meant.

In *The Elementary Forms of the Religious Life* especially (but in his other writings on religion as well), Durkheim presents religion as "a system of ideas with which the individuals represent to themselves the society of which they are members, and the obscure but intimate relations which they have with it" ([1912] 1965:257). Thus, religion is something to be interpreted and deconstructed, not taken as given. Far from treating religion as a manifestation of the status quo or conflict, he regards it as the product of "immense cooperation" (p. 29). "Social life, in all its aspects and in every period of its history, is made possible only by a vast symbolism," Durkheim writes (p. 264), "but one must know how to go *underneath* the symbol to the reality which it represents and which gives it its meaning" (p. 14; my emphasis). Durkheim preceded the postmodernists in seeking to deconstruct society and religion, but his deconstructionism does not lead to nihilism or preservation of the status quo. Beneath the symbols one finds sentiments and the will, yet "without symbols, social sentiments could have only a precarious existence" (p. 263).[3]

What is postmodern religion disclosing about the *fin de siècle* collective consciousness? As humanity heads for the end of the millennium, the postmodern generation in the United States is caught up in the collective representations that pertain to Bellah's "American civil religion," which are transparently old-fashioned, derivatives of Parsonian functionalism, at the same time that narcissism, cynicism, and cultural relativism promote egoism at the expense of religious self-abnegation (Bellah et al. 1985). Feminine archetypes are emerging in the many guises documented by Gadon (1989) in her *Goddess Within*, as well as by other feminist writers. Yet none of these contemporary feminine archetypes are on quite the same order as the Shaker movement or Mary Baker Eddy's prayers to "Our Father-Mother God, all-harmonious" (1971:16). The war between the sexes has not diminished in intensity or importance in postmodern culture. The previous *fin de siècle* ended a century of what sociologists call "the feminization of Christianity," a Romantic era in which women were regarded as the more spiritual, noble, and religious creatures compared with males.[4] The dominant characteristics attributed to Jesus were loving self-sacrifice, tenderheartedness, and willingness to forgive those who injured him. By contrast, our *fin de siècle* depicts Jesus as the warrior who must do battle with Satan for supremacy of the world, or as "the laughing Jesus" depicted in *Playboy*.

Moreover, militant metaphors abound in postmodern culture, with holy wars being declared and waged on drugs, AIDS, potholes, hunger, alcoholics, poverty, crime, mental illness, the recession, and just about anything else that is considered to be threatening or evil. Slightly more than a generation following the Vietnam War, which seems to have inspired Bellah's famous 1967 essay on civil religion, President Bush again invoked the notion of a just war in 1991 against Iraq, a war approved by God the Father, which was supposed to usher in "a new world order." In the present *fin de siècle*, we are witnessing a repetition of the conflict between collective representations based on the dynamo versus the Virgin that Henry Adams noticed in the previous *fin de siècle*: Americans want to be tough on crime and all other refractions of Satan at the same time that they want America to be a kinder, gentler place— and so on with many other seeming contradictions, discontinuities, and ironies that characterize postmodernism. And of course, America is important because it continues to serve as the locus of discussions concerning modernity, from Tocqueville's *Democracy in America* to Baudrillard's *America*.

With the ending of the cold war, the question that was debated in the previous *fin de siècle*, whether capitalism is superior to socialism, has reasserted itself with a new vigor in the present *fin de siècle*. Interestingly, Durkheim's sociology enables one to address this as a *religious* issue. It is difficult to avoid the conclusion that when the "evil empire"—the term that President Reagan used for the USSR—began to disintegrate, Americans began to fill the vacuum by searching for evils within the United States. Shortly after Gorbachev was depicted as a liberator, the media began to express concern with sexual molestation of preschool children, racism, drug dealing in elementary schools, and other evils that lurked within ordinary, middle-class existence. Does American civil religion need a satanic image in order to exist?

The present chapter will begin with an analysis of Bellah's famous notion of American civil religion, and the neoconservative trend it represents, contrasted with what Durkheim might have intended with his own implicit notion of civil religion, in the context of Bachofen's dramatic departure from the patriarchal view of history. We shall move to an analysis of the most important division of labor and antagonism in culture, the role of masculinity and femininity in modern life, and move to Erich Fromm's call for a reconciliation of masculine with feminine elements in religion as a possible resolution of some of the contradictions that emerge in postmodern discourse.

## TAKING BACHOFEN SERIOUSLY

I have suggested already that scholars agree that following J. J. Bachofen, the Great Mother archetype emerged as an object of study and as a mode of expression for a host of Romantic and *fin de siècle* writers. It is tempting to draw some parallels between our *fin de siècle* and the previous *fin de siècle*, to entertain the possibility that postmodernism is our Romanticism. But, if one were to take seriously the central claim that postmodernism is a rebellion against the grand narrative of modernity, one would expect the present *fin de siècle* to be exhibiting some sort of effort to reconcile patriarchal with female-centered religious symbolism or culture. While it is true that the present *fin de siècle* has its Marian apparitions at Medjugorje and elsewhere in the world, feminist critiques of chauvinist culture, and the rock star Madonna, it would be difficult to conclude that the grand narrative of modernity is in any real danger of collapsing. True, both Madonnas seem to touch on the issue that is central to postmodernist discourse: rebellion at patriarchal, Enlightenment, and sometimes oppressive grand narratives of what constitutes modernity (although, again, not everyone would agree with this summary).

But contrast these sudden eruptions of the Madonna archetype with the previously discussed essay published in 1901 by the American essayist Henry Adams, entitled "The Dynamo and the Virgin," in which he asserted that his *fin de siècle* was witnessing a fundamental shift in cultural symbols of power from the Madonna to the mechanical dynamo. In 1991, one might want to suspect that the Great Mother archetype, identified by Bachofen in the previous century, is attempting a comeback, even if it is faint and difficult to detect. Whatever constitutes postmodernism, it has definitely accompanied a marked increase in the collective attention being paid to the relationship of femininity to the modernity project and to religion. Scores of feminist writers have exposed the patriarchal bias in modern religions.[5] Yet, one feels compelled to conclude that Adams's observation still holds, that the West is still more animated by the dynamo than the Virgin, despite the challenge from a problematic and confused postmodernist discourse.

For example, Americans in particular seem obsessed with that almost living embodiment of the dynamo, the automobile. All the ecofeminist arguments in the world have not made them any more likely to consider mass transit, car pools, or other habits that would benefit Mother Earth and put a dent in their fascination with "a fast set of wheels."

One would like to turn to social theory, classical or contemporary, for guidance in assessing what postmodern religious and other cultural representations betray about our *fin de siècle* collective unconsciousness. But this is not easy when the postmodernist discourse is splintered, and contemporary textbooks and treatises continue to dismiss most classical theorists as mere chauvinists.

Moreover, the most popular contemporary writers on culture apparently draw upon the dynamo even as they critique modern culture. For example, Bellah et al. (1985) call for a return to the republican and biblical tradition despite their misgivings that these traditions might be sexist or otherwise oppressive. Bloom (1987) is unabashed in his ethnocentric defense of the Greek, Roman, and Western Enlightenment tradition. Even Christopher Lasch (1991), despite his poignant critiques of the doctrine of progress, fails to move beyond the orbit of masculine social values based on the dynamo that replaced the values associated with Adams's Virgin.

Durkheim's *The Elementary Forms of the Religious Life* ([1912] 1965), especially, tends to be read almost exclusively as a functionalist defense of masculine-sounding social order and normative consensus, the very things that many postmodernist writers criticize. It has become an automatic, unchallenged truism that Durkheim was a positivist and social engineer, and we have been resolutely challenging this misconception throughout the present book. Feminine aspects of Durkheim's sociology—especially his claim that religion is the *womb* from which all the other social institutions originate—have never been the centerpiece of the social-scientific study of religion, Durkheimian scholarship, or contemporary refractions of the Durkheimian tradition.

For example, the representation of Durkheim that is invoked in Bellah's civil religion is a Parsonian Durkheim who was supposedly interested in rational social action, social integration based on normative consensus, and social order.[6] These are the same traits that are found in the functions that American civil religion supposedly serves. The result is a tautological approach to civil religion that is essentially a closed system: a Protestant, patriarchal, American vision of essentially Protestant, patriarchal, American civil religion. This vision is self-serving and subjective in that it may appeal to some extent to contemporary Americans and Western Europeans, but cannot serve as the basis for any sort of postmodern transcendence of cultural values based on the dynamo.

## BELLAH'S CONCEPTUALIZATION OF AMERICAN CIVIL RELIGION

Robert N. Bellah's "Civil Religion in America," first published in 1967 but reprinted many times since then, became one of the most quickly accepted, misunderstood, controversial, and debated essays in sociology. Bellah defended and later formally abandoned this concept, even though it is implied in *Habits of the Heart* (Bellah et al. 1985). Over twenty years of research and discussion of American civil religion has not settled some fundamental ambiguities (see Mathisen 1989): How is American civil religion different from idolatry? Is it a liberal or a conservative "religion"? Do other nations have civil religions, or is it unique to the United States? Was American civil religion instrumental in getting the United States involved in the Vietnam War, or in getting it to end this war? How is American civil religion used by the culture industry (Adorno 1991), and why is it typically used to justify wars (see Elshtein 1986)? Of course, the positivists have objected that Bellah's notion does not stand up to empirical verification—but then, positivists routinely make this criticism, and have been unable to answer the criticisms leveled at them by postmodernist philosophers as to what constitutes genuine empirical verification.

Despite the tremendous sensitivity and complexity of thought that Bellah exhibits in some of his writings, he has not been helpful in resolving these issues. His reply to Mathisen's (1989) "Twenty Years after Bellah," in which many of the issues mentioned above were raised, was only one page long. In this reply, Bellah quips that "the argument of the [1967] article seemed obvious" and "is the sort of thing any Durkheimian would have said" (1989:147). He also confessed to growing tired of arguing with critics, and "stopped using the term civil religion" (p. 147).

But the argument is hardly obvious. Bellah claimed that American civil religion "exists alongside of and rather clearly differentiated from the churches" and that it is "not antithetical to and indeed sharing much in common with Christianity, was neither sectarian nor in any specific sense Christian" (1970:168). He also claimed that "like all religions, it has suffered various deformations and demonic distortions," including the shameful treatment of the Indians, adventures in imperialism, and several "unjust wars" (p. 179). He admits that "it has often been used and is being used today as a cloak for petty interests and ugly passions" (p. 186). But ultimately, he concludes that civil religion's central concern that "America be a society as perfectly in accord with the will of God as men can make it, and a light to all the nations" is something beneficial, benign, and functional (p. 186).[7]

My concern here is not with Bellah's notion of American civil religion per se—Bellah has apparently abandoned the concept, and that is his prerogative. Rather, and because he claims that Durkheim's sociology inspired at least part of his conceptualization of civil religion, it seems natural to want to contrast Bellah's with Durkheim's version. Additionally, President Reagan's and President Bush's invocations of American civil religion in the postmodernist 1980s and 1990s necessitate a fundamental reexamination of this concept. The popularity of Bellah's concept seems to represent a decisively neoconservative shift that is associated in some ways with postmodern tendencies to revive nostalgic, patriotic, fundamentalist, and antiliberal trends. Bellah wrote his essay during the Vietnam War, and I am writing my essay in the aftermath of the 1991 Gulf War, in the context of ongoing metaphorical wars on phenomena that range from AIDS to the recession. The United States had just "won" the cold war, but instead of turning to themes of peace, the vacuum left by the collapse of communism—the "evil empire"—was filled with a plethora of smaller evils that had to be defeated. In all these cases, the wars are being waged by using the language of American civil religion, in the name of justice, while "God is watching us." These holy wars are waged against persons or things who are depicted, in Tocqueville's words, as "enemies of the human race" ([1835] 1945:99). At the same time, the postmodern culture industry is encouraging citizens to worry about the environment (despite the terrible damage to the environment caused by wars), and to become kinder, gentler, and less racist and sexist. In sum, the coming *fin de siècle* is witnessing increasingly contradictory moral messages that reflect the contradictory discourse on postmodernism.

Bellah was on the right Durkheimian ([1912] 1965:240–43) track that a nation's political representations can constitute a religion. Suppose further that postmodernism is genuine, at least to some extent, in its claims to rebel at patriarchal, Enlightenment narratives that have been buttressing social theory for several generations now. That might necessitate a new evaluation of the supposedly obvious Durkheimian theme in Bellah's notion of civil religion.

## DURKHEIM'S CONCEPTUALIZATION OF RELIGION AS A FEMININE, SACRED COMPLEX

It is important to keep in mind Durkheim's favorable reference to Bachofen in the opening pages of *The Elementary Forms of the Religious Life*:

> Before the middle of the nineteenth century, everybody was convinced that the father was the essential element of the family; no one had dreamed that there could be a family organization of which the paternal authority was not the keystone. But the discovery of Bachofen came and upset this old conception. ([1912] 1965:18)

Consider that compared with Freud, Bellah, and many other social scientists writing on religion, Durkheim never invokes God or any other male deity in his sociology of religion. He concentrates, instead, on totemism, which he defines as the religion of an anonymous and impersonal force, without name or history, immanent in the world and diffused in a number of things (p. 216). It is not the totem that is worshipped, but the power of the sacred that lies beneath the totemic symbol and its many derivatives. Feminist writers assert that similar beliefs apply to the worship of Nature by mother-centered religions (see Gadon 1989). By extension, postmodern individuals also worship the sacred beneath their many totems, emblems, and symbols—Durkheim intended for his study of Aborigines to be relevant to "the man of today," and "to show us an essential and permanent aspect of humanity" ([1912] 1965:13). Far from making patriarchy the cornerstone for some sort of Parsonian social order, Durkheim relies on sympathy—a maternal notion—as the social glue that holds societies together. Unlike Comte and the positivists, Durkheim concludes that science will never usurp religion. Contrary to Kant, Durkheim does not bother with trying to prove or disprove the existence of God: He points out that Buddhism is a religion without a deity, and he defines religion as a matter of sacred and profane representations, without any recourse to deity. In keeping with Veblen's ([1899] 1967) social theory, Durkheim seems aware that devotional observances can be used for prestige and status seeking, as well as other selfish, pecuniary, motives found in a predatory culture. For this reason, he does *not* focus on church attendance, church membership, or other standard variables used by functionalists in a vain effort to operationalize social integration.[8]

Instead, Durkheim treats religion as culture, something that exists on a representational level outside the churches and that is accessible to all of society's members, whether or not they attend or belong to an organized church. In these and other ways, Durkheim presents one with the conceptual apparatus for constructing a softer, gentler, and less ethnocentric civil religion than the one found in Bellah's writings and most standard approaches to religion. Thus, the first significant difference between Bellah and Durkheim is that Bellah's starting point for analysis is the Protestant notion that God is a male who promotes social order, whereas Durkheim avoids deities completely in his treatment of religion and emphasizes mystic sympathy among society's members.

In Durkheim's sociology of religion, the religious and the sacred are conceptual categories that are superimposed synthetically, artificially, onto empirical, physical reality ([1912] 1965:261)—there is no room here for fundamentalist, literal interpretations of the Bible or any other holy book. Thus, for Durkheim, the reality that is the foundation of religion does *not* necessarily conform objectively to the subjective ideas that believers have of it (p. 465). And above all, "one must know how to go underneath the symbol to the reality which it represents and which gives it its meaning" (p. 14). Durkheim probably would have agreed with Jung (1959), Erich Fromm (1963), and others who broke with Freud ([1927] 1955) to follow Bachofen ([1861] 1967) that the unconscious reasons for the persistence of religion have more to do with the child's attitude toward the *mother* than the father. Finally, it is important to recall that Jung (1959) treats the concept of the unconscious itself as a feminine notion, as an aspect of the Great Mother archetype.

Thus, the *fin de siècle* Durkheim who accepted the reality of the unconscious would not assume automatically, as so many functionalists do, that the mere presence of religious beliefs leads to societal integration. I believe that Durkheim follows, instead, the psychoanalytic trajectory of social research in which the religious symbols that are used betray something that is hidden or otherwise obscured from the *collective* consciousness.[9]

Note that whereas Durkheim depicts the primary function of religion as one of symbolic expression of society's true yet hidden, psychic functioning, both Bellah and Parsons assume that the primary function of religion is the maintenance of social order (Caporale and Grumelli 1971). With Adorno and other critical theorists, I would ask: Why should all social order be considered an unqualified good? Durkheim's approach is more typically *fin de siècle* European in that he would be interested in just versus unjust social order, and the *hidden* meaning behind the patriarchal symbolism of American civil religion, whereas the American functionalists are just as typically pragmatic, in that they seek the utility of religious beliefs. It makes a world of difference which representation of Durkheim is used in analyzing religious representations.

Another one of Durkheim's most distinguishing features as a sociologist is his claim that the past is always linked to the present in an unending chain of collective representations. For example, anthropologists have documented the fact that American Indians accepted the Virgin Mary because they recognized her from their own traditional religious depictions of the Great Mother. For example, Braden (1930), Estrada (1986), Nutini (1976), and others note that the Madonna of Guadeloupe appeared on the very hillside that the Aztec goddess of fertility used for her appearances. In many developing nations today, women still turn to goddesses to attain pregnancy, goddesses are still invoked in rites meant to ensure good harvests, and in general, goddesses serve the function of protection. From this Durkheimian perspective, one has to wonder about the meaning of the fact that for American civil religion, as for Protestantism in general, a patriarchal deity has severed any and all relationship to female deities and feminine principles.

To be sure, a patriarchal religion can maintain feminine elements through its emphasis on the integrative role of the church, the pacifist aspects of Christ's teachings, and other derivatives of Jung's Great Mother archetype (Fromm and Maccoby 1970). But it is God the Father—not Jesus Christ in his many manifestations, including the compassionate Good Shepherd (see Pelikan 1985)—who is the centerpiece of

American civil religion (see Bellah 1970:170). And one cannot help notic-
ing that in Bellah's writings on American civil religion, this religion is
invoked most often for the purposes of war, from the Civil War to President Johnson's War on Poverty. For example, Easter is not invoked in
American civil religion. Could it be that the Resurrection, even the
friendly Easter Bunny, are not sufficiently militant themes?[10] In stark
contrast to Bellah, Durkheim's depiction of religion *never* relates to war.

Like Henri Bergson, William James, and other *fin de siècle* thinkers,
Durkheim conceives "religion to be like the *womb* from which come all
the leading germs of human civilization" ([1912] 1965:255, my emphasis). Durkheim's conception of religion appears to be fundamentally
feminine. Durkheim depicts all social institutions as derived from religion, and this is the source of the venerable respect, intensity, and the
good and gracious aspects attached to society (239–43). The sentiment
that lies at the basis of religion is "happy confidence" (p. 256). Religious
myths weave connections between humans and cause persons and
things to exist in "mystic sympathy" with one another (p. 174).

Let us compare each of these neglected aspects of Durkheim's sociology of religion, mentioned above, with the functionalist version that
eventually found its way into Bellah's controversial concept of American
civil religion. To begin with, the functionalists do not view religion as the
womb of civilization, but as one of several institutions whose dynamic
function is the maintenance of social order. Durkheim's feminine conceptualization of religion was completely reversed by Parsons and his
students. Moreover, this functionalist social order is not maintained by
respect, intensity, happy confidence, sympathy, or other warm and feminine aspects of being human, but through the internalization of norms,
sanctions, and utilitarian calculation that centers on rewards and punishment. In other words, the patriarchal social order is maintained by
patriarchal means, including fear. Finally, social order for the functionalists does not lead to the mystic sympathy among humans that Durkheim
hoped would lead to an international, cosmopolitan, diverse, and tolerant unity of humankind, but is far more likely to lead to ethnocentrism.[11]

Durkheim's classic on religion ends on the note that these feminine,
benign "elementary" forms will lead eventually but spontaneously and
peacefully to an international, cosmopolitan unity of humankind. One
day, the world will become one nation in which human rights will be
respected, which is a clear echo of the Great Mother archetype that
Bachofen introduced to Europe in 1861, as well as the most publicly
proclaimed cultural values in the contemporary West. But contemporary
proponents of the new world order seem unable to conceive of social
integration as based on anything but utilitarian principles, which are

hardly universal. Moreover, one has to wonder how the principle of self-interest that is unrestrained by any sort of moral framework could possibly lead to anything except the war of all against all. What a difference from Durkheim's emphasis on the unity of diversity and complementary differences that should characterize the normal and moral development of the division of labor (see Wallace 1977). Bellah admits time and time again that American republicanism opposes the liberal tradition, and that Americans view themselves as God's new chosen people. In sum, if the American way of life does triumph over most or all of the world, it will not happen spontaneously. Durkheim and the functionalists use the concept of social integration in fundamentally opposing ways to inform their respective sociologies of religion.

## IS THERE A FEMININE VOICE IN AMERICAN POSTMODERN CIVIL RELIGION?

I have already suggested that rather than perpetuate the war between the sexes, it seems more reasonable to suppose, following Jung's extrapolation of Bachofen and Durkheim, that feminine archetypes can be found in males as well as females, and most importantly, that these archetypes are woven into the very fabric of Western, Enlightenment narratives and the postmodern cultures informed by these narratives. In other words, femininity and masculinity are *collective representations*, vital ingredients of cultural makeup that shine on males and females equally.

It is important to note that my reading of the Bachofen legacy as it is traced through Durkheim and Jung leads to the conclusion that masculine archetypes or representations need to be reconciled or balanced with feminine archetypes. Fromm and Maccoby (1970) also call for a reconciliation of mother-centered with father-centered cultural aspects. Neither Durkheim nor Jung favors one voice over the other, and Jung warns that an excess of either archetype is dangerous to psychic and social well-being.

From this Durkheimian and Jungian refinement of Bachofen's original thesis, the following new perspective on American civil religion emerges: The feminine, pacifist, nonaggressive voices of religion (from Holmes 1990), which Durkheim found even among the Aborigines, have been almost completely suppressed in the postmodern version of American civil religion. If it were true that postmodernism rebels at the masculine voice of the Enlightenment that links reason with violence, and if it gives many voices a chance to be heard, these softer voices should have united to make a deafening sound. But where are today's American equivalents of Gandhi, Tolstoi, Thoreau, Schopenhauer, Buddhism, the Talmud, even the early Christian depictions of Jesus as the Good Shepherd? Bellah waffles on the question of how extensively American Protestantism draws on American civil religion, and vice versa. But the essential point is that in both "religions," God or Jesus (who are often used interchangeably by fundamentalists) battles various symbols of Satan for supremacy of the world. Turning the other cheek is definitely out of fashion among postmodernists.

Recent feminists have been resurrecting J. J. Bachofen's 1861 "myth" that in prehistory, prior to the dawning of Yahweh and other male gods, the rule of goddesses was affiliated with values that stressed a universal fraternity, and respect for life, Nature, and creation.[12] According to Jung (1959), the Great Mother archetype is associated with the qualities of sympathy, the magic authority of the female, the wisdom and spiritual exaltation that transcend reason, any helpful instinct or impulse, any helpful animal, all that is benign, that cherishes and sustains, that fosters growth and fertility. And this applies to the feminine aspect of males as well as females. Nevertheless, Bachofen's and Jung's theses have been challenged, and many feminists have opted for career track equality with males.[13]

It is certain that the myth or archetype or system of collective representations concerning femininity is extensive and spills far beyond the borders of contemporary feminism, itself factionalized into recovering versus suppressing the Great Mother archetype. Bachofen's bold revolt against the one-sided, patriarchal image of history was part of the nineteenth-century Age of Romanticism that was concerned with counter-Enlightenment alternatives to rational principles of morality that were already perceived to be heading toward bankruptcy. These alternatives included empathy, compassion, and an emotional concern for the common fate of humanity. Great care must be exhibited here in not seeking to systematize these virtues or otherwise employing the dynamic principles of social engineering to force societies to behave compassionately. This was the fault Spengler and others found with socialism, for example: "In spite of its foreground appearances, ethical socialism is *not* a system of compassion, humanity, peace and kindly care, but one of will-to-power" ([1926] 1961:361).

Many thinkers from the previous *fin de siècle* sought a balance between femininity and masculinity, even if they were chauvinists in their private lives. Thus, Nietzsche (1968) wanted Apollonian logic to be tempered with the more feminine Dionysian logic; Schopenhauer ([1818] 1977a, 1977b, 1977c) argued that the heart should inform the mind; Fromm and Maccoby (1970) called for a blend of mother-centered with father-centered principles, mercy *and* justice; Tonnies ([1887] 1963) argued that patriarchal *Gesellschaft* needs to preserve elements of *Gemeinschaft*, which is based on the mother-child relationship and is the earliest form of human association; Jung (1959) claimed that when rationality predominates, it is impoverished and leads to doctrinaire authoritarianism, while the Great Mother archetype can become devouring and excessively emotional if not tempered by reason. The feminine archetype humanizes rationality, and makes it genuine:

> Reason emits a deceptive light which illuminates only what we know already, but spreads a darkness over all those things which it would be most needful for us to know and become conscious of. The more independent reason pretends to be, the more it turns into sheer intellectuality which puts doctrine in the place of reality and shows us man not as he is but how it wants him to be. (Jung 1959:27)

Jung's proposed alternative to the excessive rationality of modernity is to make contact again with the repressed, unconscious Great Mother archetype. This contact would expose aspects of Western, Enlightenment narratives and culture that we all "know" exist, and that could inform American civil religion, but are collectively pretending do not exist at the present time, despite postmodernism: Christ's commandments to love one's neighbor as one's self, and to turn the other cheek; the tradition of benevolence, or the return of love and good actions for hatred and persecution; patience, gentleness, and the endurance of insults and affronts; the forgetting of one's desires and being reborn in God; and so on. Schopenhauer had gleaned these as the kernel of wisdom found in all the world's religions. And Sorokin (1948) proposed, with apparent seriousness, that Christ's teachings in the Sermon on the Mount ought to be the basis for modern social relations, even though he did not intend for any sort of revival of organized Christianity.[14]

Perhaps these feminine aspects of Christian love are an impractical way to deal with all the exigencies of modernity, at least not exclusively. But perhaps also they need to temper and modify the current excesses of machismo and the one-sided image of the citizen-soldier that has become the staple of American civil religion and, increasingly, of postmodern culture.

## THE SOCIAL PSYCHOLOGY OF ERICH FROMM

Throughout this book, I have been exposing linkages between Durkheim's sociology and critical theory. Erich Fromm is an important critical

theorist who complements Durkheim and Bachofen (whom he cites frequently) by insisting, contrary to Freud, that attachment to the mother—
*not* the father—is the real ground for the Oedipus complex.[15] Young-
sters crave their mothers, much like Bachofen claimed that matriarchy
precedes patriarchy, but failure to separate from the mother is at the root
of all pathology. This situation is analogous to Durkheim's insistence
that the centripetal forces of mechanical solidarity precede the modern,
centrifugal forces of organic solidarity, even though they are never eliminated. Similarly, Fromm offers an explanation of religious symbolism in
which he distinguishes between mother-centered versus father-centered
systems of social character. Like Durkheim, Fromm understands social
and individual development as a dialectical process that involves new
integration and synthesis of these opposing forces.

For example, in *Social Character in a Mexican Village*, Fromm and Maccoby argue that in Mexico "mother fixation is part of the social character,
so much so that we can consider the village to be a society which in
appearance is strictly father centered or patriarchal, but which in fact is
emotionally centered in the mother" (1970:111). Mother fixation is related to the extreme emphasis on the Madonna in Mexican Catholicism:

> The religious world is governed by the Virgin, the all-helping, all-forgiving
> merciful mother, while God and even the martyred Christ take a second
> place in the experience of the people. It is no exaggeration to say that for
> the Mexican peasant, the Virgin of Guadeloupe (and many other Virgins
> of local significance) is at the center of religious beliefs. (p. 114)

According to Fromm, the Catholic religion is more mother-centered
than other Western religions in its focus on mother Church, the role of
the Virgin Mother, and the unmarried priest, who can function as both
father and mother. In the Jewish religion, the motherly element is less
obvious, but discernible. "Protestantism seems to be the most patriarchal form of Christianity" (p. 115).

These religious differences hold affinities with forms of relatedness to
production in the secular world. This is because "the maternal principle
is unconditional love, mercy, the natural equality of children, the preva-
lence of natural law over manmade law" and equality (p. 112). On the
other hand, the fatherly principle is that of conditional love, and depends on obedience, performance, abstract thought, hierarchical structure, justice, law, and order (p. 113). Fromm does not favor one system
over the other, but a balance of both systems. In an interesting supplement to Max Weber's ([1904] 1958) thesis, Fromm argues that female-
centered Catholicism is not conducive to productive capitalism, and
fosters instead a form of dependency and passivity.

In *The Dogma of Christ* Fromm offers a psychoanalytic, Marxist analysis of the first three hundred years of Christianity up to the appearance of the cult of Mary in 326 A.D. It focuses on "the motives conditioning the evolution of concepts about the relation of God the Father to Jesus" (1963:10). According to Fromm, the earliest Christians were the downcast and oppressed masses of the uneducated poor, the proletariat of Jerusalem and peasants, who wanted to rebel against all authority. For them, Jesus symbolized a human person who was adopted by God. They could identify with the elevation of a human to divinity who suffered. But as Christianity spread to become the official religion of the Roman Empire, it became internationalized and began drawing upon the middle classes. A decisive change in dogma occurred such that a human was not elevated to a god, but a god descended to become human. According to Fromm, this changed the relationship to God from one of unconscious hostility against authority to a "tender, passive tie to the father" (p. 63).

In the fourth century, the concept of the Mother Church emerged, which had not really existed prior to that time. And suddenly, the Virgin Mary became elevated in status as being not only the mother of Christ, but the mother of God:

> Mary represents that motherly divinity grown independent by separating itself from the father god. In her, the motherly qualities, which had always unconsciously been a part of God the Father, were now consciously and clearly experienced and symbolically represented. (p. 69)

A significant aspect of Fromm's theoretical contribution is his claim that the figure of the happy, suckling baby Jesus "meant also that men had to regress to a passive, infantile attitude" (1955:71). Catholicism signified the disguised return to the religion of the Great Mother who had been defeated by Yahweh, at least for a time. Protestantism eventually turned back to the father god, and stands at the beginning of a social epoch that Max Weber ([1904] 1958) would call the spirit of capitalism. Fromm supplements Weber's analysis by noting that the shift from mother-centeredness to father-centeredness is a contrast between the passively infantile attitude of the Middle Ages and the hoarding character of the Puritans.

In the remainder of Fromm's analysis, as well as in his many other books, Fromm claims that the twentieth century exhibits a social character structure that is also passive, a kind of regression to the attitude of the Middle Ages—and this despite the victory of father-centered Protestantism! Obviously, Fromm had to return to the well-known theory of mass society promulgated by critical theorists, but using Bachofen, Adams, and Durkheim as context makes a difference in apprehending this theory. For Fromm (as for Adorno), modern humans become the eternal consumers who are eternally suckling, swallowing, devouring, and expecting. One finds refractions of Fromm's assessment of twentieth-century modernity in Veblen's ([1899] 1967) critique of the leisure class,[16] Baudrillard's (1988) disturbing portrait of postmodern consumers, Riesman's (1950) other-directedness, Daniel Bell's (1976) schizophrenic capitalist who follows the Protestant work ethic from nine to five but is anomic in the evenings and on weekends, Bellah et al.'s (1985) malignant individualists of the 1980s, and other works that criticize the narcissistic, infantile, tendencies of modern and postmodern individuals (Adorno 1991). But the important point is that Fromm suggests that this shift to medieval passivity might have occurred in the twentieth-century despite the apparent dominance of male-centered religion and modern culture in the United States and Western Europe.

Fromm is probably correct that mother-centeredness in religious symbolism is related to passive character structure in the family and the larger culture. The dominance of the cult of Mary in Eastern Europe and Russia, and the tremendous backwardness of the formerly communist countries, suggests that Fromm's analysis continues to be relevant and will apply to social changes for many years to come as Eastern Europe tries to "catch up" with the West economically.[17] Perhaps more importantly, it suggests that the West is *not* nearly as efficient, rational, and patriarchal as it appears to be to itself. In this regard, Fromm should be admitted into the postmodernist discourse, and his theories should be regarded as an important supplement to Durkheimian sociology.

## PARADOX AND PESSIMISM

Another important similarity among Durkheim, Schopenhauer, and other *fin de siècle* thinkers is their circumscription of the antirational forces in civilization. I am referring to the irony that persons often become that which they most despise, fear, and deny wanting to become. They sometimes become the *opposite* of their rational, stated goals. It is as if Schopenhauer's will gets the upper hand despite the individual's careful, rational planning. This is the essence of Schopenhauer's contribution to modern psychology, his cynicism, which found its way into works of a host of other *fin de siècle* writers (Magee 1983). It is also relevant to the seemingly contradictory depiction of postmodernity as the fragmented, alienated, and often irrational heir to modernity. It is as if modernity has become transformed into its opposite as Western humanity approaches the end of the millennium.

It is not clear to what extent Max Weber or many of his commentators are conscious of this irony in his classic *Protestant Ethic*. Weber claims that the Catholic vision of other-worldliness produced such tremendous asceticism and discipline in the material world that the Catholic Church, although claiming to seek God's heavenly city, ended up ruling the material world of the Middle Ages. On the other hand, the Protestant churches, claiming that persons must be monks within the wicked world, through their transformation of asceticism to activity within the world, ended up creating a spirit, an ethos, that was to become the seedbed for capitalism, in which the entrepreneur "gets nothing out of his wealth for himself, except the irrational sense of having done his job well" (Weber [1904] 1958:71). The Catholic ruled the very world he or she claimed to shun while the Protestant ended up serving a nonspontaneous, colorless, blandly materialistic world that he or she had intended to rule. Moreover, the postmodernist who inherited the fruits of Puritan culture has become a passive consumer not only of goods but of images such that, according to Baudrillard (1981), consumerism is the only social bond left in postmodern culture. Yet the most popular, and probably incorrect, interpretation of Weber is that he proposed the simple hypothesis that Protestantism is essential for capitalist efficiency.

Like Weber, Durkheim posited an intimate connection between religious and economic institutions. But given that modern religious representations reflect the pessimism of the collective conscience, what is the role of economics in modern life? This is a neglected chapter in Durkheimian scholarship that we shall only touch here. The versatility of Durkheim's sociology is that it enables one to find religion as soon as the sacred is distinguished from the profane. In general, Durkheim criticizes all previous economic doctrines for making the *optimistic* assumption that egoistic desires will regulate themselves of their own accord: Socialists and communists treat the state as an extension of economic interests while laissez-faire capitalists treat the state as an impediment to economic progress. Durkheim regards these strategies as appropriate to archaic, simple societies, but inappropriate for modern societies in which the relationship between means and ends is too complex for the ordinary individual to comprehend. If one takes the pessimistic and essentially religious doctrine of *homo duplex* seriously, and the constantly increasing tension based on this dualism as civilization progresses, then a new solution is required for reconciling the profane desires of economic acquisition with the forces of the sacred. Durkheim's sociology offers an alternative to the New Right and its efforts to limit the state as well as to the political Left and its emphasis on the welfare state.

Of course, contemporary economic doctrines are positivistic, and deny that economics has anything to do with religion. But for Durkheim, in principle, everything is religious. Thus, Durkheim writes:

> Whether society was conceived by the multitude with the aid of religious symbols, or by philosophers—such as Plato—under the most rational forms, it appeared to men's minds to be marked with *a sacrosanct character* (which placed it far above the inferior world of individual interests) and consequently the State, which was its highest incarnation, shared in this same characteristic. Since society was charged above all with pursuing social ends, and as these were considered as rising to ideal spheres, superior to human goals, *it was itself invested with religious dignity*. Since the economic structure had in this philosophy been deprived of all social value (because it concerned only personal egoism) it could not be a question of binding one to the other—still less of mingling them. *The very idea of such fusion was revolting—like sacrilege.* ([1928] 1958:41; my emphasis)

Socialism and communism attempted just such a sacrilege, with apparently devastating results. According to Durkheim,

> Thus between these two types of interests (social and economic) a great incompatibility existed. They were situated as the two poles of moral life. *Between them was the same distance as between the sacred and the profane.* So one could not dream of burdening the same organ with the administration of both. (p. 41; my emphasis).

But capitalism commits a similar sacrilege in assuming that one can derive a sacred moral order based on profane, egoistic acquisition—on the immoral principle of self-interest.[18] In both socialism and capitalism, proponents try to get "the most from the least, the superior from the inferior, moral rule from economic matter" (p. 240). According to Durkheim, these are contradictory and impossible aims: "As there is nothing within an individual which constrains these [economic] appetites, they must surely be contained by some force exterior to the individual, or else they would become insatiable—that is, morbid" (p. 199). In general, "however skillfully ordered, economic functions cannot co-operate harmoniously nor be maintained in a state of equilibrium unless subjected to moral forces which surpass, contain, and regulate them" (p. 197). These forces must be found outside the economic sphere of social life, in the "higher" pole of *homo duplex*, the ideals of religious society and its many manifestations. And these constraining forces are as much feminine—leading to a desire to be good—as masculine—based on a fear of punishment.

Durkheim continues to be criticized for ascribing this higher, moral role to society and, in particular, to the civil religious culture found in all societies. But the problem he posed seems relevant to postmodern economic theory and to current efforts to export democracy and free-market systems to formerly communist nations: If self-interest is basically amoral or immoral, and if self-interest is the staple of utilitarian capitalism, how in the world is capitalism going to produce and maintain a stable and moral social order? Michael Novak (1982) and other supporters of the New Right answer that despite its ruthlessness and unintended consequences, including injustice, capitalism is more beneficial for the lower classes and efficient than socialism. Even if that is true, it begs the question posed by Durkheim's sociology. Of course, the New Right wants the state to ensure the rule of law (a favorite buzzword) so that capitalism may thrive, but Durkheim's sociology would question whether this rule of law actually ensures morality in the marketplace or merely serves the interests of the ruling classes.

On the other hand, Bauman (1987, 1989, 1990) unmasks the assimilatory aspirations of the liberal welfare state as tending toward a homogeneity that actually oppresses minorities. It is important to realize that Durkheim's alternative does not fall into this trap either. He envisions a friendly, benign state whose aims should be the maintenance of individualism and diversity (see Giddens 1986). From Durkheim's perspective, the welfare state takes over economic functions that do not belong to it while the capitalist state fails to regulate economic functions. He sought an alternative that has yet to be worked out in which the division between the state and economic institutions shall reflect *homo duplex*, the division between the sacred and the profane. Integral to Durkheim's contribution is the notion that moral regulation does *not* rest primarily with the state, but with other, intermediary social institutions, among them the family, church, community, and workplace.

## IMPLICATIONS

We have uncovered several radical elements in Durkheim's sociology that are relevant to the postmodernist discourse: Durkheim regarded religion as a kind of language, a set of collective representations that aid the investigator in assessing the psychic workings of the collective conscience. In principle, everything is religious in Durkheim's sociology, and in this sense religion is the most important language. This is because religion supposes "a bipartite division of the whole universe, known and knowable, into two classes which embrace all that exists, but which radically exclude each other," namely, the sacred and the profane

(Durkheim [1912] 1965:56). Thus, "religious beliefs are the representations which express the nature of sacred things and the relations which
they sustain, either with each other or with profane things" (p. 56).

Durkheim's incredible definition enables one to consider as religious
phenomena that which other theorists would not consider: civil religion,
language, the relationship between masculinity and femininity, and the
relationship between the state and economic institutions—among others that were not addressed in this chapter. Moreover, and in line with
Bachofen, Henry Adams, and the German *fin de siècle* tradition, he regarded religion as essentially feminine, the womb from which all other
social institutions are derived. Thus, the end point of Durkheim's sociology of religion is not the modernist, Parsonian social order based on
homogeneous normative consensus, but a tolerant, diverse society unified by mystic sympathy.

Contrary to the many postmodernist depictions of cultural life as nonreferential (Baudrillard), religion always refers to *homo duplex*, the opposition between the sacred and the profane. The formula is constant,
but the representations that attach themselves to the sacred and profane
vary with societies. In this way, Durkheim offers a dynamic sociology
that nevertheless offers a reference point in the sea of circulating fictions.

## NOTES

1.   See Schoenfeld and Meštrovíc (1991) for a detailed, scholarly elaboration
of this point.
2.   For a critique of Baudrillard's position in this regard, see Gane (1991:46–
65), and particularly Gane's conclusion that "Baudrillard's arguments are also
designed to offend democratic sentiments as well as humanist ones" (p. 63).
3.   Indeed, Durkheim makes it clear that *homo duplex*, the grand opposition
between will and idea, is as much the basis for the religious distinction between
the sacred and the profane as it for understanding other social institutions
([1912] 1965:29).
4.   See Bellah et al. (1985) and Roberts (1990:286–68), among many other
sources, including Tocqueville's analysis of the role of women in America in
volume 2 of *Democracy in America*.
5.   See Atkinson et al. (1985), Condren (1989), Gadon (1989), Game (1991),
Gimbutas (1989), Goodrich (1989), and Jurkevich (1991), among many others.
6.   I agree with Bauman (1990, 1991) that these terms carry sinister and
ominous connotations.
7.   Even though Bellah does not use the term *civil religion* in *Habits of the Heart*,
Bellah et al. (1985) opt for a conservative return to the republicanism of bygone
America as opposed to the cancerous individualism that he believes is destroy-
ing contemporary American society.

8.　With the unwelcome conclusion that the most devout are often the most sexist, racist, and authoritarian; see Roberts (1990:261–81) and Bellah et al (1985), among many others.

9.　Durkheim insists that "religion is a system of ideas by which individuals represent to themselves the society of which they are members, and as such is metaphoric and symbolic" ([1912] 1965:257). In *Suicide* he writes, "Religion is in a word the system of symbols by means of which society becomes conscious of itself; it is the characteristic way of thinking of collective existence" ([1897] 1951:312).

10.　Jung regarded all friendly animals as refractions of the Great Mother archetype.

11.　Indeed, Bellah (1973, 1974, 1981, 1986, 1987) mentions many times in his writings that American civil religion has led to ethnocentric adventures and unjust wars, but he never distinguishes just from unjust wars, and he apparently does not believe that these disturbing aspects of civil religion are essential to it.

12.　Albeit these references to Bachofen are nevertheless indirect and hostile, as exemplified by Gadon (1989) and others.

13.　It is interesting to connect Jung's insight regarding helpful versus predatory animals with Veblen's ([1899] 1967) discussion of predatory versus friendly animals used in national symbols.

14.　One cannot repeat often enough that most *fin de siècle* social thinkers, among them Veblen, Spengler, Durkheim, Weber, and Simmel, were highly suspicious and critical of organized religion. But this did not prevent them from appreciating the religious element in social integration.

15.　See Fromm (1947, 1950, 1959, 1962, 1964) and the critique of Fromm's position offered by Schoenfeld (1966). Fromm's influence can also be traced through David Riesman's analysis of social culture in *The Lonely Crowd* (1950).

16.　Although today, the middle classes have taken on the characteristics of Veblen's leisure class.

17.　Note the implicit ethnocentrism in the popular beliefs that the West will redeem Eastern Europe and the USSR now that capitalism has "defeated" socialism.

18.　For a contrary view of moral capitalism, see Michael Novak's (1982) *The Spirit of Democratic Capitalism*.

Chapter 7

---

*Suicide and the Will to Life*

Suicide is the most obvious *fin de siècle* theme (Benjamin 1973). The pessimistic Schopenhauer had to touch on suicide as part of his philosophizing on the infinitely striving will to life. Because desire is infinite and insatiable, humans are condemned to perpetual unhappiness: Their desires can never be satisfied. This is the deep meaning of Durkheim's concept of anomie, missed completely in functionalist misreadings of anomie as normlessness.[1] Worse still, enlightenment exacerbates the will by expanding the horizon of desires, so that modern and postmodern humans are less happy than their ancestors were. Is desire a masculine or a feminine phenomenon? In *Seduction*, Baudrillard (1990) would have one believe that desire is strictly passive and feminine. But if that is true, how does one explain that the anomie of unlimited desires thrives within the heart of active, dynamic, modern culture? One's reply to this question will color one's perception of the nature of progress as rational, irrational, or the third option we shall present—a strange, new blend of will (feminine) *and* idea (masculine).

In some ways, Schopenhauer's early existentialism foreshadowed the postmodernist cynicism, malaise, and disguised unhappiness due to anomic, never-ending desiring. Using data from the General Social Surveys, Andrew Greeley (1989) has found that since the 1970s, Americans in general but American women in particular report an "alarming decline" in happiness. But again, Durkheim had predicted this unwelcome outcome to the utilitarian dream that fueled so much of the thinking on social progress since the previous *fin de siècle*. Prior to Durkheim's emergence on the intellectual scene, scores of writers had addressed suicide in relation to the decadence of civilization.[2] Even Durkheim's contemporaries were aware that the positivistic dream of a rational, efficient modernity was only an illusion. Thus, in *The Theory of the Leisure Class* ([1899] 1967) Veblen refracts the existentialism of Schopenhauer, Durkheim, and the *fin de siècle* spirit, even if he never mentions them or

suicide directly, in his searing exposé of the useless, wasteful, and osten-
tatious desires of modern persons.[3] A century after Veblen's classic was
published, it is evident that postmodern persons still cling to their "useless" pets, lawns, athletic wear that is hardly ever used in athletics, gas-
guzzling cars, and other nonefficient vestiges of barbarism that convey
status and prestige. Postmodern individuals tend to accumulate so
much "stuff" that newly constructed homes boast closets that are as
large as the bedrooms used to be only a generation ago. My intention in
this chapter is to show that Durkheim's sociology offers a unique and
relevant reply to the questions: Is the decadence that accompanies modernity and postmodernity essential to them, and is it desirable? Is it
really possible for the modern and postmodern person to achieve happiness in his or her life?

The relevance of Durkheim's sociology to themes that one typically
associates with the existentialists and postmodernists is hardly obvious.
Durkheim's *Suicide* is typically read as a positivistic manifesto, not an
existential statement. It has been the subject of seemingly ceaseless criticisms due to the fact that it does not and cannot fit optimistic, Enlightenment, positivistic perspectives that have been used to apprehend it,
and it has been virtually dismissed for its lack of a scientific contribution,
often harshly (see Douglas 1967; Lukes 1985). However, when read in
the context of Durkheim's *fin de siècle* outlook, his *Suicide* offers a fascinating and relevant interpretation of the role of happiness and sorrow
for societies as they pass through modernity. *Suicide* is not just about
suicide in a narrow, positivistic sense, but about morale in modern life. It
is as metaphysical and humanistic as it is scientific, though it has been
read primarily for its thin science. For example, consider Durkheim's
statement that:

> Indeed, it is wrong to believe that unmixed joy is the normal state of
> sensibility. Man could not live if he were entirely imperious to sadness.
> . . . So melancholy is morbid only when it occupies too much place in a
> life; but it is equally morbid for it to be wholly excluded from life. ([1897]
> 1951:366)

The popular 1980s song, "Don't Worry, Be Happy," seems to capture
the postmodernist version of the attempt to exclude pessimism completely from social consciousness. Scores of writers have commented on
postmodernism as the culture of fun and boosterish hyperoptimism
even as other writers comment on the apocalyptic themes found in
postmodern culture. Riesman (1950) noted this trend toward forced fun
*and* existential loneliness as early as *The Lonely Crowd*, and Erich Fromm,

Max Horkheimer, and various members of the Frankfurt school also criticized American culture for its oppressive happiness, which often hides a corrosive cynicism (see also Kanter and Mirvis 1989). From Veblen's perspective, postmodern fun is the most recent version of predatory, conspicuous leisure, which is carried out, ironically, with grim seriousness. Durkheim would have one consider that such hyperoptimism is morbid and hypocritical for the *entire* social body—all the social classes and not just the leisure class. In *The Division of Labor in Society* ([1893] 1933:337) especially, he concluded that the advancement of the division of labor leads to *less* happiness for individuals (see Mestrovic 1991:184–92). True, he never specified, in a precise, quantifiable, positivistic manner just how much melancholy is adequate, but he seems to have foreshadowed many serious criticisms of the decadence of American and postmodern society when he wrote, "Too cheerful a morality is a loose morality; it is appropriate only to *decadent* peoples and is found only among them. Life is often harsh, treacherous or empty. Collective sensibility must reflect this side of existence, too" (Durkheim [1897] 1951:366). Durkheim's melancholy pronouncements can be related easily to Schopenhauer's disturbing claim that because of the insatiability of their desires, humans can never find lasting happiness— and this applies especially to the enlightened.

In *Suicide*, Durkheim claimed that civilization in his day existed in a "state of crisis and perturbation" (p. 369) due to the happy-go-lucky ethos that he and Veblen criticized. Given all the crises—social, political, economic, and other—that have occurred since he wrote these words, it seems that he still has something to teach us in these postmodernist times. Moreover, he referred to suicide as the "ransom money" of civilization (p. 367). This is an arresting phrase reminiscent of Schopenhauer's claim that death and suffering are the "debt" humans pay to life. It is important to keep in mind that *Durkheim uses suicide as the vehicle for a much wider, existential discussion*: A positivistic understanding of suicide was never Durkheim's intent. Rather, he offered a general definition of suicide that ranged from acts of heroism and self-sacrifice to the general tendencies to self-destruction found in ordinary, everyday life, because his overall project was an existential treatise on modernity. Given all the concern given by some postmodernists to the threat of or potential for global and individual self-destruction that is part and parcel of contemporary living, it seems that it is more fruitful and relevant for our *fin de siècle* to read and apply Durkheim as he might have intended.

Let us put aside the conclusion reached by most contemporary commentators that Durkheim's *Suicide* is a bungled attempt at demonstrating positivistic methodology. He was not a positivist. Marcel Mauss

([1950] 1979a) regarded *Suicide* as a study of human *morale*, the ways in which the biological instinct for self-preservation is dependent upon the arrangement of collective representations that society uses to structure itself and communicate to its members its state of the collective conscience. Over and over again, Durkheim phrases his discussion of suicide in terms of these collective representations and "social currents." *Suicide* is part of his overall discourse of culture and communication. Jack Douglas had already arrived at this insight in *The Social Meanings of Suicide* (1967), wherein he compares Durkheim's communication theory with the symbolic interactionists. But I will not follow Douglas in assuming that Durkheim failed where the interactionists allegedly succeeded. My intent is to read Durkheim contextually and on his terms in order to learn something new and relevant to the postmodern discourse.

Perceived in this new context, one notices that Durkheim's *Suicide* is centered on an issue that is relevant to the postmodernist discourse: Is decadence merely inefficient and irrational, or does it also weaken the desire to live? Similarly, Durkheim's follower, Maurice Halbwachs ([1930] 1978), depicted *Suicide* as a book about socio-psycho-organic pain and the problem of the meaning of life. I agree with his disciples that *Suicide* is a pioneer effort in existentialism, still terribly relevant to humanity's problems as we try to survive the coming *fin de siècle*. After all, even official, positivistic rates of suicide have not abated since Durkheim's *fin de siècle*, and other forms of self-destruction that are more difficult to quantify, from drug abuse to the foolish pursuit of risk on a mass scale, and from unsafe sex to drinking and driving, occupy our postmodern attention.

But again, apart from any trace of positivistic concerns with actual suicide—some grand, rational plan to control and predict suicides—Durkheim's *Suicide* can be read as a follow-up to Schopenhauer's writings on suicide, and his doctrine on the will to life in general. Schopenhauer's famous line that "just because the suicide cannot give up willing, he gives up living" ([1818] 1977a:516) is a profound and apt summary of Durkheim's argument in his classic. Durkheim elaborates on the myriad of ways in which the postmodern person's will has been emancipated, and the many ways the postmodern person is unable to give up willing: "Our capacity for feeling is in itself an insatiable and bottomless abyss" ([1897] 1951:247). According to Schopenhauer, "the more intense the will is, the more glaring is the conflict of its manifestation, and thus the greater is the suffering" ([1818] 1977a:511). Similarly, chapter after chapter of *Suicide* treats the social causes of heightened social suffering in modern societies in relation to the all-consuming, infinitely striving will. According to Schopenhauer:

Far from being denial of the will, suicide is a phenomenon of strong assertion of will; for the essence of negation lies in this, that the joys of life are shunned, not its sorrows. The suicide wills life, and is only dissatisfied with the conditions under which it has presented itself to him. He therefore by no means surrenders the will to live, but only life, in that he destroys the individual manifestation. He wills life—*wills the unrestricted existence and assertion of the body*; but the complication of circumstances does not allow this, and there results from this great suffering. (p. 515; my emphasis)

Schopenhauer's existential assessment is deeply thought provoking. It seems unimaginable for humans embroiled in the postmodernist culture of the coming *fin de siècle* to curb their appetites and engage in the deliberate, systematic asceticism advocated by Schopenhauer, Durkheim, and Veblen in any meaningful and profound way. Similarly, one of the most enigmatic moves that Durkheim makes in *Suicide* is the linkage between suicide and various social currents that are normal, even essential to social life. For example, Durkheim depicts anomie as *both* a cause of suicide and as part of the "spirit of progress" that is necessary to society:

As soon as men are inoculated with the precept that their duty is to progress, it is harder to make them accept resignation; so the number of the malcontent and disquieted is bound to increase. The entire morality of progress and perfection is thus inseparable from a certain amount of anomie. Hence, a definite moral constitution corresponds to each type of suicide and is interconnected with it. ([1897] 1951:364)

For Durkheim, everyone in an anomic society suffers to some degree, even if only few individuals commit suicide in the strict, positivistic sense of suicide. But Durkheim's treatment of suicide continues to be misunderstood today primarily as an example of deviance, the breaking of social norms by an out-group. The popular consciousness also is exposed to the message that suicidal persons, drug addicts, and other deviants are different from the rest of society members, that *they* have a problem, while the respectable leisure class is normal and sane. Schopenhauer and Durkheim regard this neat division between the in-group and the out-group as part of the symptomatology of anomic societies. For them, one must strive to realize that one's private will is not fundamentally different from the infinitely striving will of others, that all modern individuals are deviants by virtue of the enlightened will. In this chapter, we shall explore the other, deeper, and more fruitful aspects of Durkheim's well-known but still poorly understood sociological classic as it pertains to the postmodernist dilemmas and contradictions that are being discussed.

## SUICIDE AND HUMAN MORALE AS CULTURAL PHENOMENA

Before we begin, let us review briefly how *Suicide* fits into Durkheim's overall cultural project and his discourse on communication that we have been following throughout this book. To begin with, Durkheim takes it as a given that "essentially social life is made up of representations" ([1897] 1951:312). Like language and religion, suicidal "currents" are part of "the system of symbols by means of which society becomes conscious of itself," and part of society's "characteristic way of thinking of collective existence" (p. 312). Here again, will and idea are involved. The sociologist takes on the role of the psychoanalyst who must dig beneath the surface to find what society is saying to itself about itself through an analysis of suicidal currents as well as statistics. Thus, suicide is eminently a cultural phenomenon for Durkheim. Here I disagree with Durkheimian scholars who claim that Durkheim was not concerned with culture until his classic work on religion in 1912.[4] On the contrary, from the dawn to the dusk of his career, Durkheim approached all social phenomena as cultural representations, not positivistic hard facts—and suicide is no exception to this rule.

For example, he claims that sadness comes from the group, not the individual, who merely borrows his or her individualized unhappiness from society (p. 300). Regarding this state of collective sadness or happiness, "society may generalize its own feeling as to itself, its state of health or lack of health" (p. 213). It does this through collective currents and representations that are expressed through religion, language, metaphysical systems, and all sorts of cultural artifacts:

> Thence are formed currents of depression and disillusionment emanating from no particular individual but expressing society's state of disintegration. . . . Then metaphysical and religious systems spring up which, by reducing these obscure sentiments to formulae, attempt to prove to men the senselessness of life and that it is self-deception to believe that it has a purpose. . . . On their appearance they seem to have been created out of whole cloth by their makers who are sometimes blamed for the pessimism of their doctrines. In reality they are an effect rather than a cause; *they merely symbolize in abstract language and systematic form the physiological distress of the body social.* (p. 213; my emphasis)

Given this cultural approach to suicide, Durkheim does not treat suicide as just a deviant act. Instead, "every sort of suicide is merely the exaggerated or deflected form of virtue" (p. 240). It is the virtues— altruism in primitive societies, and the anomic spirit of progress in modern societies—that are the real focus of his work, while suicide is only a vehicle for discussion. Following Durkheim's lead, we shall move the discussion in this chapter to a discussion of the role of altruism versus egoism in postmodern culture. But in general, it is important to keep in mind that Durkheim approaches suicide as a social fact in the manner that he approaches language and religion as social facts. The present chapter is a continuation of the discussion that unfolded in Chapters 4 and 5. Thus, Durkheim writes:

> It is not mere metaphor to say of each human society that it has a greater or lesser aptitude for suicide; the expression is based on the nature of things. Each social group really has a collective inclination for the act, quite its own, and the source of all individual inclination, rather than their result. It is made up of the currents of egoism, altruism or anomie running through the society under consideration with the tendencies to languorous melancholy, active renunciation or exasperated weariness derivative from these currents. These tendencies of the whole social body, by affecting individuals, cause them to commit suicide. The private experiences usually thought to be the proximate causes of suicide have only the influence borrowed from the victim's moral predisposition, *itself an echo of the moral state of society.* (p. 299; my emphasis)

## SUICIDE AND HUMAN SUFFERING

The most obvious "cause" of suicide is suffering, individual and collective. But astonishingly, this glaring aspect of suicide has been almost completely missed in the thousands of post-Durkheimian studies of suicide that try to correlate it positivistically with indicators of social control, integration, consensus, and a number of other abstractions that rest on the assumption that the cognitive acceptance of social norms by the majority spares them from the deviance that afflicts the misfits. In all these abstract misunderstandings of Durkheim's intent, social scientists have been laboring under the Enlightenment delusion that like any other social problem, suicide can be brought under rational control. The simple, powerful *fin de siècle* message of Durkheim's *Suicide* has been lost on his modern successors: Human suffering multiplies with modernization, and this is the underlying cause of a *qualitative* shift in the types of suicide that are occurring (from altruistic and fatalistic to anomic and egoistic), as well as a quantitative shift in apparently higher rates of suicide. But again, the most important aspect of Durkheim's argument is not the statistical evidence, which is always debated by social scientists, with no fruitful resolution. Rather, it is that the suicide of the relatively few is a reflection of the unconscious misery of the many who go on living.

The primary trait of modernity and civilization is anomie, and it produces symptoms that Durkheim describes with a vocabulary of human suffering: *souffrance, tourment, douleur*, frenzy, impatience, restlessness, feverishness, disenchantment, fatigue, agitation, distress, exasperation, misery, and insatiability, among other similar psychophysiological states.[5] It is important to note that for Durkheim, these derangements in emotions are related in a dialectical fashion with derangements in knowledge and cognition: Excessive, one-sided, masculine thirst for knowledge, characteristic of the Enlightenment, produces its *opposite* in the realm of feminine feeling, anomie and egoism. In his follow-up to Durkheim's *Suicide*, Maurice Halbwachs also emphasizes that "A man must have reached a rather high degree of suffering for him to decide to pass through these doors" to suicide ([1930] 1978:314), and this suffering is at its height in enlightened, civilized societies, even if it is disguised. Again, an obvious point—but scholars tend to focus instead on Halbwachs's refinements of Durkheim's statistical methodology (for example, Giddens 1971). The seemingly banal but actually profound connection between suffering and suicide seems to have been lost in contemporary versions of Durkheim's argument. It is the increase of human suffering in modernity, despite the fact that we would like to believe that modernity is always beneficial, that is interesting, and disturbing: "It even seems that the tendency to a sort of melancholy develops as we rise in the scale of social types" (Durkheim [1897] 1951:366). This is the same conclusion that Durkheim had reached earlier in *The Division of Labor in Society* ([1893] 1933:50), and is part of the general theme of civilization and its discontents uncovered by many of his colleagues. Durkheim (p. 250) simply accepts this fact, and concludes that sociologists must renounce utilitarian comparisons and approaches to the progress of the division of labor: Modernity simply does not make individuals increasingly happy.

In this thoroughly Schopenhauerian vein, Halbwachs adds:

> We can assume hat the number of suicides is a rather exact indicator of the amount of suffering, malaise, disequilibrium, and sadness which exists or is produced in a group. Its increase is the sign that the sum total of despair, anguish, regret, humiliation, and discontent of every order is multiplying. ([1930] 1978:314)

Note that for Halbwachs, like for Durkheim, the suicide of the few is a representation of the suffering of the rest of society. Durkheim implies Schopenhauer's insatiable will that has been unleashed by enlightenment when he refers to anomie as the "bottomless abyss" of human desires ([1897] 1951:247). The insatiability of passion, when unrestrained, is a source of torment in itself. Postmodern culture certainly encourages the never-ending consumption of all kinds of objects of desire, and this is bound to lead to a permanent condition of discontent. Without this state of discontent that leads to renewed conspicuous and mostly useless consumption, the capitalist order would collapse. Everyone knows this at some deeply buried level of consciousness, such that the ascetic option is never taken seriously. Society represents the collective sadness based on this insatiable desire to itself in various cultural representations and symbols, and transfers some of this sadness to its individual members: "Thence are formed currents of depression and disillusionment emanating from no particular individual but expressing society's state of disintegration" (p. 214).

## POSTMODERN NEURASTHENIA

In keeping with the Schopenhauerian assumptions that inform the *fin de siècle* spirit as well as Durkheim's classic, these collective currents of depression and disillusionment will often be unconscious or otherwise repressed, denied, or obfuscated from full, self-conscious awareness. For example, consider Durkheim's scattered discussion of *neurasthenia*, a condition that may be roughly translated into the contemporary *depression*, or sometimes, *chronic fatigue disorder*. If neurasthenia was the fashionable disease of the leisure class in Durkheim's *fin de siècle*, it has retained its high status among the "me" generation yuppies of the present *fin de siècle*. Durkheim describes the neurasthenic as delicate, extremely intelligent, sensitive, easily stimulated, unstable, and "destined to suffer." But this description corresponds to Sloterdijk's contemporary description of postmodern cynics as "borderline melancholics, who can keep their symptoms of depression under control and can remain more or less able to work" (1987:5). Translated into the vocabulary of contemporary psychologists, one could characterize Durkheim's neurasthenics as "augmenters" in opposition with "reducers" (Petrie 1967). Augmenters suffer because they are psychologically and physically overly sensitive to stimuli, whereas reducers possess the amazing ability to tune out or tone down the power of stimuli. Durkheim's sociology involves cultural and social influences upon this ability to cope with painful stimuli. Society produces more other-directed (from Riesman) augmenters with the march of modernity, in contrast with our reducer ancestors. Heightened sensitivity is a requisite for existence in a complex division of labor. Thus, "this psychological type [neurasthenia] is therefore very probably the one most commonly to be found among suicides" (Durkheim [1897] 1951:69).

But Durkheim argues that neurasthenia is not, by itself, a "cause" (in the positivistic sense) of suicide. For example, in Durkheim's time, women suffered from neurasthenia much more than men did, yet men exhibited higher suicide rates than women. This finding has been replicated repeatedly in modern times: Women continue to be more depressed than men, but still commit less suicide than men (see Kleman 1986). Obviously, Durkheim writes, "if there were a causal relation between the suicide-rate and neurasthenia, women should kill themselves more often than men" ([1897] 1951:71). But again, a positivistic cause-effect explanation does not seem to have been Durkheim's intent.

Instead, Durkheim regarded neurasthenia as the prototype of all kinds of madness, a kind of general neurosis that exhibits an affinity with suicide, broadly defined, even if it is difficult to tease out the causal mechanism. If neurasthenia or mental illness in general predisposed the individual to commit suicide, suicide rates and rates of mental illness should be related. But according to Durkheim, "the countries with the fewest insane have the most suicides" (p. 73). In addition, the same social forces that produce the social causes of suicide also tend to produce neurasthenia (p. 323). Hence,

> A given number of suicides is not found annually in a social group just because it contains a given number of neuropathic persons. Neuropathic conditions only cause the suicides to succumb with greater readiness to the current. Whence comes the great difference between the clinician's point of view and the sociologist's. (p. 323)

In summary, Durkheim denies that neurasthenia is a cause of suicide in and by itself, even though the suffering it entails predisposes the individual to suicide. The modern individual can tolerate a great deal of depression and cynicism, yet continue to live with this damaged state of morale. Additionally, society sometimes rewards this affliction. These hyperdelicate, augmenter, other-directed neurasthenics can become society's anomic innovators, and are masters of representing society to itself. According to Durkheim,

> The organic-psychic temperament most predisposing man to kill himself is neurasthenia in all its forms. *Now today neurasthenia is rather considered a mark of distinction than a weakness. In our refined societies, enamored of things intellectual, nervous members constitute almost a nobility.* (p. 181; my emphasis)

What a fascinating accompaniment to Veblen's depiction of the leisure class! For Veblen, alcoholism and neurosis are similarly prestigious:

> Drunkenness and the other pathological consequences of the free use of stimulants therefore tend in their turn to become honorific, as being a

mark, at the second remove, of the superior status of those who are able to afford the indulgence. ([1899] 1967:70)

It is still true that among society's creative neurotics, being "in therapy" is prestigious, even if many of these neurotics, like Woody Allen, joke about the fact that the therapy is ultimately useless to them. Freud, too, commented on the "secondary gains" from neurosis (see Schneider 1948). Neurosis can be transformed into a variety of constructive and destructive forms, but its fundamental mark is that these useless, neurotic members of the leisure class are ultimately society's most "useful" innovators and creators. Here Durkheim's understanding seems to be superior to Veblen's ultimate desire to impose a technical, positivistic efficiency onto society's members (discussed in Riesman 1953). Without the suicide-prone creative neurotics who do not show up in suicide statistics precisely because they can create, modern society would stagnate. A certain degree of useless, pathological anomie is absolutely essential to society's well-being, at least in Durkheim's scheme of things.

Durkheim's depiction of the social functions of useless leisure relates directly to the theme of postmodernism as rebellion against the grand narrative of hyperrational, efficient, modernity. Durkheim writes that

> Precisely because he [the neurasthenic] rebels against tradition and the yoke of custom, he is a highly fertile source of innovation. . . . They [neurasthenics] are therefore not essentially a-social types, self-eliminating because they are not born to live in the environment in which they are put down. Other causes must supervene upon their special organic conditions to give it this twist and develop it in this direction. . . . It is a field in which most varied tendencies may take root depending on the fertilization it receives from social causes. . . . *Although the degenerate multiply in periods of decadence, it is also through them that States are established; from among them are recruited all the great innovators.* ([1897] 1951:77; my emphasis)

This is hardly a ringing endorsement of decadence, but Durkheim has clearly found a benign role for what is currently referred to as postmodernist culture. The unleashed will to life, which offends and disturbs the neo-enlightenment critics of postmodernism, holds a benign as well as a malignant aspect in Durkheim's complicated social theory. Unrestrained, the will leads to senseless, seemingly unproductive anomie and unnecessary suffering. Yet indirectly, it contributes to the great cultural progress of the postindustrial age. Throughout *Suicide*, and in his other writings, Durkheim never tires of repeating that if all anomie were controlled rationally or eliminated completely, societies would thereby eliminate the spirit of progress, and would stagnate.

Interestingly, even Adorno (1991) holds that the leisure class is more capable of authentic, autonomous purity in esthetic perception and production, compared with the frugal masses (and he has been criticized by many postmodernist writers for holding to this seemingly antidemocratic sentiment). Schopenhauer, too, believed that a state of disinterested "will-lessness"—the withdrawal of practical interest in the world that is a luxury available only to the leisure class—is essential for genius and original contributions to culture. Finally, despite his positivistic leanings, Veblen (1948) also admitted that the leisure class is able to be creative precisely because it is not struggling to make ends meet, and can afford to engage in idle curiosity.

According to Durkheim, creative neurotics are unwitting societal agents who reflect back to society its "collective asthenia, or social malaise" and "they symbolize in abstract language and systematic form the physiological distress of the body social" ([1897] 1951:214). Apply Durkheim's observation to postmodernist architecture, cinema, art, music, literature, and other aspects of culture, popular as well as highbrow. There is no doubt that postmodernist culture glorifies and exhibits rebellion, decadence, neurotic instability, and pessimism. Recently built structures "waste" space, material, and money in a manner that would have astonished even the cynical Veblen (1948). Postmodern audiences take it for granted that most of the characters in the films they see will die before they walk out of the theater. New Age books turn to the crudest superstitions of the past in order to "cure" stress, escape the evils of the world, and make contact with the supernatural. Contrary to the conservative reaction to postmodernist culture, Durkheim's theory implies that a return to a supposedly more sane and rational modernity is impossible, and unwanted in any case. Yet unlike the liberal wing of writers who wholeheartedly embrace the postmodernist rebellion, Durkheim's thought sensitizes us to the fact that rebellion of any sort always entails suffering, which is a heavy price to pay for any newly won freedom.

But we are hardly alone in this plight as the millennium draws to a close. In *Moral Education*, Durkheim comments on "the veneration that so many nineteenth-century writers accorded the notion of the infinite" ([1925] 1961:36), which often results in anomie. He elaborates:

> This is why historical periods like ours, which have known the malady of infinite aspiration, are necessarily touched with pessimism. *Pessimism always accompanies unlimited aspirations.* Goethe's *Faust* may be regarded as representing par excellence this view of the infinite. And it is not without reason that the poet has portrayed him as laboring in continual anguish. (p. 40; my emphasis).[6]

What Durkheim wrote concerning the historical period in which he lived applies even more to our historical period. From the

Schopenhauerian perspective that Durkheim adopted, there is no good reason to conclude that future generations will ever be happier than we are if they continue on the path of unlimited progress. And that is a very sobering conclusion.

## PRIMITIVE ELEMENTS IN POSTMODERN CULTURE

From Adorno, other critical theorists, and David Riesman to Robert Bellah and Allan Bloom, many intellectuals have claimed that an important paradox of modern and postmodern societies is that despite the rhetoric on individualism, postcapitalist societies actually foster conformity.[7] We have seen in Chapter 1 that many writers on postmodernity are fearful of a neoconservative return to fascist, authoritarian, or other kinds of mass society. Durkheim's contribution to this discussion can be gleaned from his treatment of altruistic and fatalistic suicide in traditional societies. Again, the purpose is not to learn something new about suicide per se, but about the complexity of self-destruction within the modernization process.

I shall argue the following: Durkheim singles out militarism as a genuine throwback to past, "primitive" forms of association. This is important because the United States and the former USSR, in particular, are still heavily militaristic, and because what Bellah (1970) calls American civil religion is typically invoked in relation to wars and military phenomena. Durkheim implies that modernity ought to entail pacifism—a feminine value. Furthermore, his depiction of the high regard for the individual that he called "the cult of the individual" corresponds somewhat to the high premium placed in modern societies on human rights—at least ideally. Otherwise, Durkheim demarcates modernity from premodernity rather sharply, which leads to the conclusion that contemporary mass society is something unique, and not a throwback to past forms of group association.

Durkheim links explicitly his discussion of primitive societies to contemporary military life, which is still thriving in the United States and other postmodern nations. Like many of his *fin de siècle* contemporaries, Durkheim felt that "it is natural for some of the past to remain in the midst of the present," that "life is made of these contradictions" ([1897] 1951:238).[8] Military suicides in contemporary societies are still "the suicides of lower societies, in survival among us because *military morality itself is in certain aspects a survival of primitive morality*" (p. 238; my emphasis). In 1897, Durkheim cited Italy, Austria, and England as the nations in which one found militarism as well as customs that "most resemble the customs observed in lower societies" (p. 236).[9] The habits of passive obedience, absolute submission, tradition, and feeble individuation—which characterize military life—are a direct link to the past. They are also the characteristics that both Veblen and Spencer condemned as pertaining to barbaric societies that modern societies should have outgrown. But are these the same habits uncovered by Adorno (1991), Bellah (1985), Bloom (1987), and other commentators on postmodern conformity? The answer seems to be yes and no.

According to Durkheim, "the first quality of a soldier is a sort of impersonality not to be found anywhere in civilian life to the same degree" such that the soldier "must be trained to set little value upon himself, since he must be prepared to sacrifice himself upon being ordered to do so" ([1897] 1951:234). Along the lines of Durkheim's insight, David Riesman has remarked that during the 1991 Gulf War, Americans were not prepared to sacrifice or curb their narcissism in any appreciable way for the cause they apparently supported.[10] For example, cutting back on the use of gasoline was out of the question for most Americans. Perhaps Durkheim is correct that the modern person is far less willing to devalue him- or herself compared with the premodern or military person.

Durkheim continues, "Wrongly or rightly, the [military and primitive] habits of passive obedience, of absolute submission, of impersonalism, have proved to be more and more in contradiction with the requirements of the [modern] public conscience" and consequently have lost ground (p. 238). He foresaw that to satisfy the new sensitivity brought on by modernity, military discipline would become less rigid and less repressive of the individual. He did not think that primitive forms of association would ever disappear entirely, but he did think that they would become less important. A constant theme in his writings is that the normal development of civilization entails greater diversity and less primitive consensus.

In *Suicide*, Durkheim opposes modern egoism and anomie with primitive altruism and fatalism. These are further elaborations of his complicated concept of *homo duplex*. One might be tempted to associate egoism-anomie with masculine archetypes and altruism-fatalism with feminine archetypes. After all, Durkheim consistently associates the former with "the spirit of progress" and the latter with sacrifice and traditionalism, traits that Robert Hertz ascribed to the left side of culture. But Durkheim's dialectic is far more complicated, in that the associates egoism and anomie with *feelings*, while he associates altruism and fatalism with duty, repression, and other *objective* factors. Is Durkheim claiming that modernity entails a shift from femininity to masculinity, or vice versa?

Again, the answer is not straightforward, but involves a complicated chiasmus.

Durkheim begins the section on altruistic suicide with the statement that

> If, as we have just seen, excessive individuation [in egoism and anomie] leads to suicide, insufficient individuation has the same effects. When man has become detached from society, he encounters less resistance to suicide in himself, and he does so likewise when social integration is too strong. ([1897] 1951:217)

From a positivistic perspective, a state in which suicide varies directly and inversely with social integration at the same time is impossible. For this reason, positivists have found Durkheim's *Suicide* baffling. But for the purposes of our discussion, it is intriguing that according to Durkheim, morale or the will to life is affected by the dialectical interplay between anomic spirit of progress as well as traditional inertia.[11] This is in keeping with our interpretation of Durkheim's thought as one that tries to balance opposing forces, including the masculine and feminine aspects of social life.

Let us begin with society's representations concerning death and suicide in primitive societies. Durkheim writes of the "favorable attitude toward suicide" found in Hindu sacred texts (p. 218), the custom for the aged to kill themselves before they die naturally so that they shall not be a burden, as well as "for religious reasons," the "suicides of women on their husbands' death," and the "suicides of followers or servants on the death of their chiefs" (p. 220), among other examples. In all these cases, "for society to be able thus to compel some of its members to kill themselves, the individual personality can have little value" (p. 220). Assimilation is a distinctly primitive trait in Durkheim's scheme, even if it has been invoked in some modernist narratives (see Bauman 1990). Durkheim concedes that both the modern egoist and the traditional altruist suffer from sadness when they kill themselves because "in this respect all suicides are alike" ([1897] 1951:225). But Western Christianity supports the cult of the individual—a high regard for the individual—whereas nonmodern religions represent the individual as being much more insignificant. Thus, Durkheim writes:

> The Christian conceives of his abode on earth in no more delightful colors than the Jainist sectarian. He sees in it only a time of sad trial; he also thinks that his true country is not of this world. Yet the aversion to suicide professed and inspired by Christianity is well known. The reason is that Christian societies accord the individual a more important role than earlier ones. . . . Thus the moderate individualism in the spirit of Christianity

prevents it from favoring suicide, despite its theories concerning man and his destiny. (p. 226)

In line with our previous discussions, Durkheim argues that collective "representations function above all as an expression of a reality not of their own making" (p. 227). Language and religion serve this function more than any other systems of collective representations (p. 312). In primitive as well as modern societies, religions will express sorrow, which is an essential ingredient of life, yet modern societies will ascribe greater dignity to the individual. It is only for this reason that modernity makes suicide illegal and otherwise condemns it. Thus, Durkheim makes an interesting connection between pantheistic religious represen-tations and primitive social integration versus monotheism and Western individualism:

> If the essence of pantheism, then, is a more or less radical denial of all individuality, such a religion could be constituted only in a society where the individual counts for nothing, that is, is almost wholly lost in the group. For men can conceive [se representer] of the world only in the image of the small social world in which they live. Religious pantheism is thus only a result and, as it were, a reflection of the pantheistic organization of society. (p. 227)

Durkheim's observations serve as a corollary to our previous discus-sion of male versus female deities. It seems that female-centered so-cieties and religions will also be pantheistic. It is impossible to find a single instance of a society in which a monotheistic god was or will be exclusively female (even if the Christian Scientist God is male *and* female). And it seems to follow that postmodern conformity and mass society are fundamentally different from the lack of individualism in traditional societies. This is the important conclusion reached in this segment of the discussion: Postmodern conformity is entirely compat-ible with narcissism, which is the pathological accompaniment to indi-vidualism, and as such is fundamentally different from the premodern spirit of self-sacrifice. This conclusion is shared by Adorno (1991) but not by Riesman (1980), who believes that narcissism is a prophylactic against fascism.

Durkheim turns to religious symbolism to settle the issue. Durkheim would have one consider that even if postmodern individuals conform in a manner that led and may lead again to fascism, they would still possess an unconscious sense of dignity ascribed to the individual. Compared with our ancestors, modern and postmodern persons are far less likely to sacrifice their narcissistic aspirations for the sake of any cause. Yet, postmodern persons are capable of exhibiting the traditionalism and conformity that used to be a requisite for social life among our distant ancestors.

Durkheim writes that in traditional societies, the individual hardly has a chance to develop his or her individuality:

> Massive cohesion [means that] . . . everyone leads the same life; everything is common to all, ideas, feelings, occupations . . . collective supervision is constant, extending to everything, and thus more readily prevents divergences. The individual thus has no way to set up an environment of his own [*un milieu special*] in the shelter of which he may develop his own nature and form a physiognomy that is his exclusively. (p. 221)

Altruistic suicide is characterized by "too rudimentary individuation" and a state in which "society holds him [the individual] in too strict tutelage" (p. 221). Durkheim describes fatalistic suicide similarly, and with particularly strong pathos:

> It is the suicide deriving from excessive regulation, that of persons with futures pitilessly blocked and passions violently choked by oppressive discipline. It is the suicide of very young husbands, of the married woman who is childless. . . . To bring out the ineluctable and inflexible nature of a rule against which there is no appeal, and in contrast with the expression *anomie* which has just been used, we might call it fatalistic suicide. (p. 276)

Both altruism and fatalism are related to "the crude morality which disregards everything relating solely to the individual," which in turn illustrates "the difference between primitive peoples and the most civilized nations" (p. 227). Contrary to the efforts by Pearce (1989) and other sociologists to find examples of altruism and fatalism in postmodern societies—the fatalism of having AIDS, being depressed, extreme poverty, and other stressful situations—Durkheim would apparently not agree. This is only a surface comparison. We have stated from the outset that both postmodern and traditional persons are sad in nearly the same way. Thus, finding postmodern reasons for feeling sad in a seemingly traditional manner (altruistic and fatalistic) proves nothing that is of theoretical value. The essential criterion that Durkheim uses to distinguish modernity from traditionalism has to do with the degree of respect accorded the individual as evidenced by collective representations, *not* the degree of actual conformity. In this regard, Durkheim seems to be correct that modern and by extension postmodern societies definitely bestow greater dignity upon the individual as exemplified by collective representations expressed through law, religion, language, and other cultural systems. Yet the postmodern individual is capable of reverting to a traditional barbarism in which this high regard for the

individual momentarily ceases to be important. Such are the contradictions of postmodern culture.


## MORALE IN PRIMITIVE VERSUS MODERN SOCIETIES

Postmodernists generally avoid making Durkheim's distinction between primitive and modern societies. More than a matter of semantics,
this distinction really gets at the heart of the postmodernist debate: Does
society evolve from primitive to modern, or are these terms merely part
of the oppressive set of narratives from the Enlightenment that must be
overcome? Schopenhauer's and Durkheim's reply is complex: At the
level of the will, there is no progress, because the will exists independently of time, space, and other categories. In Solomon's words—often
quoted by Schopenhauer—there is nothing new under the sun, and
human nature is always the same. Durkheim also held that *homo duplex*
and its attendant tensions pertain to all humans in all epochs. Humans
will never outgrow the dualism of human nature. However, with regard
to the world as idea or representation, there is change and progress in
the sense that consciousness becomes more complex. Consequently,
modern and postmodern persons do experience more tension and are
less happy in comparison with our ancestors.

The positivistic reception given to Durkheim's *Suicide* addresses the
pathogenic effects of insufficient societal integration—egoism and
anomie—while it has tended to neglect the pathogenic effects of overin-
tegration, namely altruism and fatalism. As stated previously, positivists
assume that suicide cannot vary directly and indirectly with integration
at the same time. This is a serious problem when one considers that
most of the world's population lives in societies that Durkheim argued
are more likely to suffer from excessive integration, altruism, and fatalism (see Headley 1983). To comprehend the cultural problems in these
developing countries in universal terms that are really Western and
modern, namely insufficient integration, seems ethnocentric. But to assume, as Durkheim does, that developing countries are different from
modern countries, and do *not* follow the same laws, seems condescending and oppressive to some postmodernists.

Durkheim implies that, in developing countries, the individual is
ready to renounce life much more readily than in "civilized" countries
(even though this insight seems to contradict his overall conclusion that
suicide is the ransom money of civilization). We have already touched on
this issue with regard to the military, but Durkheim generalizes with
regard to all primitive life. In other words, Schopenhauer's will to life is

underdeveloped in primitive countries relative to the postmodern West. According to Durkheim, in developing nations:

> Though public opinion does not formally require them [suicides], it is certainly favorable to them. Since here not clinging to life is a virtue, even of the highest rank, the man who renounces life on the least provocation of circumstances or through simple vainglory is praiseworthy. *A social prestige thus attaches to suicide.* . . . When people are accustomed to set no value on life from childhood on, and to despise those who value it excessively, they inevitably renounce it on the least pretext. So valueless a sacrifice is easily assumed. . . . Exactly like those more explicitly prescribed by society, they arise from this state of impersonality or as we have called it, *altruism, which may be regarded as a moral characteristic of primitive man.* ([1897] 1951:222; my emphasis)

In no uncertain terms, Durkheim is implying that modern persons are more egoistic and narcissistic than primitive persons. Moreover, and contrary to the utilitarian tradition, Durkheim holds that altruism, and not egoism, is the primeval characteristic of human nature. Thus, modern suicide is not an act of renouncing life, strictly speaking, but of clinging to life too fiercely. This seemingly paradoxical state of affairs— aggravating to positivists trying to falsify Durkheim's theory—is commensurate with Schopenhauer's philosophy. Thus, both Schopenhauer and Durkheim advocate asceticism, a genuine denial of the will to live, as an antidote to the modern tendency for the will to life to become enflamed, which causes the individual to suffer from too much frustration, and some individuals to commit suicide without really renouncing life. Neither thinker regards the primitive renunciation of life as true suicide, but as sacrifice and excessive asceticism. For them, suicide is a strictly modern problem that results from excessive willing. Hence Durkheim's arresting line that "the true suicide, the sad suicide, is in the endemic state with civilized peoples" ([1893] 1933:247). Note also the implied dialectic in their theory: the will gives rise to consciousness, which "progresses" and inflames the will by expanding its horizon of desires, which gives rise to still more consciousness, and so on ad infinitum. It is for this complicated reason that Durkheim and Schopenhauer defended civilization at the same time that they cited its discontents. They foreshadowed Freud and Adorno.

We have arrived at a complicated state of affairs in Durkheim's social theory: Altruism precedes egoism in human evolution; altruism is the basis of all moral actions because it involves disinterestedness and empathy; yet altruism is a primitive trait that devalues the individual. Egoism arrives late in the development of the division of labor, and can never serve as the basis of a collective morality; egoism is distinct from individualism yet is related to the rise of individualism as a collective

representation. Thus, Durkheim arrives at the complicated conclusion
that individualism should replace altruism as the basis of morality in
modern societies at the same time that he preaches the need for old-
fashioned self-sacrifice, empathy, and other altruistic traits. Moreover,
altruism is never extinguished completely by modern egoism and
anomie. Instead, the anomic egoist "effects communion through sadness when he no longer has anything else with which to achieve it"
([1897] 1951:214).[12]

The passage that captures most of these seemingly contradictory
claims is the following from Durkheim's *Suicide*:

> Originally society is everything, the individual nothing. . . . Man is con-
> sidered only an instrument in its hands. . . . But gradually things change.
> As societies become greater in volume and density, they increase in com-
> plexity, work is divided, individual differences multiply, and the moment
> approaches when the only remaining bond among the members of a single
> human group will be that they are all men. Under such conditions the
> body of *collective sentiments* inevitably attaches itself with all its strength to
> its single remaining object, *communicating to this object an incomparable value
> by so doing*. Since human personality is the only thing that appeals unan-
> imously to all hearts, since its enhancement is the only aim that can be
> collectively pursued, it inevitably acquires exceptional value in the eyes of
> all. It thus rises far above all human aims, *assuming a religious nature*. This
> cult of man is something, accordingly, very different from the egoistic
> individualism above referred to, which leads to suicide. Far from detach-
> ing individuals from society and from every aim beyond themselves, it
> unites them in one thought, makes them servants of one work. For man,
> as thus suggested to *collective affection* and respect, is *not* the sensual,
> experiential individual . . . but man in general, ideal humanity as *conceived*
> by each people at each moment of its history. None of us wholly incarnates
> this ideal, though none is wholly a stranger to it. . . . Such an aim draws
> him beyond himself; *impersonal* and disinterested, it is above all individual
> personalities; like every ideal, it can be conceived of only as superior to
> and dominating reality. This ideal even dominates societies, being the aim
> on which all social activity depends. . . . Our dignity as moral beings is
> therefore no longer the property of the city-state; but it has not for that
> reason become our property. ([1897] 1951:337; my emphasis)

Can Durkheim have his cake and eat it too? The positivists have given
their negative reply, and made Durkheim seem consistent simply by
ignoring his high regard for individualism. For this reason, the most
dominant interpretations of Durkheim have tried to make him fit the
conservative, functionalist program. But any sensitive reader of Durkheim will eventually agree that he does not fit the conservative mold,
and that he was a champion of the individualism regarded so highly by
liberals (Giddens 1971). Yet his brand of individualism is a collective

product, opposed to utilitarian social theory, and for this reason the liberals have not embraced him either. Others have challenged his unyielding, moralistic stance that egoism cannot serve as the basis of morality (Hall 1987). But if egoism can serve morality, then it is impossible to draw the line between pathological narcissism and healthy regard for individual rights. Of course, some postmodernists want to eliminate precisely this line, while others are alarmed by the potential chaos this would create. These and other solutions that refuse to take seriously Durkheim's complexity take us into dilemmas and dead ends that are characteristic of the postmodern discourse, and that we have been striving to avoid.[13]

Let us try another tack. We shall begin by admitting Durkheim's fundamental ambivalence regarding morality and morale. He really was contradicting himself in advocating altruism at the same time that he criticized it as primitive and not conducive to individualism. And it seems terribly difficult to comprehend how one should follow him in distinguishing individualism from egoism. But perhaps this ambivalence makes him relevant to the emerging tendency to regard modernity and postmodernity as inherently ambivalent processes (Bauman 1991). Had Durkheim been consistent and neatly positivistic, his theory would have been superfluous. Postmodernists agree that contemporary individuals seek autonomy at the same time that they cling to traditions to give them a sense of rootedness. Postmodern innovation coexists with incredible revivals of nostalgia. Assimilation is stressed by Western governments at the same time that ethnic diversity and identity are supported by these same governments. Rather than criticize Durkheim by some outmoded positivistic standard that tries to impose an artificial consistency onto the modernizing process, Durkheim should be appreciated for having been ahead of his time. In some ways, his sociology applies to our *fin de siècle* more than to his.

Moreover, his ambivalent stance is consistent with several of his famous *fin de siècle* contemporaries. A careful reading of Veblen ([1899] 1967) reveals that he wanted to graft archaic, altruistic traits onto the barbaric, predatory, pecuniary interests that he thought dominated the times in which he lived—but he was not comfortable with either one in its pure state (discussed by Riesman 1953). Similarly, Tonnies ([1887] 1963) regarded the opposition between *Gemeinschaft* and *Gesellschaft* as a dialectic: Humanity would never outgrow its need for community. Rather, the archaic needs and traits would be transformed. For example, some postmodernists have assailed the shopping mall and Disney World as mere embodiments of kitsch, artificial centers of consumption and hyperreality that exclude the poor. But consider how the mall fulfills all the functions of the old-fashioned town square: Senior citizens can participate in walking or jogging groups. Christmas, Easter, and Halloween (complete with "safe" trick-or-treating at stores as opposed to the purportedly more dangerous neighborhood) are celebrated as examples of what Durkheim termed "collective effervescence," the bubbling of human emotions and collective sentiments. Primary groups form around the video arcades, coffee shops, and indoor restaurant plazas. The mall has become the focus of polls, health screening, Christmas decoration exhibits, beauty pageants, craft shops, haunted houses, horse and dog shows, automobile exhibits, antique shows—to name just some of the community events that draw on the forces of *Gemeinschaft* every bit as much as the little town squares that Tonnies idolized. And on a Durkheimian note, the mall protects the individual from the small-town gossip and surveillance that were always present in archaic societies. In the shopping mall, one preserves the relative anonymity that is supposed to characterize urbanism (from Simmel) at the same time that one finds shelter from the genuinely impersonal forces of the city. One is able to feel community and preserve one's individualism (even if some of the individualism can and does degenerate into the unhealthy consumerism criticized by Baudrillard and others).

Similarly, it seems snobbish to regard Disney World exclusively in pejorative terms, or to mock America as the Disney World culture simply because it substitutes hyperreal fantasy for reality.[14] From a Durkheimian perspective, one cannot deny the genuinely human sentiments that American and increasingly world culture have attached to this shrine erected to human innocence and childhood. In Durkheim's terms, Disney World has become a sacred site, demarcated sharply in the popular mind from everyday, profane life. In fact, it promulgates mother-centered values every bit as much as Medjugorje: Snow White is an excellent refraction of the Virgin Mary. Using Veblen, one notices that Disney World opposes the barbaric tendencies found in the rest of society's habits that pertain to liquor and intoxicants, war, hunting, and sports.

In sum, Durkheim's sociology challenges the simplistic, straight-line understanding of modern progress that positivists have been pursuing. The past never disappears entirely, but is transformed. So-called progress entails the dialectic between centripetal and centrifugal forces, masculine and feminine voices, altruism-fatalism and egoism-anomie, respectively. Individualism is a new force in human affairs, born from this dialectic, but it remains charged with the altruistic spirit of collectivism. Indeed, postmodern individuals are eager to make great sacrifices to preserve their rights, and new rights seem to be discovered all the time.

## CONCLUSIONS

We began this chapter with the observation that in taking the will to life seriously, Durkheim, like Schopenhauer, had to consider suicide as the apparent negation of the will to life. Death stands at the outset of every Romantic philosophy, and self-destruction is the most interesting form of death because it involves self-reflective consciousness, which animals supposedly lack. In pursuing this Schopenhauerian trajectory, Durkheim wrote *Suicide*, and became engaged in distinguishing primitive from modern forms of self-destruction. But he wandered far from the positivistic program, and treated suicide as the vehicle for a far-ranging discussion of human morale in relation to societal communication. He concluded that suicide, regarded in its broadest sense, is related to each society's virtues and collective representations. While he found differences between the altruistic virtues of the past and the egoistic-anomic virtues of the present, he maintained that these social currents are part of *homo duplex*, a refraction of the ever-present will *and* idea that we have been following throughout this book. As such, it seems logically consistent that he would discover a new, *altruistic individualism*, even if this seems to be an oxymoron, a positivistic aberration. He uncovered a fruitful ambivalence to the modernizing progress that makes him profoundly relevant to contemporary times, even if difficult to follow.

Durkheim concluded that modern (and by implication, postmodern) individuals will be simultaneously more autonomous and social, individualistic and group oriented, and enlightened yet sentimental, compared with our ancestors. It is not a matter of rebelling at the Enlightenment but of fusing our advanced mental lives with our hearts, with the will. He predicted that something called the cult of the individual would replace the old-fashioned, oppressive group orientation of the past. While this higher kind of individualism would necessarily imply some narcissism, egoism, and anomie—things that our ancestors knew to a far lesser extent than we—along with other unwanted aspects of individualism, it would be distinct from these lower aspects. In this manner, Durkheim overcomes some of the criticisms that have been leveled at Lasch (1991), Bellah et al. (1985), and others who fail to distinguish among various kinds of individualism, and whose criticisms of narcissism are neoconservative.

There exist many indicators that suggest that Durkheim's depiction is relevant with regard to community, nostalgia, and other conservative tendencies that are discussed in the postmodernist discourse. A kind of consensus actually exists all around us, and we need not search high

and low for some supposedly nonexistent referent. That seemingly paradoxical referent and consensus is individualism. It seems to be paradoxical because it fosters efforts to distinguish oneself from the crowd
and the average, even though these efforts seem to be the new average
trend, sanctioned by the collective conscience. Americans in particular,
and for that matter, Westerners in general, jealously guard the rights
that accompany individualism. The right to privacy, the rights of various
minority groups, the rights demanded by children that children of previous generations could not imagine, even the right to hold opinions on
nearly everything (including matters studied by sociologists)—among
many others—are sweeping contemporary social life on both sides of
the Atlantic. Slowly but surely, Eastern Europe, Asia, and the rest of the
world are also beginning to demand more democracy, because Durkheim did not regard democracy as a Western invention, but as the inevitable outcome of a constantly advancing division of labor:

> Individualism, free thought, dates neither from our time, nor from 1789,
> nor from the Reformation, nor from scholasticism, nor from the decline of
> Graeco-Latin polytheism or oriental theocracies. It is a phenomenon which
> begins in no certain part, but which develops without cessation all through
> history. ([1893] 1933:171)

It seems to be the case that individualism as a set of collective, com-
munal representations that bestow dignity upon the human person is
here to stay, and it is something that most persons in postmodern societies will agree upon. It is difficult to escape Durkheim's conclusion
that, indeed, humanity has become its own god in modern times.

If an unequivocal, unambiguous aspect of the postmodernist revolution is to be found, it seems that it lies in this curious blend of individualism and community. For example, the postmodern world is witnessing
an explosion of joining groups, from health clubs to help groups—even
help groups for those who join too many health groups. But the most
interesting aspect of this phenomenon is that the individual who joins
the group expects it to be run along democratic lines that will not inter-
fere with his or her individualism. For example, Lamaze groups exist to
integrate males into the traditionally female birthing process, but the
tone and structure in these groups is decidedly sensitive to the awk-
wardness of males trying to be helpful. This is a far cry from the authoritarian structure of groups found only a few generations ago.

In the shopping mall—denounced by many highbrow intellectuals
today like television used to be denounced a few generations ago—as in
the rest of postmodernist culture, the individual is exposed to a
seemingly constant barrage of advertised images. Yet these images are
not as random as Baudelaire ([1863] 1965, [1869] 1970) feared when he

described modernity as being the fleeting and contingent, nor as free-floating as Baudrillard (1981, 1988) thinks. On the contrary, individuals identify with certain images and develop fierce loyalties to specific brands, television personalities, and various other contemporary totems. Loyalty is definitely an altruistic matter of the heart, of societal attachment that transcends the ego. Those who bemoan the fact that modernization has killed off the unique aspects of communities and brought about a homogenized mass society—the golden arches of McDonald's can be found coast to coast and increasingly all over the world—miss the positive, archaic aspects of modernization. The world is becoming increasingly a world community and these symbols and totems function to internationalize the world and bind all of its members together emotionally. Like Disney World, McDonald's caters to nostalgic, family values with its playgrounds and other collective representations.

In sum, those who depict postmodernism as mere rebellion against Enlightenment narratives seem to miss the point that the Enlightenment narratives—including democracy and individualism—are only gaining strength as postmodernism develops, even behind what used to be the Iron Curtain. But democracy and individualism have been transformed from the previous century into communitarian, nostalgic phenomena, linked to civil religion. Rugged individualism has given way to a collective high regard for the family. On the other extreme, those who—following Tonnies—posit the alleged victory of bureaucracy and heartless abstractionism are also mistaken. Evidence abounds that postmodern individuals are more sentimental than our ancestors could imagine. Witness the explosion of businesses that deal in sentimental, *useless* (from Veblen [1899] 1967) things like greeting cards, Victorian decor, souvenir spoons, nostalgia channels, synthetic flowers, toys, and other aspects that are arrogantly dismissed by some as kitsch. Durkheim's sociology would have us consider that all these things embody human sentiment and the altruistic tendency to think beyond terms of egoistic efficiency. A completely new version of community is emerging in the postmodern world, a new synthesis of will and idea.

## NOTES

1. Moreover, one finds this notion of unlimited desires in the works of a host of Durkheim's predecessors and contemporaries, even if they never used the precise word *anomie*, from Tocqueville ([1835] 1945) to Veblen ([1899] 1967) and Spengler ([1926] 1961).

2.   Reviewed in Douglas (1967), Ellenberger (1970), and Masaryk ([1881] 1970), among others.

3.   David Riesman wrote of Veblen's thesis, "to view modern civilization as still barbaric at its core seems less funny today than to those who laughed in 1899 (at the end of the splendid little war with Spain) at *The Theory of the Leisure Class*" (1964:391).

4.   A claim made by Jeffrey Alexander (1988) and others. Alexander assumes that a significant hiatus exists in Durkheim's sociology. For a contrary view, see Robert N. Bellah (1973), who claims that Durkheim was one of those intellectuals who writes one book throughout his career, but in many different versions.

5.   For a more extensive discussion, see Mestrovic (1988:54–75).

6.   As an aside, Schopenhauer admired greatly his friend Goethe, and both thinkers were instrumental in developing the Romantic theme of the infinite as it pertains to the shift from traditional to modern thinking.

7.   This is also an important theme in Alexis de Tocqueville's *Democracy in America*. Equality makes all individuals feel small and helpless, because they cannot rely on the aristocratic spirit for self-esteem. It is a short step from Tocqueville to David Riesman's "lonely crowd."

8.   Compare with Veblen ([1915] 1964, 1917) on militarism and the persistence of barbaric "mental habits" from the past.

9.   Compare with Veblen ([1915] 1964), who cited Germany and Japan as much more militaristic than England. This contrast is worth discussing. Consider also Riesman's (1964:395) trenchant observation that "before the [first world] war, Veblen plainly regarded American capitalists as latter day barbarians; how is it that he suddenly sees the Germans as the real barbarians?"

10.   Riesman made this remark to me during a private conversation in February 1991.

11.   Again, compare with Veblen's (1948) treatment of progress versus the inertia of traditional "habits," and the conflict between centripetal and centrifugal forces discussed earlier.

12.   This is an interesting foreshadowing of Freud's dictum that neurotics are relating socially even in the midst of their narcissism.

13.   For example, Bellah et al. (1985) seek to promote a healthy cultural relativism and high regard for the individual at the same time that they call for a renovation of the Biblical and republican traditions—which were often hostile to the individual. They seem to fail to distinguish between the two sorts of individualism, one healthy and the other pathological, that is the centerpiece of Durkheim's thought.

14.   Baudrillard (1986) mocks America as an extension of Disney World in this manner. Chris Rojek's unpublished essay on Disney and postmodern culture was also helpful to me.

# Chapter 8

## *Conclusions*

A consistent theme in this book has been that postmodern contradictions are not new, but are nevertheless real and deserve to be taken seriously. In this regard, we take issue with Anthony Giddens, who claims that "rather than entering a period of post-modernity, we are moving into one in which the consequences of modernity are becoming more radicalised and universalised than before" (1990:3). Contrary to Giddens, we have argued that so much attention and cultural effervescence would not have been given to the idea of postmodernity if it did not represent, however imperfectly, a widespread social awareness that something has gone wrong with the modernist project. Admittedly, the awareness is often unconscious, and it is difficult to specify what went wrong. But one of the things that went wrong is that contrary to the expectations of globalization, the victory of liberal democracy, and universal modernization, much of the contemporary world is moving in traditional, centripetal directions.

For example, it is already apparent that the fall of communism in the late 1980s has not ushered in the "golden age of capitalism" that is eagerly awaited in the pages of *The Wall Street Journal*. Instead, capitalism and the modern world order are in serious trouble on both sides of what used to be the Iron Curtain. Capitalism is based on the doctrine of self-interest, which does not inspire faith of any sort, and cannot replace old-fashioned asceticism and self-sacrifice as the basis for collective morality. Instead of the integrity of the nation-state being preserved, the first two years of the 1990s have witnessed the formation of a plethora of new nations that were apparently submerged beneath the borders erected by the modernists. Giddens, and other defenders of the modernist project, cannot account for the formation of new nations for the simple reason that they failed to account for the traditional power of human sentiment—what Schopenhauer termed the heart—and overestimated the power of the mind.

On the opposite end of the modernist discourse one finds Jean Baudrillard, the high priest of postmodernism. Baudrillard would have one believe that contemporary, postmodern existence is dominated by the circulation of fictions and signs that have no referent, origin, or permanence. In opposition to Baudrillard, we have uncovered many traditional referents that continue to operate in postmodern cultures, from the right-left distinction discussed by Robert Hertz to the Great Mother archetype discussed by Bachofen, Jung, Henry Adams, and others.

Thus, we chose to steer a middle course between those who follow Giddens, the last modernist, and Baudrillard, the prophet of cultural apocalypse. The neglected sociology of Emile Durkheim was used as the vehicle for discussion, but not the Durkheim of the functionalists and positivists, who served as a prop for the modernist defenders of social order or as the straw man for its critics. Rather, we used the contextual, *fin de siècle* Durkheim who was primarily a student of culture, not of an abstract society conceived as a social system. And in pursuing this project, we drew Durkheim into an orbit of other students of culture who were inspired by the *fin de siècle* spirit, among them Jung, Adorno, Henry Adams, Sorokin, and Veblen.

For example, in 1930, Jung was already reminiscing on the actual origins of psychology versus the one-sidedness and dogmatism that were beginning to distort its nature and mission in the world:

> Psychology, which once eked out a modest existence in a small and highly academic backroom, has, in fulfillment of Nietzsche's prophecy, developed in the last few decades into an object of public interest which has burst the framework assigned to it by the universities. In the form of psychotechnics it makes its voice heard in industry, in the form of psychotherapy it has invaded wide areas of medicine, in the form of philosophy it has carried forward the legacy of Schopenhauer and von Hartmann, it has quite literally rediscovered Bachofen and Carus, through it mythology and the psychology of primitives have acquired a new focus of interest, it will revolutionize the science of comparative religion, and not a few theologians want to apply it even to the cure of souls. Will Nietzsche be proved right in the end with his *"scientia ancilla psychologiae?"* At present, unfortunately, this encroaching advance of psychology is still a welter of chaotic cross-currents, each of the conflicting schools attempting to cover up the confusion by an all the more vociferous dogmatism and a fanatical defence of its own standpoint. (Jung 1966:84)

Jung's old-fashioned reference to psychology actually included what is now demarcated as sociology, along with other, former "moral philosophies," which used to share the same back room with psychology. All of them succumbed to positivistic dogmatism, and have lost sight of their initial mission to interpret culture in all its aspects, and to substitute a balanced, secular morality for crumbling Christianity. And yet, ironically, contemporary positivism is like religious fundamentalism in its strict insistence on what will be admitted into discourse and what will be absolutely forbidden. The forbidden includes the theorists and topics mentioned by Jung: Schopenhauer, Bachofen, mythology, and the curing of souls. In fact, Jung's "mystical" psychology is still forbidden in postmodern Universities.[1] This repression applies to all the refractions of the other side of the mind that positivism abhors: Schopenhauer's will, Durkheim's society as Being, Henry Adams's forces of the Virgin, Veblen's archaic society of peace, Freud's Eros, Hertz's left-side orientation, among many other aspects of the former *fin de siècle* spirit. Instead of fostering dialogue, the positivistic attitude toward these things seems to be: Let the humanists and theologians have their "soft science" and talk about these "fuzzy" things as they "muck about" about in "left field"; we will emulate the hard sciences, like physics and chemistry, and stick to "hard facts." The net result has been an increasing irrelevance of formal sociology to the most pressing problems of our times. Enrollments in sociology are at an all-time low, and two major sociology departments have been closed in the United States.[2]

Thus, the "end of modernity" cited by the postmodernists has accompanied the near extinction of the sociological enterprise. This is not meant to imply that either modernity or sociology will really end. Both will be transformed. For example, some of the most interesting sociological work in the present era is being done by nonsociologists: historians, linguists, journalists, philosophers, and other humanists. And this is not surprising, given that a century ago sociology was established by *philosophers* who sought to extend philosophy's domain to include culture. In this book, we have followed this original inspiration for sociology, as exemplified in the works of Emile Durkheim—who was a philosopher by training.

Throughout this work, we have invoked forbidden theorists and topics into the social scientific discourse on postmodernity as part of the overall aim to restore balance and objectivity into a discussion that assumes progress and enlightenment even as it purports to challenge them. We have cited sufficient sources to convince an objective and impartial reader that the social sciences were born in a Romantic frenzy of collective effervescence that paid attention to the other side of the mind, and that tried to balance the heart with the mind. As for the artificial distinction between the hard and soft sciences, closer inspection reveals that this, too, is part of the cultural bias of our age. For example, Henry Adams was among the first to realize that Schopenhauer's notion of the will "slipped readily over to the idea of Energy, taught by Kelvin and Clausius" (cited in Partenheimer 1988:343).

Magee (1983) also draws many connections between Schopenhauer's humanism and contemporary physics. Up to the previous *fin de siècle*, it was commonplace to consider humanistic and scientific knowledge as a unity even if today it is routine to consider them separated by an unbridgeable gap.

But the most important motivation for resurrecting the forbidden other side of the social scientific legacy is that the postmodern rebellion is a repetition—albeit unwitting and quite unconscious—of many of the debates, themes, and unfinished business of the previous *fin de siècle*: socialism versus capitalism, metaphysics versus positivism, spirituality versus materialism, fragmentation versus holism, among others. Postmodernism also purports to challenge the tidy but repressive borders that delineate academic paradigms: "One of the key aspects of postmodernism is its tendency to subvert and explode boundaries between disciplines and subdisciplines and to create a multidisciplinary, multidimensional perspective that synthesizes ideas from a range of fields" (Ritzer 1991:238).

If this were entirely true, one would expect that postmodern scholars would be as interested as scholars from the previous *fin de siècle* in synthesizing and integrating academic knowledge—including the forbidden, nonpositivistic knowledge. But because of the dominant positivistic bias in our *fin de siècle* academic world, postmodern discourse has misapprehended the problem of the Enlightenment, and has degenerated into a contradictory, fragmented, and often nihilistic discourse that is nevertheless tending in a neoconservative direction.[3] Postmodernists begin their discussions with the incorrect premise that the Enlightenment narratives are as unequivocal, unilateral, and one-sided as the positivists have depicted them. The central aim of this book has been to uncover what Durkheim and his *fin de siècle* discovered about the grand narratives of the Enlightenment: that these narratives are themselves ambivalent, dualistic, and dialectical, that the entire world, including the social world, is will *and* idea. Whereas most participants in the postmodernist discourse deny an objective referent or ground to social reality, Durkheim and many of his contemporaries claimed that they found it in phenomena that range from society to the will to life.

Reconceptualized in this way, the entire tenor of the postmodern discourse changes dramatically. First, Enlightenment narratives are *not* universally valid hard facts, but artificial human constructions, cultural artifacts. Thus, progress is not real in the positivistic sense, but is a human conceptual category, an invention that balances the good and ill that comes with social development and seeks to conclude that overall, things have become better. But decadence, degeneration, and decline always accompany so-called progress, and progress always creates new problems, even if modern humans do not wish to dwell on this truth (Bailey 1958). Few have captured these rich dimensions of progress better than Park and Burgess, who begin their chapter on progress with the line, "It seems incredible that there should have been a time when mankind had no conception of progress" (1921:953). They conclude, and I think correctly, that

> The conception of progress in general involves a balancing of the goods against the ills of life. It raises the question whether the gains which society makes as a whole are compensation for the individual defeats and losses which progress inevitably involves. One reason why we believe in progress, perhaps, is that history is invariably written by the survivors. . . . Progress, in so far as it makes the world more comfortable, makes it more complicated. (p. 954)

Second, if the ground or referent for the mind is not the mind itself in a tautological, Kantian sense, but is the will or society, then one no longer has the option of rebelling at Enlightenment narratives. One cannot rebel meaningfully at Necessity, at Nature. If the world is will and idea, then it involves centripetal as well as centrifugal forces, and the task of the individual is to recognize these forces and attempt to balance them to the extent that he or she is able. Durkheim summarizes this insight well:

> This does not mean that civilization has no use, but that it is not the services that it renders that makes it progress. It develops because it cannot fail to develop. Once effectuated, this development is found to be generally useful, or at least, it is utilized [but] we must notice that the good it renders in this direction is not positive enrichment, a growth in our stock of happiness, but it only repairs the losses that it has itself caused. ([1893] 1933:337)

If the world is not just idea, as taught by the Kantians as well as most contemporary writers on postmodernism, but is instead will *and* idea, then we have discovered the ground or referent that has been perceived to be missing by postmodernists. Durkheim's society seems to fulfill the role of ground or referent for ideas that Schopenhauer's will fulfilled following Kant. But to claim that the will is the referent that fills the gap that Baudrillard depicts in his vision of the world as a mess of circulating fictions is not to reassert the oppression of Enlightenment narratives in a new disguise. On the contrary, the will is always changing. One cannot use the will to gain the positivistic sense of permanence and security that is still being sought. And if the postmodernists are correct that there is a connection between male chauvinism and so-called objectivity, what should be done about it? Durkheim and many of his contemporaries perceived the other side of the objective idea, its ground or referent, its will, as *feminine*, and sought to reconcile objectivity with subjectivity, masculine with feminine modes of relating.

To recognize the will as the ground for culture is to be open to the task of reconciling the tough, right-handed, egoistic mind with the will's many derivatives: with the forces of the Virgin described by Henry Adams; with the archaic, matriarchal, and peaceable habits discovered by Veblen; with altruism, empathy, and other sympathetic elements that are essential to social solidarity, as taught by Durkheim; with the unconscious, which Jung regarded as primarily feminine; and in general, with all that is subsumed by Schopenhauer and Bachofen under the rubric of the heart.

For those who would take Durkheim seriously in this regard, the postmodernist debate would shift from its present state of infighting between liberals versus conservatives, from the unwelcome alternatives of chaos versus maintenance of the status quo, and from a rebellion at Enlightenment narratives that often seems to lead headlong into hostility against science and all objectivity. The new agenda uncovered by the Durkheimian analysis in this book is actually old: It treats Western culture as a resume of wisdom that was accumulated through the ages and refracted in its religion, philosophy, language, and other cultural representations. Like Schopenhauer, Durkheim felt that at least since Plato, Western culture has been focusing on *homo duplex* as the always changing formula that necessitates constant readjustment in balancing the forces based on the will versus the idea. While it is true that Schopenhauer also considered Buddhism and Hinduism in this vein, and that Durkheim considered the Aborigines, it is also true that they refused to conclude that the Western formula for *homo duplex* was either superior to others or universal. They were neither ethnocentric nor iconoclastic, but sought to uncover the benign as well as harmful elements of Western culture.

What has been misunderstood as Durkheim's positivism betrays actually a longing to find a new sense of psychic wholeness. Adams, Veblen, Jung, and some of Durkheim's other contemporaries that we have been invoking in this book shared Durkheim's general orientation toward balance, and constantly looked backward in history to make sense of their present, and of the future. It is not the case that they were conservative—because they were all radical critics of the status quo— but that they realized that to address the fragmentation of their present and future societies (our present), one had to integrate the culture of the present with the accumulated wisdom of the past. They looked backward in order to move forward, because they denied the radical break from the past that has become the staple of modern, positivistic thinking and the fragmentation of postmodernity.[4]

Thus, in the conclusion to *The Elementary Forms of the Religious Life*, Durkheim concludes—against the positivists—that we do not derive our certainty in scientific concepts from methodology, but "we get [concepts] from language, that is to say, from common experience" ([1912] 1965:486). He elaborates:

> A collective representation presents guarantees of objectivity by the fact that it is collective: for it is not without sufficient reason that it has been able to generalize and maintain itself with persistence. If it were out of accord with the nature of things, it would never have been able to acquire an extended and prolonged empire over intellects. At bottom, the confidence inspired by scientific concepts is due to the fact that they can be methodically controlled. But a collective representation is necessarily submitted to a control that is repeated indefinitely; the men who accept it verify it by their own experience. Therefore, it could not be wholly inadequate for its subject. It is true that it may express this by means of imperfect symbols; *but scientific symbols themselves are never more than approximate*. It is precisely this principle which is at the basis of the method which we follow in the study of religious phenomena: we take it as an axiom that religious beliefs, howsoever strange their appearance may be at times, contain a truth which must be discovered.
>
> On the other hand, it is not at all true that concepts, even when constructed according to the rules of science, get their authority uniquely from their objective value. *It is not enough that they be true to be believed. If they are not in harmony with the other beliefs and opinions, or in a word, with the mass of the other collective representations, they will be denied; minds will be closed to them; consequently it will be as though they did not exist.* Today it is generally sufficient that they bear the stamp of science to receive a sort of privileged credit, because we have faith in science. But this faith does not differ essentially from religious faith. (p. 486; my emphasis).

Durkheim regards science itself as a cultural activity whose ground or referent is society conceived as will and idea. Rather than searching after positivistic causes, he sought the ground or referent for the idea of cause in the metaphysical notion of social forces. He thought and wrote in terms of *affinities* among various phenomena for each other, not positivistic causes and effects. His perspective explains why geniuses who are ahead of their time will be ignored, even if subsequent generations are finally able to "fit" their discoveries into the rest of the cultural outlook.[5] Science does not derive its authority from itself, but from the degree to which it harmonizes with the rest of culture. Truth does not, and cannot, speak for itself.

Similarly, the new world order touted by the New Right cannot really be grounded in some fictitious, a priori principle of inherent, universal rationality that emerged with the so-called end of history (Fukuyama 1992), but in the empirical, perceptual, total category that is society. This is not only because the Enlightenment notion of rationality is not universal—plenty of postmodernists have made that criticism. Additionally, Enlightenment rationality is egoistic, aimed at maximizing the individual's pleasure and interests, and one cannot derive social solidarity from egoism. By contrast, Durkheim's version of the new world order finds the seeds of internationalism in the very empathy and mystic sympathy that is the basis of all social solidarity, from archaic to modern and postmodern. Religion eventually spills over the borders of one's tribe and nation. The international aspect of religion reflects the international aspect of society. In Durkheim's words:

> There is nothing in this situation which is peculiar to Australian societies. There is no people and no state which is not a part of another society, more or less unlimited, which embraces all the peoples and all the States with which the first comes in contact, either directly or indirectly; there is no national life which is not dominated by a collective life of an international nature. In proportion as we advance in history, these international groups acquire a greater importance and extent. Thus we show how, in certain cases, this universalistic tendency has been able to develop itself to the point of affecting not only the higher ideas of the religious system, but even the principles upon which it rests. ([1912] 1965:474)

If Durkheim's insight is ignored again in the coming end of the century, there exists every possibility that victorious capitalism will mirror the effects of the ruthless Bolshevik system in its insensitivity to the other side of the mind: nationalism, religion, traditionalism, all the centripetal forces that turn human attention to the home, the soil, the past—and the mother. These centripetal forces must work with the centrifugal forces of internationalism, and cannot be severed or ignored in some hyperrational, transnational, assimilatory dream of a new world order held together by left-wing or right-wing ideology. It is important to realize that communism, socialism, and capitalism share the same modernist dream of conquering the centripetal aspects of human nature.

Durkheim would have held that even postmodern culture does not outgrow the need to harmonize scientific representations of reality with the rest of society's collective representations. Central to his sociology is the claim that society and culture are made possible by collective representations that express sympathy, empathy, and bonding. His insight helps to explain why fragmented, anomic, postmodern culture is reflected in the fragmented, compartmentalized, intellectually anomic state of contemporary science and society.

The radical Durkheim was trying to teach us that cultural analysis is every bit as scientific as the controlled experiment. Culture presents one with all the hard data that is necessary to draw conclusions about the psychic state of the collective consciousness. And he singled out religious culture as the most important indicator. From his study of religion, he did not arrive at some positivistic formulas concerning societal integration and deviance (which is what the functionalists derive from Durkheim), but at *homo duplex* as the basis for religion. And from this insight, he drew conclusions about individualism, progress, spirituality, the future of Western civilization, and other phenomena that have resurfaced in the postmodern discourse, and that we have been following throughout this book.

Finally, and following Durkheim, we have been aiming at restoring all sorts of harmonies and pointing to interesting affinities throughout this book. One is the harmony between Durkheim and his contemporaries, as well as the collective representations that dominated his *fin de siècle*. Durkheim fits in with Veblen, Adams, Jung, Freud, and his other illustrious contemporaries, but does not really fit the positivistic program of deductive reasoning and hypothesis testing. We have also exposed many affinities between the contemporary postmodern discourse and the previous *fin de siècle* spirit, although we noted differences as well. The notion of harmony also exposes the soft side of Durkheim's sociology, his left-handed insistence that empathy—*not* right-handed, rational, cognitive, consensus—is the glue that holds societies together. Here again, we detect a connection with the faint outline of an emerging collective consciousness fostered by *some* (but not all) fragmented, postmodern philosophy that humanity is a unity, and that humanity needs to be mindful of Mother Earth—ideas that Durkheim had foreshadowed with his vision of a united nation of the world. Finally, the idea of harmony brings to mind the longing for peace. It is worth emphasizing that in contradistinction to the many instances of brutality and violence with which the Enlightenment has been associated, Durkheim's thought constitutes a pacifist sociology. He abhorred war as it manifests itself in political as well as economic, religious, domestic, academic, and other social institutions, and sought a peaceful social solidarity based on justice and mercy. Here again, Murphy (1989) and Bauman (1987, 1989, 1990) have exposed the tendency in some—but not all—postmodern discourse to emphasize liberty, diversity, tolerance, and justice. But postmodern discourse is just as likely to support violence and war.

I have tried to emphasize that Durkheim's understanding of compassion is different from its fake, ornamental imitations: pity, kindliness, smug but guarded concern, and the middle-class habit of being nice. Nietzsche, Veblen, Riesman, and other cynics are right to criticize the egoistic motives that often lurk beneath the surface of these imitations of compassion. Durkheim's understanding of the empathy that holds society together has an affinity with Schopenhauer's understanding of compassion as cosuffering. Genuine compassion is an involuntary, nonegoistic reaction to the insight that we all share in the struggle to survive entailed by the will to life. If the postmodern programs of saving the Earth and protecting the oppressed succeed at all, they will need genuine compassion as ground or referent, not just the boosterish, fun atmosphere of being nice that has characterized "We Are the World" and other postmodern spectacles of raising consciousness (and money).

## DURKHEIM AND VEBLEN ON CHRISTIAN
## MORALS AND MODERNITY

In this section, we shall compare and contrast Durkheim and Veblen on the role of Christian morals in the modernity project in order to highlight Durkheim's contribution to the moral import of postmodern discourse. We have already exposed Durkheim's contribution in this regard, in this book and elsewhere, as part of his quest to establish sociology as a science of morality (Meštrović 1988, 1991). But the dominant reaction by positivists to this verifiable trait in Durkheim's sociology is so hostile—it is still forbidden to invoke values in a scientific discussion, despite C. Wright Mills (1959) and Gouldner (1958, 1970)— that it requires further explication. Veblen has already been labeled as an iconoclast, the precursor to C. Wright Mills, so that comparing Durkheim with Veblen will help to accentuate further the radically pacifist elements in Durkheim's sociology. And it should go without saying that many of Durkheim's and Veblen's contemporaries were heading in a similar direction.

Veblen was consistently critical of Christianity when it reduces itself to an appendix to the leisure class. Riesman summarizes well Veblen's feeling that Christianity is "a patriarchal religion of futile subservience to extravagant earthly representations of a leisure-laden heavenly hierarchy" (1953:66). But in his 1910 essay entitled "Christian Morals and the Competitive System" especially (and less clearly elsewhere), Veblen isolates and praises Christian morality as an essential habit in Western culture. It teaches brotherly love, self-abnegation, and humility, the habits that Durkheim subsumes under altruism and asceticism, the essential elements of any system of morality that leads to nonoppressive social solidarity. But "Western civilization is both Christian and competitive (pecuniary)" according to Veblen, so that if these two tendencies seem contradictory, "the student of this culture might have to face the question: Will western civilization dwindle and decay if one or the other, the morals of competition or the morals of Christianity fall into abeyance?" (1943:200). Veblen's approach is essentially a refraction of Durkheim's discovery of the coexistence of altruism and egoism as part of *homo duplex*. In a rather sharp contrast with Veblen and Durkheim, Max Weber ([1904] 1958) portrays Protestant culture almost exclusively in terms of competitive, egoistic, pecuniary culture, and is hardly mindful of the opposing, empathetic tendencies toward brotherly love.

In any case, Veblen locates the origins of Christianity in the late Roman period[6] and that of competitive morals in the principle of natural rights, which dates from the eighteenth century. Durkheim and the other theorists we have been following in this book would agree, but Veblen adds another layer of complexity. Even though he argues that the Christian habits of self-abnegation were a radical departure from Greco-Roman paganism, Judaism, and even subsequent Islam—and are in this respect somewhat unique in human culture—he argues also that these habits are archaic. According to Veblen, a form of the Christian principle to love thy neighbor as thyself "seems, in its elements at least, to be a culturally atavistic trait, belonging to the ancient, not to say primordial, peaceable culture of the lower savagery" (1943:215). Here we touch on Veblen's subscription to Bachofen's myth, such that "throughout all the vicissitudes of cultural change, the golden rule of the peaceable savage has never lost the respect of occidental mankind, and its hold on men's convictions is, perhaps, stronger now than at any earlier period of the modern time" (p. 215). Durkheim, too, held the seemingly contradictory position that altruism preceded egoism in human development at the same time he felt that primitive forms of solidarity are inferior when compared to the greater social solidarity in advanced societies.

One way to resolve this apparent contradiction in Veblen and Durkheim is to suggest that ideal (but not vulgar) Christianity offers a distilled, purified version of the selfless, altruistic tendency that is essential to the sustained and vigorous existence of all societies. Similarly, modern, enlightened egoism is also much more potent than archaic self-interest. In Veblen's words, "these two codes of conduct, Christian morals and business principles, are the institutional by-products of two different cultural situations" (p. 214), which are peculiar to the West even if they are built upon the *homo duplex* formula, which is universal. Consider the following passage from Durkheim's *Moral Education* as a point of comparison with Veblen:

> The principal obligations [in primitive religions] are *not* to respect one's neighbor, to help him, to assist him; but to accomplish meticulously prescribed rites, to give to the Gods what is their due, and even, if need be, to sacrifice one's self to their glory. . . . But gradually things change. Gradually, human duties are multiplied, become more precise, and pass to the first rank of importance; while others, on the contrary, tend to become attenuated. One might say that Christianity itself has contributed most to the acceleration of this result. *An essentially human religion*, since its God

dies for the salvation of humanity, Christianity teaches that the principal duty of man toward God is to love his neighbor. Although there are religious duties—rites addressed only to divinity—the place they occupy and the importance attributed to them continue to diminish. ([1925 1961:6; my emphasis)

But all habits of thought must harmonize with habits of life, according to Veblen. The habits of life that gave rise to both Christian and competitive morals are defunct, and are not valid for all time. Clinging to them constitutes cultural lag. Here we are reminded of Durkheim's insistence in *The Rules* that social facts are normal only when they fit a culture's particular phase of development. Veblen argues that egoism was appropriate to eighteenth-century craftsmanship because it was restrained by small, personal, primary groups and by the Christian notion of fair play. But "times have changed since the eighteenth century, when this system of pecuniary egoism reached its mature development," Veblen writes (1943:213). He elaborates:

The excellence and sufficiency of an enlightened pecuniary egoism are no longer a matter of course and of common-sense to the mind of this generation, which has experienced the current era of machine industry, credit, delegated corporation management, and distant markets. (p. 214)

Durkheim had also warned that old-fashioned capitalism and socialism, erected as they were on the principles of egoistic self-interest, would become pathological in the modern era. It is almost a truism in our cynical age that, according to opinion polls, most Americans do not believe that economic professionals operate on the principle of fair play (Kanter and Mirvis 1989). Moreover, "the ancient Christian principle of humility, renunciation, abnegation, or non-resistance has been virtually eliminated from the moral scheme of moral Christendom," Veblen (1943:216) wrote in 1910. While one can debate whether postmodern Christianity still subscribes to these principles officially, one is likely to concur with Veblen that these ancient virtues are no longer taught or followed as if they were common sense. And this is precisely the same anomic state of immorality that Durkheim described and criticized in his sociological writings. Both thinkers predicted the eruption of the "me" generation, unrestrained by altruistic motives, which characterizes postmodern culture in the present *fin de siècle*.

Here we arrive at Veblen's conclusion. He observes that both Christian and competitive habits of thought "are in process of disintegration" (p. 218). But he predicted that humankind would realize that pecuniary self-interest is no longer appropriate in a complex, modern society.[7] For reasons he never explained, Veblen ends his essay with the claim that while competitive morals will disintegrate, "the Christian principle of brotherhood should logically continue to gain ground at the expense of the pecuniary morals of competitive business" (p. 218).

It is difficult to defend Veblen in this regard, or even to trace his conclusion to the argument that precedes it. Rather, one is likely to agree with Riesman (1953) that here Veblen simply followed Marx's own overly idealistic and utopian conclusions. No commentator on postmodern culture has uncovered any semblance of the alleged victory of Christian morals over pecuniary self-interest, although many suggest the contrary (especially Bellah et al. 1985). In fact, postmodern philosophers tend to ignore Christian morals, as if these were part of the oppressive narratives they purport to rebel against, or perhaps because they still subscribe to the positivistic fact-value distinction. Of course, it is an open question whether Marx and Veblen will prove to be correct some centuries into the future.

Durkheim agrees with Veblen up to the point that both self-interest and Christian morality are disintegrating as systems of collective representations that could harmonize with contemporary needs.[8] But in contrast with Veblen, Durkheim anticipated a radically new morality, which would be like an alloy of these two dominant strands of Western culture, egoism and altruism. He predicted the emergence of a new cult of the individual, a new morality that would transform the old morals of egoism and self-abnegation. This new individualism would not be like the old egoism, and the new humility would have as its object of worship the rights and dignity that every individual deserves and obtains from *society*, the referent and ground of Being, not some Kantian a priori principle. This new religion of the future will have as its object "the general interests of humanity—that is to say, committing itself to an access of justice, to a higher morality" (Durkheim [1925] 1961:77).

I shall leave open for discussion the question whether the postmodern revolution, if it can be called that, is tending—however imperfectly—in the direction of the new world order as imagined by Durkheim. The objective investigator will have to account for the "me" generation, narcissistic tendencies of pecuniary egoism that apparently continue to operate as habits in postmodern culture. Veblen regarded these as throwbacks to barbarism. And as of this writing, the high priests of old-fashioned, laissez-faire capitalism—which is based on outmoded habits of thought that both Veblen and Durkheim criticized—are predicting total victory over socialism, and domination of the world economy. If they are correct, a new system of ruthless modernity will replace a defunct system of ruthless modernity (communism; see Bauman 1991:222), at least for a while. But if Durkheim and Veblen are correct, victorious capitalism will eventually fail like socialism, because both modern systems are insensitive to the other side of human nature, the heart.

But in defense of Durkheim, one can point to extremely faint outlines of a moral code that seems to resemble his cult of the individual. The popularity of Lamaze classes testifies to the radical departure from the chauvinistic assumption that operated from barbaric times to only a generation ago that birth is strictly woman's business. The preservation of the dignity of *all* the family's members is only beginning to emerge as a legislative agenda. Up to now, laws favored the working male "head of the family." Similarly, it is possible to interpret the explosion of litigation in the past decade as more than pecuniary self-interest on the part of lawyers and litigants (although that is certainly an important ingredient). It could also be the case that postmodern individuals are more aware than any previous generations of their rights, and duties. Suddenly, it seems, almost everyone's rights and duties are being specified very carefully: pregnant women, medical doctors, students, professors, children, parents, and so on for increasingly more social roles. (Although, following Durkheim's criticisms, it still seems true that the business profession remains tardy in this general trend toward professional ethics.) Murphy (1989) sees in postmodern social philosophy a deep and genuine thirst for justice by all of society's members, especially the members who have been neglected and exploited up to now. Overall, however, the contemporary situation is too tumultuous too predict whether the next millennium will begin tending toward egoism, altruism, or a reconciliation between these two extremes.


## POSTMODERNISM AND THE EPISTEMOLOGICAL
## IMAGINATION REQUIRED BY SOCIOLOGY


We have seen that postmodern philosophy undercuts its viability and import by treating as unequivocally oppressive all objective ground and reference points that are necessary for communication and social life. It tends to deconstruct and demystify social existence into nothingness, a nihilistic fantasy of chaotic, circulating fictions that is seen by many as liberating. Our age is characterized by heightened consciousness concerning the environment and social justice, at the same time that it perpetuates destruction of the environment, neoconservatism, and the social injustice that has led to heightened racial tensions. We have pointed to Durkheim's apparent solution to this problem, that society, as an important manifestation of the will to life, is the ground or referent for the vast symbolism that constitutes communication and social life. To be sure, it is a dynamic ground that cannot yield permanent truths and natural laws. We have taken great efforts to distinguish Durkheim's benign, social order from the oppressive versions of social order that postmodernism questions. Nevertheless, the prejudice against holistic thinking is so widespread in this regard that we have probably not convinced the skeptic. Margaret Thatcher claimed that there is no such thing as society, that there are only individual men and women and families. She probably represents the dominant view among laypersons and professionals—sadly, even sociologists. Imagine C. Wright Mills (1959) trying to convince postmodernists to use the sociological imagination! Many postmodern philosophers take delight in deconstructing the notion of society.

It is a curious contradiction in our postmodernist age that whereas social unity is denied in favor of liberating fragmentation, the physical universe is admitted to be congruent and whole. Everyone knows and accepts that the universe is constantly changing, yet everyone is able to work with an ever-changing force of gravity and other physical forces, even the dismal knowledge that the universe will eventually disintegrate. Durkheim felt that the sociological knowledge of society's hidden forces would similarly grant authentic freedom and autonomy to the individual:

> There was a time when the human mind did not know that the physical universe had its laws. Was it then that man held greatest sway over things? No doubt, the sorcerer or the magician believed that he could transmute at will various bodies one into another; but the powers which he thus attributed to himself were, we know today, purely imaginary. On the contrary, since the positive natural sciences were established (and they too were established by taking the determinist postulate as a foundation), what changes we have introduced into the universe! Until yesterday we believed that all this was arbitrary and contingent, that legislators or kings could, just like the alchemists of yore, at their pleasure change the aspect of societies, make them change from one type to another. In reality, these supposed miracles were illusory; and how many grave errors have resulted from this yet too widespread illusion! On the contrary, it is sociology which by discovering the laws of social reality will permit us to direct historical evolution with greater reflection than in the past; for we can change nature, whether moral or physical, only by conforming to its laws. ([1906] 1978:75)

Durkheim spoke too soon. Sociologists continue to criticize him for allegedly depriving the individual of autonomy by his so-called overestimation of social forces. Other social scientists also cling to outmoded, eighteenth-century, egoistic starting points of analysis in which social life begins and ends with the individual. Thus, contemporary linguists are much more likely to study the mathematical precision of ideal sen-

tence structure without paying sufficient attention to the social context
that is the ground for any meaningful conversation. Religion is still
studied by social scientists as something that flows from the individual's
need for meaning. Economists suffer the most from intellectual cultural
lag by insisting that utilitarian self-interest is the dynamo that drives and
should drive the economy. All of these are derivatives of one-sided
Enlightenment narratives that postmodernism purports to rebel against,
but that continue to dominate contemporary academic life, even postmodern discourse. And all the social sciences continue to operate as if
society were not a totality, but a fragmented domain that each discipline
can reduce to its own egoistic paradigm. Most important of all, the new
world order is still envisaged in outmoded, eighteenth-century terms as
being motivated by rational self-interest, as if this egoistic tendency
were capable of the mighty task of envisioning a holistic unity to the
world that transcends the solitary individual at every turn.

When the social sciences are characterized by extensive intellectual
anomie, there is no good reason to hope that laypersons are going to
grasp Durkheim's solution to the postmodern tendency toward nihilism and fragmentation. Durkheim is not a household word like Freud.
The sociology section in academic as well as nonacademic bookstores
is more likely to be stocked with New Age books, even Shirley Mac-
Laine's autobiographical musings on reincarnation, than works that
focus on how the holistic knowledge of social laws can liberate the
individual. Most social problems are apprehended in society at large as
things that can be solved by individual effort. "Just say no" to drugs
became a popular, kitsch solution to a devastating postmodern problem
in the 1980s. Enormous government attention was focused on interdict-
ing drugs and drug dealers, and hardly any attention was paid to the
reasons why postmodern individuals crave drugs. The most interesting
sociological aspect of how postmodern individuals approach social
problems—they declare war on them—draws hardly any attention.
Postmodernists declare war on crime, cancer, AIDS, potholes, poverty,
the recession, and other social problems without reflecting on the total
state of the social body that is producing these pathological and ineffec-
tual reactions. For example, the war on mental illness took to deinstitutionalization as the panacea to the problem of hospitalizing the mentally
ill. But it is now evident that the "community" that was supposed to
receive the mentally ill has shunned them—because *Gemeinschaft* no
longer exists in modern societies—and that treatment is more costly
than ever (see Johnson 1990).

From Durkheim's and Veblen's perspectives, contemporary social
thought places burdens on the solitary, egoistic individual that he or she
may have been able to bear in the relatively community oriented

eighteenth-century, but cannot sustain in a complicated, postmodern society. The relationships between an individual's goals and means, self-interest versus the interest of others, and other aspects of old-fashioned utilitarianism are no longer clear and simple. More importantly, Durkheim felt that it is impossible for the isolated, modern individual to spontaneously feel disinterested empathy for the common good. Yet, without collective effort, and without a sociological imagination, contemporary social problems are too overwhelming to be solved on the basis of egoistic self-interest.

But to be true to the Durkheimian program that is being pursued here, one has to conclude that humankind will not be convinced to abandon the defunct principle of egoistic self-interest on the basis of sound and logical reasoning. Logic and reason have to harmonize with the hidden intent of society and one's historical epoch. My intent in this book has been to suggest that a Durkheimian reading of the postmodern rebellion at oppressive Enlightenment narratives leads to the hopeful conclusion that humankind is at the brink of realizing the epistemological revolution necessary for genuine, constructive social change. Postmodernist discourse has begun, finally, to raise questions about progress, assimilation, and enlightenment that will hopefully lead to a new synthesis of the cultural forces that gave rise to the Enlightenment in the first place. But the present state of postmodern discourse is so chaotic that it is equally likely that right-hand thinking will emerge more victorious than ever, and that the left-hand—Western culture's archaic symbol for the other, feminine side of rationality—will remain mutilated and deformed for some time to come.

## OVERCOMING BARBARISM

It is difficult for the postmodern individual to admit that he or she lives in a modern culture based on barbarism that turns to violence to solve social problems. After all, postmodern culture is predicated on the fun-system, as noted by Baudrillard (1981) and others. In *The Lonely Crowd*, David Riesman (1950) had warned that the drawback to an other-directed culture geared toward fun is that it disallows genuine indignation. If everyone is always portrayed in the media as friendly, tolerant, and happy—even when they are engaged in wars—that leaves no room for *sincere* conviction. In sum, the collective representations pertaining to the metaphorical wars betray a contradictory state that reflects the discrepancies and hypocrisies we have uncovered in postmodern discourse. Oppressive modernity continues to emerge, with all its linkages to violence, assimilation, and the maintenance of social order at almost any cost. At the same time, postmodern wars are fought with a sense of moral urgency, even concern and sympathy for general well-being.

Freud did not believe that civilization, the League of Nations (and by extension, the United Nations), or any other system of ideas could ultimately control human aggression in the sense of eliminating the possibility of war. With regard to the United Nations, which was erected on the ashes of the bankrupt League of Nations, he is certainly correct. One could conclude that Freud was postmodern before his time, that from 1915 to 1932 he seems to have abandoned his remaining strands of faith in Enlightenment narratives that aggression can be controlled by reason. Some other solution must be sought. Freud's many *fin de siècle* colleagues also rebelled at one-sided Enlightenment narratives, and began to suspect the model that society, or any of its organs, could hold back the terrifying forces that modernity was only beginning to unleash. Durkheim, Veblen, Adorno, and Adams are to be counted among these famous colleagues. They were seeking an alternative to the Enlightenment narratives that persist into our *fin de siècle*. Were they right? Is the Enlightenment bankrupt, finally?

This is the important question to which the present book leads, but given the confusing state of the contemporary postmodernist discourse, it is almost impossible to answer decisively. One's answer hinges on whether one assumes—along the trajectory established by thinkers from Schopenhauer to Durkheim, Veblen, Horkheimer, and Adorno—that enlightened, heartless reason is the culprit in human aggression, or whether one takes the positivistic tack that humanity has not become sufficiently enlightened. More significant is the fact that in the present *fin de siècle*, Freud and his pessimistic colleagues, Durkheim, Veblen, and Simmel, are passé. University social science courses continue to refer to a boosterish, postmodernist version of Enlightenment narratives: to rational social action, rational choice theory, cognitive psychology, and other testimonials to the mind's supposed power over passion—minus the doubts, reservations, and fears expressed from Hobbes to Freud. Our *fin de siècle* morality is still derived from the works of Habermas, Kohlberg, Piaget, and other disciples of the Enlightenment, not Durkheim, Bergson, Schopenhauer, Veblen, and other thinkers from the previous *fin de siècle* who were seeking to ground morality in the heart, not the mind.

For example, at least since the 1980s, Lawrence Kohlberg's (1981) Enlightenment-based understanding of moral development has been challenged (albeit not effectively) by Carol Gilligan's (1982) feminist approach. In brief, the controversy is as follows: Kohlberg presents subjects with a moral dilemma that should be resolved with a decision, for example, whether or not one should *steal* a drug for a just cause, in this case, to save someone's life. Gilligan found that compared with 1960s males, females questioned why stealing should be an option at all, and actively sought alternatives to committing a crime for the sake of a just cause.[9] The alternatives center on negotiation, caring, and trying to get all the parties involved to understand each other's point of view. Kohlberg's scoring procedure tends to find that because women stress caring more than universal principles of justice, they are less moral than males. Gilligan has rightfully challenged this chauvinistic conclusion, and suggests that women may use a system of moral reasoning that is separate from male reasoning.[10] I am drawing the obvious analogy that for Kohlberg as for modern thinking on moral crusades that has survived into the postmodern era, the masculine view of morality makes the commission of violence for the sake of a just cause seem axiomatic. For example, the late 1980s and beginning of the 1990s in the United States have witnessed a dramatic "get tough" attitude in the war on crime, including more use of the death penalty, a lessening of constitutional protection, and longer sentences.

But, as noted in Chapter 2, other feminist writers have criticized the notion of a caring feminine voice as a weak, even false alternative to the masculine, Enlightenment voice. Here is the last, and most puzzling aspect of war—real or metaphorical—in postmodern times: The feminine, pacifist, nonaggressive voices have been almost completely suppressed.

Jung's proposed solution to modern barbarism is to make contact again with the repressed, unconscious Great Mother archetype. Bachofen's, Jung's, and other Romantics' sensitivity to the Great Mother archetype casts a new light on the postmodernist debate. The postmodernist version of the counter-Enlightenment merely throws off the shackles of reason, but does nothing to offset, contain, even recognize the barbaric habits of the fight that coexist with modernity. In rebelling against all grounds and referents for social reality, postmodernism has thrown out the feminine, Christian referents that Durkheim and Veblen felt should offset modernity. Postmodern fragmentation and circulation of fictions is not morally liberating, not even morally neutral. On the contrary, the results seem to include: neoconservative, reactionary sentiments; schizoid culture that sees only what it wants to see; the retreat to a fantasy version of the world as a fun paradise where the "good guys" live; the psychic withdrawal into a narcissistic strategy of survival; the increasing denial of the distinction between the real and unreal; and above all, the continuation of the assimilatory, violent, status quo tendencies associated with the Enlightenment project.

By contrast, the previous *fin de siècle* efforts at countering the negative aspects of the Enlightenment sought to complement reason with the feminine unconscious, to reconcile the mind with the heart, to temper morality based on rational principles of justice with the tender-hearted impulse in humans to feel compassion, even for one's enemies and the objects of one's hatred. Schopenhauer brings out these Romantic aspects of morality most forcefully in *On the Basis of Morality* ([1841] 1965). Schopenhauer exposed the hypocrisy of his bourgeois culture in pretending to be just when it tolerated vicious cruelty toward women, children, animals, and all others it defined as not-me. His critique is still relevant.

Consider the consequences of the new, Durkheimian perspective on American civil religion, Robert N. Bellah's controversial phrase for the new religion of Americanism that coexists and competes with bona fide religions.[11] Like Freud, Bellah focuses too exclusively on the masculine aspects of God as all-knowing, all-powerful, rational, and judging. Freud ([1927] 1955) ridiculed this modernist version of God, and implied—almost in spite of himself—a more relevant and complete image of God as Father *and* Mother (see Schoenfeld 1966, Vitz 1988). In a sense, Jung, Fromm, and Freud's other followers completed the *fin de siècle* implications of Freud's thought, even if they claimed to rebel at his patriarchy. One of my intentions in this book has been to suggest that despite the functionalist misreadings of Durkheim, Durkheim's sociology portrays society as Father *and* Mother, and culture as the language with which one may apprehend society.

My intent has been to contrast the right-handed, modern understanding of the new world order and civil religion that is dominating our *fin de siècle* collective consciousness, and that is commensurate with Bellah's analysis, with Durkheim's understanding of these same phenomena. Despite the postmodern rhetoric of choice, tolerance, kindness, and justice (Bauman 1990, 1991), it would seem that right-handed, neoconservative social forces dominate postmodern culture in the present *fin de siècle*. In this sense, postmodernism extends the modernist project even as it purports to rebel against it.

By contrast, in establishing sociology as a science of morals a century ago, Durkheim was seeking a new world order that would preserve right-handed progress and capitalist efficiency, but that would be balanced with left-handed, mystic sympathy and sense of international social solidarity. This Durkheimian goal still seems reasonable and appropriate as the millennium draws to a close, because the moral problems of our *fin de siècle* have not changed appreciably from Durkheim's time. He felt that his society was undergoing a stage of transition and moral mediocrity in which the old gods were dead or dying, but new ones had not yet been born. The same can be said of postmodern culture.

Finally, the reader will have missed entirely the point of this book if he or she concludes that we are calling for a new program of social engineering in which left-handed compassion is systematized. Nothing could be further from our intentions. From the moment that any virtue is systematized, it loses its left-handed character and becomes an aspect of right-handed oppression. The intent in this book has been to argue for the legitimacy of spontaneous and free, left-handed thinking and feeling, and for admitting these into the postmodern discourse.

## NOTES

1. For example, I had to take courses on Jung at the Harvard Divinity School, because none were offered in the psychology department.
2. At Washington University and the University of Rochester.
3. Consider Douglas Kellner's conclusion, for example, that "Baudrillard's fin de siècle exhaustion [is a] capitulation to the hegemony of the Right and a secret complicity with aristocratic conservatism" (1989:215).
4. Consider, for example, the influence of Edward Bellamy's *Looking Backward* ([1888] 1951) upon Veblen's social theory in this regard (Leathers 1986).
5. And in this sense, Durkheim was way ahead of his time, even our time.
6. Compare with Erich Fromm (1963) and Oswald Spengler ([1925] 1961) on the cultural origins of Christianity.
7. Here he mirrors or was influenced by Edward Bellamy's amazing optimism.
8. See Durkheim's ([1887] 1976b) review of Guyau's *Non-religion of the Future*.
9. I found no such gender differences in my 1991 university classes.
10. It should be noted that Gilligan waffles on the issue whether she is comparing males with females, or feminine with masculine reasoning.
11. We again leave civil religions in non-American societies for another discussion.

# References

Adams, H. [1900] 1983. "The Dynamo and the Virgin," Pp. 1068–75 in *The Education of Henry Adams*, New York: Viking,

Adorno, T. W. 1991. *The Culture Industry*, London: Routledge,

Alexander, J. C. 1988. *Durkheimian Sociology: Cultural Studies*. Cambridge: Cambridge University Press.

Alpert, H. 1937. "France's First University Course in Sociology." *American Sociological Review* 2:311–17

———. 1938. *Emile Durkheim and His Sociology*. New York: Columbia University Press.

———. 1939. "Explaining the Social Socially." *Social Forces* 17(3):361–65.

———. 1941. "Emile Durkheim and the Theory of Social Integration." *Journal of Social Philosophy* 6(2):172–84.

Atkinson, C. W., Buchanan, C. H., and Miles, M. 1985. *Immaculate and Powerful: The Female in Sacred Image and Social Reality*. Boston: Beacon Press.

Bachofen, J. J. [1861] 1967. *Myth, Religion, and Mother Right*. Princeton, NJ: Princeton University Press.

Bailey, R. B. 1958. *Sociology Faces Pessimism: A Study of European Sociological Thought Amidst a Fading Optimism*. The Hague: Martinus Nijhoff.

Baillot, A. 1927. *Influence de la philosophie de Schopenhauer en France (1860–1900)*. Paris: J. Vrin.

Balbus, I. 1981. "Habermas and Feminism: Male Communication and the Evolution of Patriarchal Society." *New Political Science* 13:27–47.

Baudelaire, C. [1863] 1965. *The Painter of Modern Life and Other Essays*, translated by J. Mayne. New York: Phaidon.

———. [1869] 1970. *Paris Spleen*, translated by Louise Varese. New York: New Directions Books.

Baudrillard, J. 1981. *Critique of the Political Economy of the Sign*. St. Louis, MO: Telos Press.

———. 1986. *America*. London: Verso.

———. 1988. *Selected Writings*. Stanford: Stanford University Press.

———. 1990. *Seduction*. New York: St. Martin's Press.

Bauman, Z. 1987. *Legislators and Interpreters: On Modernity, Post-Modernity, and Intellectuals*. Ithaca, NY: Cornell University Press.

_____. 1989. *Modernity and the Holocaust*. Ithaca, NY: Cornell University Press.

_____. 1990. *Modernity and Ambivalence*. Ithaca, NY: Cornell University Press.

_____. 1991. *Intimations of Postmodernity*. London: Routledge.

Bell, D. 1976. *The Cultural Contradictions of Capitalism*. New York: Basic Books.

_____. 1988. *The End of Ideology*. Cambridge, MA: Harvard University Press.

Bellah, R. N. 1967. "Civil Religion in America." *Daedalus* 96:1–21.

_____. 1970. *Beyond Belief*. New York: Harper & Row.

_____. 1973. "Civil Religion in America." *Archives de sciences sociales des religions* 18:7–22.

_____. 1974. "The New Religious Consciousness and the Secular University." *Daedalus* 103(4):110–15.

_____. 1981. "Democratic Culture or Authoritarian Capitalism?" *Society* 18(6):41–50.

_____. 1985. "Creating a New Framework for New Realities: Social Science as Public Philosophy." *Change* 17(2):35–39.

_____. 1986. "Are Americans Still Citizens?" *Tocqueville Review* 7:89–96.

_____. 1987. "Legitimation Processes in Politics and Religion." *Current Sociology* 35(2):89–99.

_____. 1989. "Reply to Twenty Years after Bellah." *Sociological Analysis* 50(2):149.

Bellah, R. N., Madsen, R., Swidler, A., Sullivan, W. M., and Tipton, S. M. 1985. *Habits of the Heart*. Berkeley: University of California Press.

Bellamy, E. [1888] 1951. *Looking Backward, 2000–1887*. New York: Random House.

Benjamin, W. 1968. "The Work of Art in the Age of Mechanical Reproduction." Pp. 219–66 in *Illuminations*, edited by Hannah Arendt. New York: Harcourt, Brace & World.

_____. 1973. *Charles Baudelaire: A Lyric Poet in the Era of High Capitalism*, translated by H. Zohn. London: NLB Press.

Bergson, H. [1932] 1954. *The Two Sources of Morality and Religion*, translated by R. A. Audra and C. Brereton. Garden City, NJ: Doubleday.

_____. 1944. *Creative Evolution*. New York: Modern Library.

Birch, C. 1988. "Eight Fallacies of the Modern World and Five Axioms for a Postmodern Worldview." *Perspectives in Biology and Medicine* 32(1):12–30.

Bloom, A. 1987. *The Closing of the American Mind*. New York: Simon and Schuster.

Blum, L. A. 1988. "Gilligan and Kohlberg: Implications for Moral Theory." *Ethics* 98(3):172–91.

Bocock, R. J. 1979. "The Symbolism of the Father—A Freudian Sociological Analysis." *British Journal of Sociology* 30:205–17.

Bougle, C. 1938. *The French Conception of "Culture Generale" and Its Influences upon Instruction*. New York: Columbia University Press.

Braaten, J. 1991. *Habermas's Critical Theory of Society*. Albany, NY: SUNY Press.

Braden, C. S. 1930. *Religious Aspects of the Conquest of Mexico*. Durham, NC: Duke University Press.

Burston, D. 1986. "Myth, Religion and Mother Right: Bachofen's Influence on Psychoanalytic Theory." *Contemporary Psychoanalysis* 22(4):666–87.

Brzezinski, Z. 1989. *The Grand Failure: The Birth and Death of Communism in the Twentieth Century*. New York: Scribner's.

Cantarella, E. 1982. "J. J. Bachofen Between History and the Sociology of Law." *Sociologia del Diritto* 9(3):111–36.

Caporale, R., and Grumelli, A. 1971. *The Culture of Unbelief*. Berkeley: University of California Press.

Cartwright, D. 1984. "Kant, Schopenhauer, and Nietzsche on the Morality of Pity." *Journal of the History of Ideas* 45(1):83–98.

———. 1987. "Kant's View of the Moral Significance of Kindhearted Emotions and the Moral Insignificance of Kant's View." *Journal of Value Inquiry* 21:291–304.

———. 1988a. "Schopenhauer's Compassion and Nietzsche's Pity." *Schopenhauer Jahrbuch* 69:557–67

———. 1988b. "Schopenhauer's Axiological Analysis of Character." *Revue International de Philosophie* 42:18–36.

Cassirer, E. 1946. *Language and Myth*. New York: Dover.

———. 1972. *Philosophy of Symbolic Forms*. New Haven, CT: Yale University Press.

Clark, P. 1975. "Suicide, societe et sociologie: De Durkheim a Balzac." *Nineteenth-Century French Studies* 3:200–12.

Collier, J. L. 1991. *The Rise of Selfishness in America*. New York: Oxford.

Condren, M. 1989. *The Serpent and the Goddess: Women, Religion, and Power in Celtic Ireland*. New York: Harper Collins

Cortese, A. J. 1984. "Moral Judgment in Chicano, Black and White Young Adults." *Sociological Focus* 7:189–99.

———. 1989. *Ethnic Ethics: The Restructuring of Moral Theory*. Albany, NY: SUNY Press.

Cortese, A. J., and Mestrovic, S. G. 1990. "From Durkheim to Habermas: The Role of Language in Moral Theory." *Current Perspectives in Social Theory* 10:63–91.

Crawford, R. 1984. "The Savage and the City in the Work of T. S. Eliot." Unpublished doctoral dissertation, Oxford University.

Daly, M. 1978. *The Metaethics of Radical Feminism*. Boston: Beacon Press.

De Wolf, M. 1970. "One of the More Elementary Forms of Symbolization: The Meaning of Left and Right." *Cahiers internationaux de symbolisme* 19:87–112.

Dinneen, F. P. 1967. *An Introduction to General Linguistics*. New York: Holt, Rinehart, and Winston.

Doroszewski, W. 1932. "Quelque remarques sur les rapports de la sociologie et de la linguistique: Durkheim et F. de Saussure." *Journal de Psychologie* 80:82–91.

Douglas, J. 1967. *The Social Meanings of Suicide*. Princeton, NJ: Princeton University Press.

Dugger, W. M. 1984. "Veblen and Kropotkin on Human Evolution." *Journal of Economic Issues* 18:971–85.

Durkheim, E. [1885] 1978. "Review of Albert Schaeffle's *Bay und Leben des Sozialen Korpers*." Pp. 93–114 in *Emile Durkheim on Institutional Analysis*, edited by M. Traugott. Chicago: University of Chicago Press.

———. [1887] 1976a. "La Science positive de la morale en allemagne." Pp. 267–343 in *Textes*, edited by V. Karady, Vol. 1. Paris: Les Editions de Minuit.

_____. [1887] 1976b. "L'avenir de la religion." Pp. 149–65 in *Textes*, edited by V. Karady, Vol. 2. Paris: Les Editions de Minuit.

_____. [1889] 1978. "Review of Tonnies' *Community and Society*." Pp. 115–22 in *Emile Durkheim on Institutional Analysis*, edited by M. Traugott. Chicago: University of Chicago Press.

_____. [1893] 1967. *De la Division du travail social*. Paris: Presses Universitaires de France.

_____. [1893] 1933. *The Division of Labor in Society*, translated by George Simpson. New York: Free Press.

_____. 1895. *Les Regles de la methode sociologique*. Paris: Alcan.

_____. [1895] 1982. "The Rules of Sociological Method." Pp. 31–163 in *Durkheim: The Rules of Sociological Method and Selected Texts on Sociology and Its Method*, edited by S. Lukes. New York: Free Press.

_____. [1897] 1951. *Suicide: A Study in Sociology*, translated by John A. Spaulding and George Simpson. New York: Free Press.

_____. [1897] 1963. *Incest: The Nature and Origin of the Taboo*, translated by E. Sagarin. New York: Stuart Lyle.

_____. 1908. "Remarks in L'inconnu et l'inconscient en histoire." *Bulletin de la Societe Francaise de Philosophie* 8:217–47.

_____. [1912] 1965. *The Elementary Forms of the Religious Life*, translated by J. Swain. New York: Free Press.

_____. [1914] 1973. "The Dualism of Human Nature and Its Social Conditions." Pp. 149–66 in *Emile Durkheim on Morality and Society*, edited by R. Bellah. Chicago: University of Chicago Press.

_____. [1925] 1961. *Moral Education*, translated by Everett K. Wilson and Herman Schnurer. Glencoe, IL: Free Press.

_____. [1928] 1958. *Socialism and Saint-Simon*, translated by Charlotte Sattler. Yellow Springs, OH: Antioch Press.

_____. [1938] 1977. *The Evolution of Educational Thought*, translated by Peter Collins. London: Routledge & Kegan Paul.

_____. [1950] 1983. *Professional Ethics and Civic Morals*, translated by Cornelia Brookfield. Westport, CT: Greenwood Press.

_____. [1955] 1983. *Pragmatism and Sociology*, translated by J. C. Whitehouse. Cambridge: Cambridge University Press.

Durkheim, E., and Fauconnet, P. [1903] 1982. "Sociology and the Social Sciences." Pp. 175–208 in *The Rules of Sociological Method and Selected Texts on Sociology and Its Method*, edited by S. Lukes. New York: Free Press.

Eagleton, T. 1991. *Ideology*. London: Verso.

Eddy, M. B. 1971. *Science and Health with Key to the Scriptures*. Boston: First Church of Christ, Scientist.

Eff, E. A. 1989. "History of Thought as Ceremonial Genealogy: The Neglected Influence of Herbert Spencer on Thorstein Veblen." *Journal of Economic Issues* 23:689–716.

Eisler, R. 1987. *The Chalice and the Blade: Our History, Our Future*. New York: Harper & Row.

Ellenberger, H. 1970. *The Discovery of the Unconscious*. New York: Basic Books.

Elshtein, J. B. 1986. "Citizenship and Armed Civic Virtue: Some Critical Questions on the Commitment to Public Life." *Soundings* 69(1–2):99–110.

Engels, F. [1884] 1972. *The Origin of the Family, Private Property and the State.* London: Lawrence & Wisehart.

Espinas, A. [1878] 1977. *Animal Societies.* New York: Arno Press.

Estrada, I. 1986. "Our Lady of Guadaloupe: Expression of the Integration Process in Mexico." *Social Compass* 33(1):23–55.

Farr, R. M., and Moscovici, S. 1984. *Social Representations.* Cambridge: Cambridge University Press.

Filloux, J. 1977. *Durkheim et le socialisme.* Paris: Droz.

Fluehr, L. 1987. "Marxism and the Matriarchate: One Hundred Years After the Origin of the Family, Private Property and the State." *Critique of Anthropology* 7(1):5–14.

Fraser, C., and Gaskell, G. 1990. *The Social Psychological Study of Widespread Beliefs.* Oxford: Clarendon.

Fraser, N., and Nicholson, L. 1988. "Social Criticism Without Philosophy: An Encounter Between Feminism and Postmodernism." *Theory, Culture and Society* 5(2–3):373–98.

Frazer, J. [1890] 1981. *The Golden Bough.* New York: Avenel.

Freud, S. [1912] 1950. *Totem and Taboo.* New York: Norton.

———. [1925] 1959. *An Autobiographical Study.* New York: W. W. Norton.

———. [1927] 1955. *The Future of An Illusion.* New York: W. W. Norton.

———. [1933] 1965. *New Introductory Lectures on Psychoanalysis.* New York: W. W. Norton.

Frisby, D. 1984. *Georg Simmel.* London: Tavistock.

———. 1986. *Fragments of Modernity: Theories of Modernity in the Work of Simmel, Kracauer and Benjamin.* Cambridge, MA: MIT Press.

Fromm, E. 1947. *Man for Himself.* New York: Rinehart.

———. 1950. *Psychoanalysis and Religion.* New Haven, CT: Yale University Press.

———. 1955. *The Sane Society.* Greenwich, CT: Fawcett.

———. 1959. *Sigmund Freud's Mission.* New York: Harper.

———. 1962. *Beyond the Chains of Illusion.* New York: Simon & Schuster.

———. 1963. *The Dogma of Christ and Other Essays on Religion, Psychology and Culture.* New York: Holt, Rinehart, and Winston.

———. 1964. *The Heart of Man: Its Genius for Good and Evil.* New York: Harper.

Fromm, E., and Maccoby, M. (1970) *Social Character in a Mexican Village: A Sociopsychoanalytic Study.* Englewood Cliffs, NJ: Prentice-Hall.

Fukuyama, F. 1989. "The End of History?" *The National Interest* 16(Summer):3–19.

———. 1990. "Are We at the End of History?" *Fortune* 121(January 15):75–77.

———. 1992. *The End of History and the Last Man.* New York: Free Press.

Gadon, E. W. 1989. *The Once and Future Goddess.* New York: Harper Collins.

Game, A. 1991. *Undoing the Social: Towards a Deconstructive Sociology.* Toronto: University of Toronto Press.

Gane, M. 1991. *Baudrillard: Critical and Fatal Theory.* London: Routledge.

Garrett, C. 1977. "Women and Witches: Patterns of Analysis." *Signs* 3(2):161–70.

Giddens, A. 1971. "The Individual in the Writings of Emile Durkheim." *European Journal of Sociology* 12:210–28.

———. 1986. *Durkheim on Politics and the State.* London: Polity.

———. 1990. *The Consequences of Modernity.* Stanford: Stanford University Press.

———. 1992. "Uprooted Signposts at Century's End." *The Higher* (January 17):21

Gilligan, C. 1982. *In a Different Voice.* Cambridge, MA: Harvard University Press.

Gimbutas, M. 1989. *The Language of the Goddess.* New York: Harper and Row.

Girard, R. 1972. *Violence and the Sacred.* Baltimore: Johns Hopkins University Press.

———. 1987a. *Job, the Victim of His People.* Stanford: Stanford University Press.

———. 1987b. "Generative Scapegoating." Pp. 73–148 in *Violent Origins: Ritual Killing and Cultural Formation,* edited by R. G. Hamerton-Kelly. Stanford: Stanford University Press.

Glassner, B. 1989. "Fitness and the Postmodern Self." *Journal of Health and Social Behavior* 30(2):190–97.

Godel, R. 1969. *A Geneva School Reader in Linguistics.* Bloomington: Indiana University Press.

Goodrich, N. L. 1989. *Priestesses.* New York: Harper Collins.

Gouldner, A. 1958. "Introduction." Pp. v–xxviii in *Socialism and Saint-Simon,* by Emile Durkheim. Yellow Springs, OH: Antioch Press.

———. 1970. *The Coming Crisis of Western Sociology.* New York: Basic Books.

Graybeal, J. 1990. *Language and the Feminine in Nietzsche and Heidegger.* Bloomington: Indiana University Press.

Greeley, A. M. 1989. "The Declining Morale of Women." *Sociology and Social Research* 73(2):53–58.

Greenwood, S. 1990. "Emile Durkheim and C. G. Jung: Structuring a Transpersonal Sociology of Religion." *Journal for the Scientific Study of Religion* 29:482–95.

Greisman, H. 1981. "Matriarchate as Utopia, Myth, and Social Theory." *Sociology* 15(3):321–36.

Guyau, J. [1885] 1907. *Esquisse d'une morale sans obligation ni sanction.* Paris: Alcan.

———. [1887] 1909. *L'irreligion de l'avenir.* Paris: Alcan.

Habermas, J. 1984. *The Theory of Communicative Action.* Boston: Beacon Press.

———. 1987. *The Philosophical Discourse of Modernity.* Cambridge, MA: MIT Press.

Halbwachs, M. [1930] 1978. *The Causes of Suicide.* London: Routledge & Kegan Paul.

———. [1938] 1960. *Population and Society: Introduction to Social Morphology,* translated by Otis Dudley Duncan and Harold W. Pfautz. Glencoe, IL: Free Press.

Hamlyn, D. 1980. *Schopenhauer.* London: Routledge & Kegan Paul.

Harris, R. 1985. "Saussure and the Dynamic Paradigm." Pp. 167–83 in *Developmental Mechanisms of Language,* edited by C. Bailey. Oxford: Pergamon.

Harvey, D. 1989. *The Condition of Postmodernity.* London: Basil Blackwell.

Headley, L. 1983. *Suicide in Asia and the Near East.* Berkeley: University of California Press.

Hermand, J. 1984. "All Power to the Women: Fascist Concepts of Matriarchy." *Argument* 26:53–54.

Hertz, R. [1907–1909] 1960. "The Pre-eminence of the Right Hand: A Study in Religious Polarity." Pp. 89–113 in *Death and the Right Hand,* translated by R. and C. Needham. Aberdeen: Cohen & West.

Holmes, R. L. 1990. *Nonviolence in Theory and Practice.* Belmont, CA: Wadsworth.

Holub, R. C. 1991. *Jurgen Habermas: Critic in the Public Sphere.* London: Routledge.

Horkheimer, M. 1947. *The Eclipse of Reason.* New York: Oxford University Press.

Horkheimer, M., and Adorno, T. 1972. *Dialectic of Enlightenment.* New York: Continuum Press.

Hubert, H. [1925] 1934. *The Rise of the Celts.* New York: Knopf.

Ingram, D. 1988. "The Postmodern Kantianism of Arendt and Lyotard." *Review of Metaphysics* 42(1):51–77.

Isambert, F. A. 1982. "On Definitions: Reflections on the Durkheimian Strategy for Determination of the Object." *L'Annee sociologique* 32:163–92.

James, W. [1896] 1931. *The Will to Believe, and Other Essays in Popular Philosophy.* New York: Longmans.

Janik, A., and Toulmin, S. 1973. *Wittgenstein's Vienna.* New York: Simon and Schuster.

Johnson, A. B. 1990. *Out of Bedlam: The Truth About Deinstitutionalization.* New York: Basic Books.

Jones, E. 1981. *The Life and Work of Sigmund Freud,* Vols. 1–3. New York: Basic Books.

Jung, C. G. 1959. *Four Archetypes.* Princeton, NJ: Princeton University Press.

––––––. 1966. *The Spirit in Man, Art, and Literature.* Princeton, NJ: Princeton University Press.

Jurkevich, G. 1991. *The Elusive Self: Archetypal Approacches to the Novels of Miguel de Unamuno.* Columbia: University of Missouri Press.

Kaern, M. 1985. "Georg Simmel's Sociology of Als-Ob." Ph.D. dissertation, University of Pittsburgh.

Kaern, M., Phillips, B. S., and Cohen, R. S. 1990. *Georg Simmel and Contemporary Sociology.* Boston: Kluwer.

Kandal, T. R. 1988. *The Woman Question in Classical Sociological Theory.* Miami: University Presses of Florida.

Kanter, D. L., and Mirvis, P. H. 1989. *The Cynical Americans.* San Francisco: Jossey-Bass.

Kellner, D. 1988. "Postmodernism as Social Theory." *Theory, Culture, and Society* 5(2–3):239–70.

––––––. 1989. *Jean Baudrillard: From Marxism to Postmodernism and Beyond.* Stanford: Stanford University Press.

Kennedy, G. 1987. "Fin de Siecle Classicism: Henry Adams and Thorstein Veblen, Lew Wallace and W. D. Howells." *Classical and Modern Literature* 8(1):15–21.

Kleman, G. L. 1986. *Suicide and Depression.* Washington, DC: American Psychiatric Association Press.

Kohlberg, L. 1981. *Essays in Moral Development.* San Francisco: Harper & Row.

Kramer, F. W., Jell, B., and Werts, D. 1985. "Empathy—Reflections on the History of Ethnology in Pre-fascist Germany: Herder, Creuzer, Bastian, Bachofen, and Frobenius." *Dialectical Anthropology* 9:337–47.

Kroker, A., and Cook D. 1986. *The Postmodern Scene: Excremental Culture and Hyper-Aesthetics.* New York: St. Martin's Press.

Laquer, T. 1990. *Making Sex: Body and Gender from the Greeks to Freud.* Cambridge, MA: Harvard University Press.

Lasch, C. 1991. *The True and Only Heaven: Progress and Its Critics.* New York: W. W. Norton.

Lash, S. 1986. "Postmodernity and Desire." *Theory and Society.* 14(1):1–31.

———. 1988. "Discourse of Figure? Postmodernism as a Regime of Signification." *Theory, Culture and Society* 5(2–3):311–36.

Lears, T. J. 1983. "In Defense of Henry Adams." *Wilson Quarterly* 7:82–93.

Leathers, C. G. 1986. "Bellamy and Veblen's Christian Morals." *Journal of Economic Issues* 20:107–19.

Leroy, M. 1965. "Individualist Tendencies in Linguistics." *Diogenes* 51:168–85.

Levy, M. 1989. *Our Mother-Tempers.* Berkeley: University of California Press.

Levy-Bruhl, L. (1890) *L'Allemagne depuis Leibniz.* Paris: Hachette.

———. 1895. "La Crise de la metaphysique en Allemagne." *Revue des Deux Mondes* 15:341–67.

———. 1899. *The History of Modern Philosophy in France.* Chicago: Open Court Publishing.

———. 1903a. *La morale et la science des moeurs.* Paris: Alcan.

———. 1903b. *The Philosophy of Auguste Comte,* translated by Kathleen de Beaumont-Klein. London: Swan Sonnenschein.

Littre, E. [1863] 1963. *Dictionnaire de la langue francaise.* Paris: Gallimard.

Logue, W. 1983. *From Philosophy to Sociology.* De Kalb: Northern Illinois University Press.

Logue, W., and Bazon, M. 1979. "Sociology and Politics: The Liberalism of Celestin Bougle." *Revue francaise de Sociologie* 20(1):141–61.

Lukacs, G. 1980. *The Destruction of Reason,* translated by Peter Palmer. Atlantic Highlands: Humanities Press.

Lukes, S. 1982. "Introduction." Pp. 1–27 in *Durkheim: The Rules of Sociological Method and Selected Texts on Sociology and Its Method,* edited by S. Lukes. New York: Free Press.

———. 1985. *Emile Durkheim: His Life and Work.* Stanford: Stanford University Press.

Lyotard, J. 1984. *The Postmodern Condition.* Minneapolis: University of Minnesota Press.

Magee, B. 1983. *The Philosophy of Schopenhauer.* New York: Oxford University Press.

Mann, T. [1939] 1955. "Introduction." Pp. iii–xxiii in *The Works of Schopenhauer,* edited by W. Durant and T. Mann. New York: Frederick Ungar.

Masaryk, T. [1881] 1970. *Suicide and the Meaning of Civilization.* Chicago: University of Chicago Press.

Matarasso, M. 1973. "Robert Hertz, Our Precursor: Sociology of the Left and of Death, Pre-structuralism and Asymmetry." *L'Annee sociologique* 24:119–47.

Mathisen, J. A. 1989. "Twenty Years after Bellah: Whatever Happened to American Civil Religion?" *Sociological Analysis* 50(2):29–46

Mauss, M. [1920] 1969. *Oeuvres.* Vols. 1–3. Paris: Les Editions de Minuit.

———. [1950] 1979a. *Sociology and Psychology.* London: Routledge & Kegan Paul.

———. [1950] 1979b. *Seasonal Variations of the Eskimo: A Study in Social Morphology.* London: Routledge & Kegan Paul.

Meillet, A. 1906. "Comment les mots changent des sens." *L'Annee sociologique* 9:1–39.

Menand, L., and Schwartz. S. 1982. "T. S. Eliot on Durkheim: A New Attribution." *Modern Philology* 79:309–15.

Merton, R. K. 1957. *Social Theory and Social Structure.* New York: Free Press.

Meštrovíc, S. G. 1988. *Emile Durkheim and the Reformation of Sociology.* Totowa, NJ: Rowman & Littlefield.

———. 1991. *The Coming Fin de Siecle: An Application of Durkheim's Sociology to Modernity and Postmodernism.* London: Routledge.

Mill, J. S. 1968. *Auguste Comte and Positivism.* Ann Arbor: University of Michigan Press.

Mills, C. W. 1959. *The Sociological Imagination.* New York: Oxford University Press.

Mitzman, A. 1977. "Anarchism, Expressionism and Psychoanalysis." *New German Critique* 10:77–104.

Moreland, K. 1989. "Henry Adams, the Medieval Lady, and the 'New Woman.'" *Clio* 18:291–305.

Mounin, G. 1975. *La Linguistique du XXe siecle.* Paris: Presses Universitaires de France.

Muller, M. F. [1879] 1965. *Lectures on the Science of Language.* Delhi: Munshi Ram Manohar Lal.

Murphy, J. W. 1989. *Postmodern Social Analysis and Criticism.* New York: Greenwood Press.

Nandan, Y. 1970. *Emile Durkheim: Contributions to L'Annee Sociologique.* New York: Free Press.

Nietzsche, F. [1874] 1965. *Schopenhauer as Educator.* South Bend, IN: Gateway.

———. [1901] 1968. *The Will to Power.* New York: Random House.

———. 1968. *The Portable Nietzsche,* translated by W. Kaufmann. New York: Viking Library.

Novak, M. 1982. *The Spirit of Democratic Capitalism.* New York: Simon and Schuster.

———. 1991. "Transforming the Democratic/Capitalist Revolution." Paper presented at the Karl Brunner Symposium, Interlaken, Switzerland.

Nutini, H. 1976. "Syncretism and Acculturation: The Historical Development of the Cult of the Patron Saint in Tlaxcala, Mexico (1519–1670)." *Ethnology* 15(3):301–21.

O'Keefe, D. L. 1982. *Stolen Lightning: A Social Theory of Magic.* New York: Random House.

Park, R. E., and Burgess, W. E. 1921. *Introduction to the Science of Sociology.* Chicago: University of Chicago Press.

Parsons, T. 1937. *The Structure of Social Action.* Glencoe, IL: Free Press.

Partenheimer, D. 1988. "The Education of Henry Adams in German Philosophy." *Journal of the History of Ideas* 49:339–45.

Pearce, F. 1989. *The Radical Durkheim.* London: Unwin Hyman.

Pelikan, J. 1985. *Jesus Through the Centuries: His Place in the History of Culture.* New Haven, CT: Yale University Press.

Petrie, A. 1967. *Individuality in Pain and Suffering.* Chicago: University of Chicago Press.

Posnock, R. 1987. "Henry James, Veblen and Adorno: The Crisis of the Modern Self." *Journal of American Studies* 21(1):31–54.

Ranulf, S. 1939. "Scholarly Forerunners of Fascism." *Ethics* 50:16–34.

Renouvier, C. 1892. "Schopenhauer et la metaphysique du pessimisme." *L'Annee philosophique* 3:1–61.

Ribot, T. 1874. *La Philosophie de Schopenhauer.* Paris: Librairie Gerner Bailliere.

———. 1896. *The Psychology of Attention.* Chicago: Open Court Press.

Riesman, D. 1950. *The Lonely Crowd.* New Haven, CT: Yale University Press.

———. 1953. *Thorstein Veblen: A Critical Interpretation.* New York: Charles Scribner's Sons.

———. 1956. *Constraint and Variety in American Education.* Lincoln: University of Nebraska Press.

———. 1964. *Abundance For What?* Garden City, NY: Doubleday.

———. 1980. "Egocentrism." *Character* 1(5):3–9.

Ritzer, G. 1991. *Metatheorizing in Sociology.* Lexington, MA: Lexington Books.

Roberts, K. 1990. *Religion in Sociological Perspective.* Belmont, CA: Wadsworth.

Rojek, C. 1990. "Baudrillard and Leisure." *Leisure Studies* 9(1):7–20.

Rosenau, P. M. 1992. *Post-modernism and the Social Sciences.* Princeton, NJ: Princeton University Press.

Saussure, F. [1916] 1959. *Course in General Linguistics,* translated by W. Baskin. New York: Philosophical Library.

Schlegel, A. 1984. "Hopi Gender Ideology of Female Superiority." *Quarterly Journal of Ideology* 8(4):44–52.

Schneider, L. 1948. *The Freudian Psychology and Veblen's Social Theory.* Morningside Heights, NY: King's Crown Press.

Schoenfeld, C. G. 1966. "Erich Fromm's Attacks upon the Oedipus Complex—A Brief Critique." *Journal of Nervous and Mental Disease* 141(5):580–85.

Schoenfeld, E., and Mestrovic, S. G. 1989. "Durkheim's Concept of Justice and Its Relationship to Social Solidarity." *Sociological Analysis* 50(2):111–27.

———. 1991. "With Justice and Mercy: Instrumental-Masculine and Expressive-Feminine Elements in Religion." *Journal for the Scientific Study of Religion* 30(4):363–80.

Schopenhauer, A. [1813] 1899. *On the Fourfold Root of the Principle of Sufficient Reason and On the Will in Nature.* London: G. Bell and Sons.

———. [1818] 1977a. *The World as Will and Idea,* translated by R. Haldane and J. Kemp. Vol. 1. New York: AMS Press.

———. [1818] 1977b. *The World as Will and Idea,* translated by R. Haldane and J. Kemp. Vol. 2. New York: AMS Press.

———. [1818] 1977c. *The World as Will and Idea,* translated by R. Haldane and J. Kemp. Vol. 3. New York: AMS Press.

———. [1841] 1965. *On the Basis of Morality.* Indianapolis, IN: Bobbs-Merrill.

Simmel, G. [1907] 1986. *Schopenhauer and Nietzsche.* Amherst: University of Massachusetts Press.

_____. 1971. *On Individuality and Its Social Forms.* Chicago: University of Chicago Press.

Sloterdijk, P. 1987. *Critique of Cynical Reason,* translated by Michael Eldred. Minneapolis: University of Minnesota Press.

Sorokin, P. 1948. *The Reconstruction of Humanity.* Boston: Beacon Press.

Spengler, O. [1926] 1961. *The Decline of the West. Vol. 1. Form and Actuality,* translated by Charles F. Atkinson. New York: Alfred A. Knopf.

_____. [1928] 1961. *The Decline of the West. Vol. 2. Perspectives on World-History,* translated by Charles F. Atkinson. New York: Alfred A. Knopf.

Stone, G. P., and Farberman, H. 1967. "On the Edge of Rapprochement: Was Durkheim Moving Toward the Perspective of Symbolic Interactionism?" *Sociological Quarterly* 8(2):149–64.

Tarde, G. 1969. *On Communication and Social Influence.* Chicago: University of Chicago Press.

Tocqueville, A. [1835] 1945. *Democracy in America.* Vol. 1. New York: Vintage.

Tonnies, F. [1887] 1963. *Community and Society,* translated by C. Loomis. New York: Harper & Row.

_____. [1921] 1974. *Karl Marx: His Life and Teachings,* translated by C. Loomis and I. Paulus. Lansing: Michigan State University Press.

Traugott, M. 1978. *Emile Durkheim on Institutional Analysis.* Chicago: University of Chicago Press.

Turner, B. 1984. *The Body and Society.* London: Blackwell.

Turner, R. 1987. "Six, Sex, Sin, and Sorcery: The Social Construction of Gendered Religion." *Free Inquiry in Creative Sociology* 15:129–37.

Vaihinger, H. [1924] 1935. *The Philosophy of As If.* London: Routledge.

Veblen, T. [1899] 1967. *The Theory of the Leisure Class.* New York: Penguin Books.

_____. [1910] 1943. "Christian Morals and the Competitive System." Pp. 200–28 in *Essays in Our Changing Order,* edited by L. Ardzrooni. New York: Viking.

_____. [1915] 1964. *Imperial Germany and the Industrial Revolution.* New York: Sentry Press.

_____. 1917. *An Inquiry Into the Nature of Peace and the Terms of Its Perpetuation.* New York: Macmillan.

_____. 1943. *Essays in Our Changing Order.* New York: Viking.

_____. 1948. *The Portable Veblen,* edited by Max Lerner. New York: Viking.

_____. 1973. *Essays, Reviews, and Reports.* New York: Sentry Press.

Vitz, P. C. 1988. *Sigmund Freud's Christian Unconscious.* New York: Guilford Press.

Wallace, R. A. 1977. "Emile Durkheim and the Civil Religion Concept." *Review of Religious Research* 18(3):287–90.

Waller, W. T. 1988. "The Concept of Habit in Economic Analysis." *Journal of Economic Issues* 22:113–26.

Weber, M. [1904] 1958. *The Protestant Ethic and the Spirit of Capitalism,* translated by T. Parsons. New York: Charles Scribner's Sons.

Wells, H. G. 1906. *The Future in America: A Search After Realities.* New York: Harper and Brothers.

Willer, J. 1968. "The Implications of Durkheim's Philosophy of Science." *Kansas Journal of Sociology* 4(4):175–90.

Woodman, M. 1985. *The Pregnant Virgin: A Process of Psychological Transformation.* Toronto: Inner City Books.

Wundt, W. 1907. *The Principles of Morality and the Departments of the Moral Life.* New York: Macmillan.

———. [1887] 1916. *Elements of Folk Psychology: Outlines of the Psychological History of the Development of Mankind.* London: Allen and Unwin.

———. 1907. *The Principles of Morality and the Departments of the Moral Life.* New York: Macmillan.

Zimdars-Swartz, S. L. 1989. "Popular Devotion to the Virgin: The Marian Phenomena at Melleray, Ireland." *Archives desciences sociales des religions* 31: 125–44.

# Additional Readings

Abrams, P. 1988. "Notes on the Difficulty of Studying the State." *Journal of Historical Sociology* 1:58–89.

Alpert, H. 1940. "Celestin Bougle (1870–1940)." *Journal of Social Philosophy* 5(3):270–73.

Arsleff, H. 1982. *From Locke to Saussure: Essays on the Study of Language and Intellectual History.* Minneapolis: University of Minnesota Press.

Ash, T. G. 1990. "Eastern Europe: The Year of Truth." *New York Review of Books* 37(2):17–22.

Bailey, J. 1988. *Pessimism.* London: Routledge.

Barnouw, D. 1988. *Weimar Intellectuals and the Threat of Modernity.* Bloomington: Indiana University Press.

Baudrillard, J. 1991. "The Reality Gulf." *Guardian,* January 11, p. 25.

Bell, D. 1977. *The Coming of Post-Industrial Society: A Venture in Social Forecasting.* New York: Basic Books.

———. 1981. "First Love and Early Sorrows." *Partisan Review* 48(4):532–51.

———. 1985. "The Revolt Against Modernity." *Public Interest* 81:42–63.

———. 1987. "The World and the United States in 2013." *Daedalus* 116(3):1–31.

Bellah, R. N. 1972. *Emile Durkheim on Morality and Society.* Chicago: University of Chicago Press.

Bellah, R. N., and Hammond, P. E. 1980. *Varieties of Civil Religion.* New York: Harper & Row.

Berman, M. 1982. *All That Is Solid Melts Into Air: The Experience of Modernity.* New York: Simon and Schuster.

Bougle, C. 1896. *Les Sciences sociales en Allemande.* Paris: Alcan.

———. [1908] 1971. *Essays on the Caste System.* Cambridge: Cambridge University Press.

———. 1909 *Darwinism and Sociology.* Pp. 465–76 in *Darwin and Modern Science,* edited by A. C. Seward. Cambridge: Cambridge University Press.

———. 1918. *Chez les prophetes socialistes.* Paris: Alcan.

———. 1926. *The Evolution of Values,* translated by Helen Sellars. New York: Henry Holt.

———. 1930. "The Present Tendency of the Social Sciences in France." Pp. 64–83 in *The New Social Science,* edited by Leonard D. White. Chicago: University of Chicago Press.

———. 1935. *Bilan de la sociologie francaise contemporaine.* Paris: Alcan.

Bowler, P. J. 1988. *The Non-Darwinian Revolution: Reinterpretation of a Historical Myth.* Baltimore: Johns Hopkins University Press.

Bringmann, W. G. and Tweney R. D. 1980. *Wundt Studies: A Centennial Collection.* Toronto: C. J. Hogrefe.

Brown, M. 1970. "A Sociolinguistic Study of Choctaw." *Southern Quarterly* 9:41–49.

Byrnes, J. F. 1988. "Explaining the Mary Cult: A Hypothesis and Problems." *Journal of Religion* 68:277–85.

Cahoone, L. E. 1988. *The Dilemma of Modernity: Philosophy, Culture, and Anti-Culture.* Albany, NY: SUNY Press.

Calinescu, M. 1987. *Five Faces of Modernity.* Durham, NC: Duke University Press.

Callinicos, A. 1990. *Against Postmodernism: A Marxist Critique.* New York: St. Martin's Press.

Carroll, M. P. 1985. "The Virgin Mary at LaSalette and Lourdes: Whom Did the Children See?" *Journal for the Scientific Study of Religion* 24:56–74.

———. 1987. *The Cult of the Virgin Mary: Psychological Origins.* Princeton: Princeton University Press.

Cartwright, D. 1989. "Schopenhauer as Moral Philosopher—Towards the Actuality of His Ethics." Paper presented at the bicentennial of Schopenhauer's birth, New Orleans, LA.

Chamboredon, J. C. 1981. "Emile Durkheim: Le social object de science." *Critique* 10:110–31.

Clinch, B. J. 1906. "Our Lady of Guadalupe." *American Catholic Quarterly Review* 31:240–67.

Curro, C. 1983. "The Cult of Saints as Protectors Against Earthquakes in Salerno." *Sociologia* 17(3):155–89.

Davis, L. 1989. "A Postmodern Paradox? Cheerleaders at Women's Sporting Events." *Arena Review* 13(2):121–33.

Denzin, N. 1987. "On Semiotics and Symbolic Interactionism." *Symbolic Interaction* 10(1):1–19.

———. 1989 "Reading/Writing Culture: Interpreting the Postmodern Project." *Cultural Dynamics* 2(1):9–27.

Deploige, S. [1911] 1938. *The Conflict Between Ethics and Sociology,* translated by Charles C. Miltner. London: B. Herder.

Deutsch, K. W. 1963. *The Nerves of Government: Models of Political Communication and Control.* New York: Free Press.

Dijkstra, B. 1986. *Idols of Perversity: Idols of Feminine Evil in Fin de Siècle Culture.* London: Oxford.

Durant, W. 1981. *The Story of Philosophy.* New York: Simon and Schuster.

Durkheim, E. [1886] 1990. "Review of Fouillee's *La Propriete sociale et la democratie (1884),*" translated by R. Jones. *Durkheim Studies* 2:27–32.

———. [1888] 1976. "Introduction a la sociologie de la famille." Pp. 13–34 in *Textes,* edited by V. Karady, Vol. 3. Paris: Les Editions de Minuit.

———. [1897] 1982. "Marxism and Sociology." Pp. 167–74 in *Durkheim: The Rules of Sociological Method and Selected Texts on Sociology and Its Method*, edited by S. Lukes. New York: Free Press.

———. [1897] 1986. "Socialism and Marxism." Pp. 121–45 in *Durkheim on Politics and the State*, edited by A. Giddens. London: Polity.

———. [1900] 1973. "Sociology in France in the Nineteenth Century." Pp. 3–22 in *Emile Durkheim on Morality and Society*, edited by R. Bellah. Chicago: University of Chicago Press.

———. [1906] 1978. "Review of Marianne Weber." Pp. 139–44 in *Emile Durkheim on Institutional Analysis*, edited by M. Traugott. Chicago: University of Chicago Press.

———. [1920] 1978. "Introduction to Morality." Pp. 191–202 in *Emile Durkheim on Institutional Analysis*, edited by M. Traugott. Chicago: University of Chicago Press.

———. [1924] 1974. *Sociology and Philosophy*, translated by D. F. Pocock. New York: Free Press.

Durkheim, E., and Mauss, M. [1902] 1975. *Primitive Classification*, translated by R. Needham. Chicago: University of Chicago Press.

Eliade, M. 1957. *Myths, Dreams, and Mysteries*. New York: Harper & Row.

Elias, N. 1982. *The Civilizing Process*. Oxford: Basil Blackwell.

Fauconnet, P. 1920. *La Responsabilite: Etude sociologique*. Paris: Alcan.

Featherstone, M. 1988. "In Pursuit of the Postmodern." *Theory, Culture and Society* 5(2–3):195–216.

Filloux, J. 1970. *La Science sociale et l'action*. Paris: Presses Universitaires de France.

Foulquie, P. 1978. *Dictionnaire de la langue philosophique*. Paris: Presses Universitaires de France.

Fox, M. 1980. *Schopenhauer: His Philosophical Achievement*. Totowa, NJ: Barnes & Noble.

Freud, S. [1901] 1965. *The Psychopathology of Everyday Life*. New York: Norton.

———. [1915] 1958. "Thoughts for the Times on War and Death." Pp. 206–35 in *Sigmund Freud on Creativity and the Unconscious*. New York: Harper & Row.

———. [1930] 1961. *Civilization and Its Discontents*. New York: W. W. Norton.

———. [1932] 1963 "Why War?" Pp. 134–47 in *Sigmund Freud on Character and Culture*, edited by P. Rieff. New York: Collier.

Gane, M. 1981. "Institutional Socialism and the Sociological Critique of Communism." *Economy and Society* 10(3):301–30.

———. 1984. "Durkheim: The Sacred Language." *Economy and Society* 12(1):1–47.

Gehrig, G. 1979. *American Civil Religion: An Assessment*. Storrs, CT: Society for the Scientific Study of Religion.

Giddens, A. 1987. *Social Theory and Modern Sociology*. Stanford: Stanford University Press.

Gisbert, P. 1959. "Social Facts in Durkheim's System." *Anthropos* 54:353–69.

Godel, R. 1969. *A Geneva School Reader in Linguistics*. Bloomington: Indiana University Press.

Goodwin, P. 1967. "Schopenhauer." Pp. 325–32 in *The Encyclopedia of Philosophy*, edited by P. Edwards, vol. 7. New York: Macmillan.

Gordon, S. 1990. *Prisoners of Men's Dreams: Striking Out for a New Feminine Future.* Boston: Little, Brown.

Greeley, A. M. 1987. "Review Essay: The Cult of the Virgin Mary." *Sociology and Social Research* 71(3):172–73.

———. 1988. "Evidence That a Maternal Image of God Correlates with Liberal Politics." *Sociology and Social Research* 72(3):150–54.

Habermas, J. 1970. *Toward a Rational Society.* Boston: Beacon Press.

———. 1979. *Communication and the Evolution of Society.* Boston: Beacon Press.

———. 1981. "Modernity versus Postmodernity." *New German Critique* 22:3–14.

Halbwachs, M. [1912] 1974. *La Classe ouvriere et les niveaux.* London: Gordon & Breach.

———. 1918. "La doctrine d'Emile Durkheim." *Revue philosophique* 85:353–411.

———. 1925. "Les origines puritaines du capitalisme." *Revue d'histoire et de philosophie religieuses.* 5:132–57.

———. 1935 *Sources of Religious Sentiment.* New York: Free Press.

———. 1939. "Individual Conscience and Collective Mind." *American Journal of Sociology* 44:812–22.

———. 1958. *The Psychology of Social Class,* translated by Georges Friedman. Glencoe, IL: Free Press.

Hall, J. A. 1988. *Liberalism: Politics, Ideology, and the Market.* Chapel Hill: University of North Carolina Press.

Hall, R. T. 1987. *Emile Durkheim: Ethics and the Sociology of Morals.* New York: Greenwood Press

Hartley, C. G. 1914. *The Position of Woman in Primitive Society: A Study of the Matriarchy.* London: Eveleigh Nash.

Hegel, G. W. F. [1899] 1965. *The Philosophy of History.* New York: Dover.

Hertz, R. 1922. "Le peche et l'expiation dans les societes primitives." *Revue de l'histoire des religions* 86:5–60.

Hodson, C. E. 1971. "Nuestra Senora de Guadalupe: Appearance Before an Indian." *Catholic World* 54:727–34.

Hubert, H., and Mauss M. [1899] 1964. *Sacrifice: Its Nature and Function.* Chicago: University of Chicago Press.

———. [1904] 1972. *A General Theory of Magic.* New York: W. W. Norton.

Hunter, J. D. 1983. *American Evangelicalism: Conservative Religion and the Quandary of Modernity.* New Brunswick, NJ: Rutgers University Press.

Izzo, A. 1980. "Durkheim and Socialism." *Critica Sociologica* 55:19–26.

James, W. [1890] 1950. *The Principles of Psychology.* New York: Dover.

———. [1902] 1961. *The Varieties of Religious Experience.* New York: Collier Books.

———. 1948. *Essays in Pragmatism.* New York: Hafner.

Janaway, C. 1989. *Self and World in Schopenhauer's Philosophy.* New York: Oxford.

Jay, M. 1988. *Fin de Siecle Socialism and Other Essays.* London: Routledge.

Jovanovic, R. 1975. "Durkheim's Conception of Corporate Socialism." *Sociologija* 17(1):151–67.

Jung, C. G. 1961. *Memories, Dreams, Reflections.* New York: Pantheon.

———. 1973. *Man and His Symbols.* New York: Dell.

Kalberg, S. 1987. "The Origin and Expansion of *Kulturpessimismus:* The Relationship Between Public and Private Spheres in Early Twentieth Century Germany." *Sociological Theory* 5:150–65.

———. 1990. "The Rationalization of Action in Max Weber's Sociology of Religion." *Sociological Theory* 8:58–84.

Kant, I. [1784] 1963. *On History.* Indianapolis, IN: Bobbs-Merrill.

———. [1788] 1956. *Critique of Practical Reason.* Indianapolis, IN: Bobbs-Merrill.

Kennedy, P. 1990. "Fin de Siecle America." *New York Review of Books* 37(11):31–40.

Knapp, P. 1985. "The Question of Hegelian Influence upon Durkheim's Thought." *Sociological Inquiry* 55:1–15.

Koerner, E. 1972. *Bibliographica Saussureana 1878–1970.* Ithaca, NY: Cornell University Press.

Kristeva, J. 1977. "Chinese Women: The Mother at the Center." *Liberation* 20(3):10–17.

Kroker, A., and Kroker M. 1991. *Ideology and Power in the Age of Lenin in Ruins.* New York: St. Martin's Press.

Kurzweil, E. 1990. *The Freudians: A Comparative Perspective.* New Haven, CT: Yale University Press.

Lacroix, B. 1981. *Durkheim et le politique.* Paris: Presses de la Fondation Nationale des Sciences Politiques.

Lacroix, B., and Landerer B. 1972. "Durkheim, Sismondi and the Socialists of the Chair." *L'Annee sociologique* 23:159–201.

Lalande, A. [1926] 1980. *Vocabulaire technique et critique de la philosophie.* Paris: Presses Universitaires de France.

Landowski, P. 1943. *Peut-on enseigner les beaux arts?* Paris: Editions Baudiniere.

Lasch, C. 1977. *Haven in a Heartless World.* New York: Basic Books.

———. 1979. *The Culture of Narcissism.* New York: W. W. Norton.

———. 1985. "Historical Sociology and the Myth of Maturity: Norbert Elias's 'Very Simple Formula.'" *Theory and Society* 14(5):705–20.

———. 1986. "The Communitarian Critique of Liberalism." *Soundings* 69(1–2):60–76.

Lash, S. 1990. *The Sociology of Postmodernism.* London: Routledge.

Lefevre, S. R. 1978. "Durkheim's Discussion of Socialism and Communism." *Social Science Journal* 15(2):131–42.

Loizos, P. 1989. "The Virgin Mary and Marina Warner's Feminism." *LSE Quarterly* 2(2):175–92.

Lovaton, L. 1971. "La Virgen de las Mercedes en la isla de Santo Domingo." *Journal of Inter-American Studies* 13:53–61.

Love, N. 1986. *Marx, Nietzsche, and Modernity.* New York: Columbia University Press.

Luft, E. 1988. *Schopenhauer: New Essays in Honor of his 200th Birthday.* Lewiston, NY: Mellen.

Malinowski, B. 1966. *The Father in Primitive Psychology.* New York: W. W. Norton.

Mansbridge, J. 1990. *Beyond Self-Interest.* Chicago: University of Chicago Press.

Marcus, S. 1984. *Freud and the Culture of Psychoanalysis: Studies in the Transition From Victorian Humanism to Modernity.* Boston: Allen and Unwin.

Markowitz, H. M. 1991. "Markets and Morality." *The Wall Street Journal,* May 14, p. A16.

Marx, K. [1858] 1977. *Capital.* Vol. 1. New York: Random House.

———. 1983. *The Portable Karl Marx,* edited by E. Kamenka. New York: Penguin.

Mauss, M. 1906. "Review of Wilhelm Wundt's Volkerpsychologie." *L'Annee Sociologique* 2:53–68.

———. 1983. *Sociologie et anthropologie.* Paris: Presses Universitaires de France.

Meillet, A. 1982. *Linguistique Historique et Linguistique Generale.* Paris: Champion.

Mestrovic, S. G. 1989a. "Rethinking the Will and Idea of Sociology in the Light of Schopenhauer's Philosophy." *British Journal of Sociology* 40:271–93.

———. 1989b. "Moral Theory Based on the Heart Versus the Mind: Schopenhauer's and Durkheim's Critiques of Kantian Ethics." *Sociological Review* 38:431–57.

———. 1989c. "Searching for the Starting Points of Scientific Inquiry: Durkheim's *Rules of Sociological Method* and Schopenhauer's Philosophy." *Sociological Inquiry* 59(3):267–86.

———. 1989d. "Reappraising Durkheim's *Elementary Forms of the Religious Life* in the Context of Schopenhauer's Philosophy." *Journal for the Scientific Study of Religion* 28(3):255–72.

Michel, P. 1980. "Polish Catholicism: Sociological Approaches." *Archives de sciences sociales des religions* 25:161–75.

———. 1981. "Popular Cults in Poland: Material for a Political Symbolism." *Archives de sciences sociales des religions* 26:101–19.

Mirowski, P. 1987. "The Philosophical Bases of Institutionalist Economics." *Journal of Economic Issues* 21:1001–37.

Molitierno, A. 1989. "Georg Simmel's Cultural Narcissism: A Non-ideological Approach." *Midwest Quarterly* 30(3):308–23.

Mulnix, M. 1983. "Ivan Mestrovic in Vienna." *Journal of Croatian Studies* 24:36–50.

Nandan, Y. 1977. *The Durkheimian School: A Systematic and Comprehensive Bibliography.* Westport, CT: Greenwood Press.

Neuhaus, R. J. 1991. "The Pope Affirms the New Capitalism." *The Wall Street Journal,* May 2, p. A12.

Niebuhr, R. 1957. *Love and Justice.* Philadelphia: Westminster Press.

Nisbet, R. A. 1974. *The Sociology of Emile Durkheim.* New York: Oxford University Press.

Oliver, D. W. 1989. *Education, Modernity, and Fractured Meaning: Toward a Process Theory of Teaching and Learning.* Albany, NY: SUNY Press.

O'Neill, J. 1988. "Religion and Postmodernism: The Durkheimian Bond in Bell and Jameson." *Theory, Culture and Society* 5(2–3):493–508.

Parsons, T. 1971. "Belief, Unbelief, and Disbelief." Pp. 207–46 in *The Culture of Unbelief,* edited by R. Caporale and A. Grumelli. Berkeley: University of California Press.

Pels, D. 1981. "A Fellow-Traveller's Dilemma: Sociology and Socialism in the Writings of Durkheim." *Acta-Politica* 19(3):309–29.

Piaget, J. 1926. *The Language and Thought of the Child.* London: Routledge.

———. [1932] 1965. *The Moral Judgment of the Child.* New York: Free Press.

Pickering, W. S. F. 1984. *Durkheim's Sociology of Religion: Themes and Theories.* London: Routledge & Kegan Paul.

Ponce, C. 1988. *Working the Soul: Reflections on Jungian Psychology.* Berkeley: North Atlantic Books.

Popper, K. R. [1934] 1961. *The Logic of Scientific Discovery.* New York: Science Editions.

Popson, S. 1986. "From Symbolic Exchange to Bureaucratic Discourse: The Hallmark Greeting Card." *Theory, Culture and Society* 3(2):99–111.

Preston, J. J. 1982. *Mother Worship.* Chapel Hill: University of North Carolina Press.

Proto, M. 1971. "Durkheim and Labriola." *International Review of Sociology* 7(2):911–57.

Riba, T. 1985. "Romanticism and Nationalism in Economics." *International Journal of Social Economics* 12:52–68.

Ribot, T. 1899. *German Psychology of Today,* translated by James M. Baldwin. New York: Charles Scribner's Sons.

Riesman, D. 1976. "Liberation and Stalemate." *Massachusetts Review* 17(4):767–76.

———. 1977. "Prospects for Human Rights." *Society* 15(1):28–33.

———. 1980. *On Higher Education: The Academic Enterprise in an Era of Rising Student Consumerism.* San Francisco: Jossey-Bass.

———. 1981. "The Dream of Abundance Reconsidered." *Public Opinion Quarterly* 45(3):285–302.

Riesman, D., and Riesman, E. T. 1967. *Conversations in Japan: Modernization, Politics, and Culture.* Chicago: University of Chicago Press.

Rochberg-Halton, E. 1986. *Meaning and Modernity: Social Theory in the Pragmatic Attitude.* Chicago: University of Chicago Press.

Roche, S. 1988. "Insecurity, the Feeling of Insecurity and Social Recomposition: Comparable Ends to Two Centuries." *International Review of Community Development* 19:11–20.

Rodriguez, Z. 1973. "Durkheim: His Conception of the State and the First World War." *Revista Espanola de la Opinion Publica* 32:119–53.

Rojek, C. 1985. *Capitalism and Leisure Theory.* London: Tavistock.

———. 1989. *Leisure for Leisure.* New York: Routledge.

Ronhaar, J. H. 1931. *Woman in Primitive Motherright Societies.* The Hague: J. B. Walters.

Rundell, J. F. 1987. *Origins of Modernity: The Origins of Modern Social Theory from Kant to Hegel to Marx.* Madison: University of Wisconsin Press.

Russell, J. C. 1981. "Family Experience and Folk Catholicism in Rural Ireland." *Journal of Psychoanaltic Anthropology* 7(2):141–70.

Savramis, D. 1986. "The Cult of the Virgin Mary as an Ideology That Is Hostile to Women." *Osterreischische Zeitschrift fur Soziologie* 11(3):145–49.

Schoenfeld, C. G. 1984. *Psychoanalysis Applied to the Law.* Port Washington, NY: Associated Faculty Press.

Schoenfeld, E. 1987. "Militant Religion." Pp. 125–37 in *Religious Society,* edited by W. Swatos. Westport, CT: Greenwood Press.

_____. 1989. "Justice: An Illusive Concept in Christianity." *Review of Religious Research* 30:236–45.

Schopenhauer, A. 1985. *Early Manuscripts (1804–1818)*. Oxford: Berg.

Schorske, C. 1980. *Fin de Siecle Vienna: Politics and Culture*. New York: Alfred A. Knopf.

Schwartz, H. 1990. *Century's End: A Cultural History of the Fin de Siecle*. New York: Doubleday.

Segady, T. W. 1987. *Values, Neo-Kantianism and the Development of Weberian Sociology*. New York: Peter Lang.

Showalter, E. 1990. *Sexual Anarchy: Gender and Culture at the Fin de Siecle*. New York: Viking.

Sica, A. 1988. *Weber, Irrationality, and Social Order*. Berkeley: University of California Press.

Silverman, I. J., and Dinitz, S. 1974. "Compulsive Masculinity and Delinquency: An Empirical Investigation." *Criminology* 11(4):498–515.

Simic, A. 1983. "Machismo and Cryptomatriarchy: Power, Affect, and Authority in the Contemporary Yugoslav Family." *Ethos* 11:66–86.

Sonn, R. D. 1989. *Anarchism and Cultural Politics in Fin de Siecle France*. Lincoln: University of Nebraska Press.

Sorokin, P. 1957. *Social and Cultural Dynamics*. New York: American Book Company.

Spencer, H. 1864. *First Principles*. New York: D. Appleton.

_____. 1899. *The Principles of Ethics*. New York: D. Appleton.

Staud, J. R. 1976. "From Depth Psychology to Depth Sociology: Freud, Jung, and Levi-Strauss." *Theory and Society* 3(3):303–38.

Steeman, T. M. 1963. "Durkheim's Professional Ethics." *Journal for the Scientific Study of Religion* 2:163–81.

Stokes, J. 1989. *In the Nineties*. Chicago: University of Chicago Press.

Sutter, C. 1972. "Introduction to the Study of Four Columbian Ethnic Groups." *Ethnopsychologie* 27(1):129–52.

Teich, M., and Porter, R. 1990. *Fin de Siecle and Its Legacy*. Cambridge: Cambridge University Press.

Thompson, C. 1985. "The Power to Pollute and the Power to Preserve: Perceptions of Female Power in a Hindu Village." *Social Science and Medicine* 21(6):701–11.

Thurow, R. 1991. "Yugoslav Secessions Underscore the Forces Tearing Nation Apart." *The Wall Street Journal*, June 26, p. A1.

Tomasic, D. 1948. *Personality and Culture in Eastern European Politics*. New York: George W. Stewart.

_____. 1953. *The Impact of Russian Culture on Soviet Communism*. Glencoe, IL: Free Press.

Tosti, G. 1898. "The Delusions of Durkheim's Sociological Objectivism." *American Journal of Sociology* 4:171–77.

Tufts, J. H. 1896. "Recent Sociological Tendencies in France." *American Journal of Sociology* 1:446–56.

Turner, B. 1990. *Theories of Modernity and Postmodernity*. London: Sage.

Turner, S. 1986. *The Search for a Methodology of Social Science: Durkheim, Weber, and the Nineteenth Century Problem of Cause, Probability, and Action.* Dordrecht, Holland: D. Reidel.

Vattimo, G. 1988. *The End of Modernity: Nihilism and Hermeneutics in Postmodern Culture.* Baltimore: Johns Hopkins University Press.

Veblen, T. [1919] 1961. *The Place of Science in Modern Civilization.* New York: Russell & Russell.

Vendreys, J. 1921. "Le caractère social du langage et la doctrine de Ferdinand de Saussure." *Journal de Psychologie* 18:617–24.

Wallach, M. A., and Wallach, L. 1983. *Psychology's Sanction for Selfishness.* San Francisco: W. H. Freeman.

Warner, M. 1976. *Alone of All Her Sex: The Myth and Culture of the Virgin Mary.* London: Weidenfeld & Nicholson.

Warnes, H. 1979. "Cultural Factors in Irish Psychiatry." *Psychiatric Journal of the University of Ottawa* 4(4):329–35.

Weber, E. 1987. *France, Fin de Siecle.* Cambridge, MA: Harvard University Press.

Wells, H. G. 1928. *The Way the World is Going.* London: Benn.

———. 1935. *The New America: The New World.* London: Cresset.

———. 1939. *The Fate of Man.* New York: Longmans.

Whimster, S., and Lash, S. 1987. *Max Weber, Rationality and Modernity.* Boston: Allen & Unwin.

White, S. K. 1988. *The Recent Work of Jurgen Habermas: Reason, Justice, and Modernity.* Cambridge: Cambridge University Press.

Wistrich, R. S. 1976. *Revolutionary Jews from Marx to Trotsky.* London: Harrop.

Wolfe, S. J., and Stanley, J. 1980. "Linguistic Problems with Patriarchal Reconstructions of Indo-European Culture." *Women's Studies International Quarterly* 3:227–37.

Wolff, K. 1983. *Beyond the Sociology of Knowledge.* Lanham, MD: University Press of America.

———. 1991. *Survival and Sociology: Vindicating the Human Subject.* New Brunswick, NJ: Transaction Books.

Wundt, W. [1886] 1902. *Ethics: An Investigation of the Facts and Laws of the Moral Life.* New York: Macmillan.

———. [1887] 1916. *Elements of Folk Psychology: Outlines of the Psychological History of the Development of Mankind.* London: Allen and Unwin.

Zimdars-Swartz, S. L. 1989. "Popular Devotion to the Virgin: The Marian Phenomena at Melleray, Ireland." *Archives de sciences sociales des religions* 31: 125–44.

# Author Index

Adams, Henry, ii, v, 7–10, 12,
16–17, 22–25, 27, 32, 38–
39, 52, 55, 93–96, 106, 110,
140–141, 144, 147, 156, 161

Adorno, Theodor, 7–8, 10–12, 15,
18, 39, 48–49, 52, 55–57,
60–61, 66, 79–81, 123, 125–
128, 131, 140, 156, 161

Bachofen, Johann J., v, 8, 16–28,
35, 55, 76, 83–86, 97–106,
110–111, 140–144, 149,
156–157, 161

Baudrillard, Jean, i–ii, v, 1–3, 6–
7, 10, 13, 15, 24, 28, 39, 43,
45–46, 48–49, 51, 58, 66–
67, 69–70, 84, 88, 91, 93,
107, 110, 134–138, 140–143,
155, 161, 173

Bauman, Zygmunt, 1, 9, 48, 56,
69, 80, 109–110, 127, 133,
147, 151, 161–162

Bell, Daniel, 10, 28, 43, 55, 106,
162, 173

Bellah, Robert N., 11, 67, 92–102,
110–111, 125–126, 135, 138,
151, 162, 173

Bergson, Henri, 27–28, 32, 34, 39,
100, 106, 156, 162

Bloom, Allan, 67, 78, 89, 95, 125–
126, 162

Comte, Auguste, 27, 30–31, 35,
39, 44, 63, 80, 98, 163

Durkheim, Emile, i–v, 3–8, 10,
12, 16, 18–25, 27–40, 43,
45, 47–48, 58–61, 63–66,
70–82, 88, 92, 96–101, 104,
106–111, 130–131, 134–137,
140–155, 159, 163–164,
174–175

German influence on his
thought, 8, 17, 41, 51–52,
74, 89

Liberal aspect of his thought,
5, 8, 11, 64, 85, 132

Writings typical of the *fin de siècle*, 35, 38–39, 41, 115

Eisler, Riane, 4–5, 15, 18, 164

Ellenberger, Henri, v, 12, 21, 30–
34, 38, 40, 44, 49, 138, 164

Engels, Friedrich, 20, 25, 165

Freud, Sigmund, 5, 8, 12, 20–21,
27–32, 36, 39–44, 52, 59,
66, 81, 91, 97–98, 104, 123,
131, 138, 147, 154, 156,
165, 175

Fromm, Erich, v, 20–21, 26, 33,
39, 55, 73, 78, 93, 98, 101–
106, 111, 114, 159, 165

Giddens, Anthony, v, 1, 91, 109,
120, 132, 139–140, 166, 175

Habermas, Jürgen, 11, 16, 28, 53,
61, 69–70, 88, 156, 166, 176

Halbwachs, Maurice, 67, 116, 120,
    166, 176
Hegel, G. F. W., 8, 9, 12, 30, 52,
    176
Hertz, Robert, 25, 35, 75, 83–88,
    126, 141, 166–167, 176

James, William, 27, 32, 36, 39, 53,
    81, 100, 167, 176
Jung, Carl G., ii–iii, v, 5–8, 12,
    16–21, 24, 27–28, 31–33,
    55–56, 66–69, 98–103, 111,
    140–141, 144, 147, 156–157,
    167, 176

Kant, Immanuel, v, 8–9, 12, 31,
    34, 51, 54, 65, 67, 89, 98,
    143, 177

Mann, Thomas, 12, 25, 31, 32,
    33, 39–40, 48, 168
Marx, Karl, 2, 20, 22, 151, 178
Mauss, Marcel, 30, 32, 63, 72–73,
    83, 115, 168–169, 178
Mills, C. Wright, 6, 169

Nietzsche, Friedrich, iii–v, 1–9,
    12–13, 17, 20–21, 27–28,
    32, 38, 52–53, 66, 102, 140,
    147, 169

Parsons, Talcott, 6–7, 29, 39, 41–
    46, 53, 80, 92, 99, 110, 169,
    178

Riesman, David, v, 7, 13, 19, 25,
    42, 48, 55, 58, 64, 106, 111,
    114, 121, 125–126, 128,
    133, 138, 147–148, 151,
    155, 170, 179

Saint-Simon, Henri, 30, 44
Saussure, Ferdinand, 70–73, 86–
    89, 170
Schopenhauer, Arthur, iii, 2–6, 8,
    11, 17, 23–29, 31–37, 42–
    49, 52, 55, 59–61, 70–75,
    80, 82, 86–89, 102–103,
    106, 113, 117, 121, 130,
    138–143, 147, 156, 170, 180
  relevance to postmodernism,
    iv, v, 7, 29
  critique of Kant, 12, 34, 54, 65
  and Durkheim's sociology, v, 4,
    8, 30–35, 38, 58, 120, 131,
    135
Simmel, Georg, iii–iv, 3–9, 12,
    18, 20, 27–29, 36–43, 66,
    111, 134, 156, 170–171
Sorokin, Pitirim, 8, 13, 61, 103,
    140, 171
Spengler, Oswald, 3–4, 8, 13, 25,
    52, 67, 79, 111, 137, 159,
    171, 180

Tocqueville, Alexis, v, 11, 52–53,
    67, 93, 97, 110, 137–138,
    171

Veblen, Thorstein, iii–v, 2, 5–12,
    15, 17–28, 37, 39, 46, 48–
    49, 52, 56–57, 64–67, 86–
    89, 98, 106, 111–117, 122,
    124, 126, 133–138, 140–151,
    154, 156, 159, 171

Weber, Max, iii, 5, 27, 39, 43, 52,
    104–107, 111, 149, 171
Wundt, Wilhelm, 30, 32, 36, 39,
    70, 73, 89, 172, 181

# Subject Index